PILSUDSKI

Marschall Piłsudski

PILSUDSKI

A Biography by

His Wife

ALEXANDRA PILSUDSKA

WITH FRONTISPIECE

NEW YORK

DODD, MEAD & COMPANY

1941

WESTPORT
PRINTED IN THE UNITED STATES OF AMERICA
BY THE VAIL-BALLOU PRESS, INC., BINGHAMTON, N. Y.

PREFACE

I HAVE written this book not for Poles, who know the history of their country, but especially for foreigners, giving them the fragments of my personal recollections against an historical background. The work was rather difficult because I had left many of my books and documents in Poland. The conditions under which I wrote this book, in collaboration with Mrs. Jennifer Ellis, were also difficult. I know no English, Mrs. Ellis no Polish. I had to tell her my story in French, she wrote it in English, and then every chapter had to be read to me in Polish so that I could judge it and make final suggestions.

I have tried to draw both the faults and good qualities of my country and its people and I think that English and American people will be able to find some characteristics of ours which are common also to themselves. I shall be very happy if this book can contribute a little towards the mutual understanding of our nations.

The fate of the war has not yet been decided. I began my story with the guns of Poland still echoing in my ears. We wrote the last chapter while the anti-aircraft shells were bursting in the sky over London. Polish forces are continuing the fight on land and sea and in the air. As long as there is one soldier left under arms our faith and confidence in the final issue remains unshaken. As my husband said once before . . . "Our faith is our greatest strength. . . ."

ALEXANDRA PILSUDSKA

CONTENTS

PART ONE

★

BLIGHTED HARVEST

"To be vanquished and not surrender—that is victory"
                                        MARSHAL PILSUDSKI

CHAPTER I

THERE WAS not a cloud to darken the sky on that morning
of the sixth of August in the year nineteen hundred and
thirty-nine, and as I motored along the road from Warsaw to
Cracow the riches of the Polish countryside lay spread out
before me. Field upon field of wheat and barley threaded with
the scarlet of poppies and the deep blue of lupins stretching
far across the plains to the distant horizon; acres of gently
rolling pastureland fringed with forests of pine and oak; the
pale, ethereal beauty of flax ready to be gathered and sent to
the great looms of Wilno; the homeliness of farms and peasant holdings, of earth reclaimed from the barren plains, tilled
and cultivated into fertility, of tomatoes ripening in the sun,
and wine-red cabbages still glistening with the morning's dew.
There had never been such a harvest within living memory,
said the old people. Even the fruit trees lining the road between Warsaw and Kielce were laden almost to the ground
with their burden of apples, cherries and plums; every cottage garden was a blaze of sunflowers and sweet peas.

Dawn was just breaking as I left the outskirts of Warsaw
and for the first few miles I drove through a silent world of
grey shadows and sleeping villages. Then the sun rose over
the distant hills dappling the long avenues of chestnuts and
beeches, and with much crowing of cocks and lowing of cattle
the country awoke to a new day.

As the morning wore on, the roads became crowded with
carts and farm wagons of every description. Some of them
were primitive affairs, rough wooden benches stretched across
creaking wheels, but the floor of each one had been lined
with fresh straw and covered with a carpet of rainbow hue
woven by the women of the household. The horses had been
brushed and groomed for the occasion with a care that might
have been expended on a racing stable, and tossed their heads
in the sunlight as though conscious of the significance of the

flowers and ribbons plaited into their glossy manes. The Polish peasant's most cherished possession is his horse, and in hard times he and the rest of the family will uncomplainingly go short of food so that they can afford its upkeep.

We passed through thriving manufacturing towns where looms were silent while the workpeople streamed out into the squares and cafés bent on the fullest enjoyment of the holiday, and through little villages decorated with flags and triumphal arches and gay with the laughter of peasants in traditional gala dress, for it was a great day in Poland. The twenty-fifth anniversary of the Legions.

I had promised to be present at the celebrations in Cracow, and as I drove over the familiar road from Warsaw my thoughts went back to that other time when the first Polish Legions had crossed the frontier, driven back the Russian troops and regained the land that had been stripped from us. Twenty-five years ago, though it seemed only yesterday! I could re-member almost every inch of the way. There had been no laughing crowds then, only men and women, silent and grimly determined, knowing that they were braving death or exile to Siberia, their eyes straining into the distance after the little force that had gone forth with my husband riding at its head to meet the Czar's picked regiments. Not even to ourselves would we admit how slender had seemed its chance of success that day. Ill-equipped, only half-trained, the cavalry on their sorry mounts, the infantry shouldering the old out-dated rifles which the Austrian Government had thought good enough for the Polish Franc Tireurs. The poorest and the shabbiest army in Europe, but the first that Poland had raised and sent into the field since the long past days of her splendour, and all our hopes were centred on it. Hour after hour we had waited for news in an agony of suspense, but none had come and so it had needed some resolution to carry out our plan. For it had been decided that I and one or two other women chosen to act as couriers and carry out various duties behind the lines, in order to release every available man for service in the field, were to cross the frontier later that day in the wake of the army. The more we had thought of it the less we had liked the prospect of that silent and empty road lying

ahead of us. The road that might lead to Siberia. But we
had had to face it, and just as the sun began to sink we, too,
had set forth into the unknown, a straggling little company
of civilians, looking neither heroic nor dignified, packed tightly
into a country cart with our baggage piled up around us.

So long ago! Yet I remembered it all so vividly that I
could still feel the hard outline of the printing press I had
taken with me in the cart digging into my knees. How we
had laughed at the funny picture we presented for we had
been young then, and the young can always laugh in the face
of danger and uncertainty. Our confidence had been justified
for at Słomniki we had come upon a small band of Legionaries
who had told us that the road ahead was clear. The Russian
patrols were in flight.

Yet as I sat back in the car I was glad that those days
of storm and striving were over and that I would not have to
live through them again. The intervening years had brought
peace and prosperity to Poland for the little army that had
gone forth to challenge the might of Russia had been victorious. The old frontier we had crossed twenty-five years ago
was abolished, the lands that had once lain beyond it on both
its borders were Polish territory again. Those fields of yellow
ripening wheat covered the scars of battle; the young men
and girls who waved to us from the orchards were the new
generation which had known neither the turmoil of the fight
nor the sweets of victory, for the freedom we had won so
hardly was their heritage. I turned my eyes from the glowing
plains to the monument standing by the roadside to the men
of the Polish Legions who had fallen in the war. On that anniversary morning they seemed no longer dead, they were still
one with the new Poland which they had created and never
lived to see.

My thoughts came back to the present when we reached
Cracow and drove through the wide market-place with its
mediæval arcades lined with shops selling a variety of wares.
There, too, were flags and decorations and holiday crowds;
business men and their families, soberly-attired clerks and
students from the University, Legionaries proudly escorting
admiring womenfolk in gala dress of embroidered bodices and

voluminous frilled skirts, young farmers stiff and self-conscious in their Sunday suits and tight boots, tall mountaineers from the Zakopane in their picturesque white breeches, sheepskin coats and sandals.

We drove through the noise and bustle of the market-place to the field just outside the town where the Legions, eighteen thousand men, had assembled to hear Mass which was celebrated at an altar erected on the grass. I looked at them as they knelt there in their ranks, dressed in their grey-blue uniforms, their Maciejowka caps held in their hands, their heads bowed in prayer, and that picture will be for ever engraved on my memory for never again was I to see them thus. White-haired men, veterans who had served under my husband, round-faced boys straight out of the military training schools, they knelt there, side by side, while the priest prayed for peace. An army born of sorrow and oppression and the longings of an enslaved people. An army that was so soon to know the bitterness of defeat.

The Mass was followed by a parade at which Marshal Rydz-Smigly took the salute and gave a short address. He spoke of the coming issue when Poland would have to make her choice between submission and the surrender of everything she had gained, and fighting for her independence however great the cost. He was answered in one voice from those thousands . . . "Let us fight." There was no bravado in the words, only an unshakable determination. I looked at the men who had uttered them and thought once again of those first Legions who had crossed the frontier twenty-five years before. Their faces, too, had reflected that same resolution. They had conquered and laid aside their arms believing that they had secured peace and the right to freedom for those who came after them. But it had only been a brief respite, for now another generation would have to take up the sword.

Several of our Ministers were present at the official luncheon which was held after the parade, although they were anxious to hurry back to Warsaw where the defence preparations were being put through with the utmost speed. Those who talked to me did not attempt to hide the gravity of the situation. None of them believed that there was any possibility

of averting war. Colonel Beck, who was still making ceaseless
efforts to negotiate with Germany, had repeatedly intimated
the willingness of Poland to arrive at a peaceful settlement
over the question of Danzig, but neither Hitler nor von Ribben-
trop had shown the slightest desire to compromise. It was obvious that Danzig was merely a pretext to cloak Hitler's designs,
and that even if we were prepared to cede it we could only
expect a repetition of Czechoslovakia's fate. The attacks upon
us in the Nazi press were almost identical with those launched
against the Czechs the year before, and the whole campaign
had evidently been planned on parallel lines.

Thus the stage was already set for that war with Germany
which had been my husband's constant dread, for he had
known it to be inevitable sooner or later. We had never had
any illusions as to the perils of Poland's position since her geographical situation made her a barrier to the expansion of both
Germany and Russia. Under my husband's guidance all our
foreign policy had been directed towards maintaining a balance
between these two Powers, but he never lost sight of the menace
behind Germany's insistent clamour for the return of Danzig
and the Corridor. Again and again he played for time to enable Poland to build up her defences. Even in the last years
of his life when his health was beginning to fail he rallied all
his energies to establish some lasting basis for peace, and with
the signing of the ten-year non-aggression pact with Hitler
he believed he had succeeded. After his death Marshal Rydz-
Smigly and Colonel Beck had pursued the same line of policy
and our relations with Germany had been friendly enough,
at least on the surface. Then without warning Hitler had revived the old demand for Danzig, a pretext for forcing us into
a war for which we were unprepared.

We had existed as an independent state for twenty-five years
only, and twenty-five years is a short time in the history of nations. We had had to struggle for our very survival and devote
such resources as we had to repairing the havoc of the last war,
not preparing for another. Without credit, without an exchequer, without at first even a currency, we had had neither
the money to pay for elaborate defences nor the time in which
to construct them. And now, with so much still left undone,

we were to be faced with a foe many times our strength.

Later that afternoon I drove up the hill to the ancient Wawel Castle, which has been the setting for so many of the scenes in Poland's stormy history, and the last resting-place of her kings and heroes. My husband's tomb is there and I wanted to visit it on this of all days.

Afterwards I went on to the terrace and stood looking down at the city spread out below encircled with its green girdle of trees. It was beautiful, I thought, seen thus with the rays of the sun blending its green and red roofs into a shimmering opal, gilding the spires and domes of its many churches. And for miles beyond it stretched fields and orchards interspersed with villages, clusters of lime-washed houses, blue and white and shining like alabaster.

From down below came the sound of music and the laughter of the crowds determined, because it was a holiday and the sun had never shone more brightly, to forget the menacing shadow of Germany. The city of Cracow has sent forth its sons to fight in many wars. It might have been just such a summer's day as this, I thought, in the year 1410 when they had ridden out to give battle to the Order of the Teutonic Knights at Grünwald. Now Poland would go to war again in a new cause that was still the old cause. But could history repeat itself in an age when the issue of battles was decided not by valour but by numbers and economic resources? I remembered how often my husband had deplored the modern system of mass warfare with its elimination of the personal element and its vast wastage of "cannon-fodder." Only a few days before I had been going through some of his papers which I was collecting for publication and had found these notes. . . .

"Mass strategy which has for its essential the uniting of millions of combatants in a constantly collaborating mass . . . gave no definite results in the World War. After various attempts it petered into immobility and impotence. Movement was overcome by the power of the trench and by the material forces which the adversaries were able to bring against one another. Consequently there was the struggle against the trench, the struggle against the obstacle to movement, the power of which had been so considerably restricted. . . . Every at-

tempt to break down the trench system and revert to a war
of movement was made at the price of sacrifices that were beyond computation enormous. . . . I remember Maréchal Pé-
tain one day showing me the blood-stained hills round Verdun
and telling me that nearly a million men were lying on those
shell-swept slopes. A million men gone without a trace, so utterly eliminated that often the very bones of the adversaries
were intermingled! . . . These were the gigantic hecatombs
necessary for the re-creation of a war of movement which has
been lost in the sombre gulf of the trenches! . . . I thought in
that moment that not only was war degenerating but that it
should disappear for ever. From the moment that movement,
once the main factor of victory, had been lost sight of, war became a foul absurdity, a savage method of exterminating men. I
could not think that humanity would be capable of passing
through such an experience again or that it would ever again
consent to upset the life of a whole country for the sole purpose
of feeding the trench! Strategy and tactics would with veiled
faces be reduced to taking account of the slain, and only from
this appalling balance could some idea of victory be obtained.

"I was happy in those days in the trenches because I thought
that war was destined to disappear and the nightmare which
had for so long hung over so many generations of men would
end by destroying itself. War would so profoundly degenerate
that through the very horror of this mechanical massacre of
men art, which could not make a lovely thing of war, would
rouse against war even its most fervent partisans. And so war,
with all its terrible consequences, would disappear. This would
be some consolation, too, for my country which had been so
conspicuous a victim of war!

"But at the same time I regretted the passing of the art which
has been part of the history of man for so many thousands of
years. The art of war which has produced so many great men,
men in whom the conception of brute force had forged so wonderful a power that out of the victories which they won were
born legends which have endured for centuries. Would humanity find some other means to simplify the historic art of
warfare? How many times in the mud of the trenches I asked
myself that question!" . . .

After the Fête of the Legions I went with my daughters to our little country estate at Kamienny Dwor. In the peace of the garden with its scent of lime trees and jasmine, surrounded by the simple life of the village, it was easy to forget the shadow of war. The harvest had just been gathered and in observance of a custom so old that it probably had its origin in some dim pagan rite, the first sheaf of wheat had been carried into the house with great ceremony and laid by the hearth, covering the sheaf of the previous year . . . to ensure twelve months of plenty and good crops.

Our return was celebrated with a harvest supper to which the farm labourers and tenantry had been looking forward for weeks, for the life of the Polish peasant is hard, and festive occasions are few and much prized. The proceedings opened with a procession to the house which was led by the youngest and prettiest of the girl reapers who presented me with a big bouquet of wheat and flowers, while the rest stood in a circle and sang the old traditional song of the harvest. Then we all repaired to the garden where tables set out under the trees were laden with pink home-cured hams, country cheeses of the dimensions of cartwheels, enormous pies and cakes and bowls of kissel, foaming jugs of home-brewed beer and cider. After plates had been emptied and more songs had been sung the village band—two violins, a double bass and a concertina— got out their instruments and struck up the first mazurka which was led by my daughter Wanda and the blacksmith. It was followed by a waltz, then a polka, then another mazurka, for the modern wave of jazz has not yet reached the Polish country districts and the name of Gershwin is still unknown. But the band were not conscious of any limitation in their repertoire and neither were the young people, for they danced on the lawn till the light of the stars was dimmed by the faint glimmer of dawn.

As I watched them whirling in the gay lilt of the mazurka, I thought that here was a part of the real wealth of Poland, these young peasants with their happy faces and strong bodies: these and the rich fertile lands that they tilled. But then there rose before my eyes the vision of the vast armament works of Skoda and Essen, of machines that were never silent, of mighty furnaces pouring out night and day their streams of molten iron and steel to be fashioned into weapons of destruction. Was this generation, too, doomed even as mine had been?

The days passed in a round of simple tasks and simple pleasures. We baked bread and cakes, made jam and preserved fruit and vegetables, brewed cider from the apples in the orchard and liqueurs from sloes and peaches.

There was great rejoicing when one of my maidservants was married from the house. Weddings, christenings and funerals are the main interests of the countryside and peasants from miles around arrived for the festivities. Every one in the district who had a cart of any description lent it for the occasion so that the procession to the church should be an imposing one, a good augury for the future.

After the bride had been dressed with due ceremony and escorted downstairs by all the young girls in the party, the chief bridesmaid presented the bridegroom with the customary bouquet of myrtle, and the procession was ready to start for the church. In that part of Poland there is a strict precedent for this stage of the proceedings. The bride has to remain standing at the front door and see that each guest in turn is seated in the long row of carts. When the last cart is filled she must ask formally: "Is all ready and in order?" and on receiving an affirmative reply she must give the signal for the procession to start. Only then can she take her own place in the cart.

Maria, my maid, being a stranger to the neighbourhood and knowing nothing of the custom, got into the first of the carriages and was driven off with her bridegroom before the guests had even begun to seat themselves, a flouting of tradition which spread dismay and confusion throughout the whole wedding-party. A wrinkled old grandmother came up to me shaking her head ominously. . . . "She has not fulfilled the order, Madame, and now her life will be disordered. I have seen it happen before and always trouble has come of it." . . .

I told her not to be so foolish and said that the poor girl could not possibly be blamed for breaking a tradition she had not even heard of. But I could see that she did not believe me.

Scarcely a week later I heard sobs and lamentations in the kitchen and went out to investigate. Maria, the bride, was seated on a chair, her apron over her head as she rocked herself to and fro in an abandonment of grief. Her husband had gone to join his regiment. He and most of the other young men in the village had received mobilization orders that morning.

I hurried to the telephone and put through a call to Warsaw. All lines were engaged and I had to wait several hours, but at length I managed to speak to one of our friends, a colonel, who later played an heroic part in the defence of Lwow. He could only confirm Maria's news. The Germans had concentrated immense numbers of troops along the frontier even though negotiations were still proceeding. The attack could be expected at any moment and we were mobilizing with all possible speed.

War was upon us.

CHAPTER II

MY DAUGHTERS and I decided to go back to Warsaw immediately for the various women's organizations to which we belonged would be needing all their helpers. We packed a few necessities and caught the next train. It was hours behind time and so crowded with reservists recalled to the colours and families whose summer holidays had been interrupted hurrying back to their homes that we despaired of getting into a compartment, until three soldiers gave up their seats to us and joined the long queues in the corridor. At every stopping-place the confusion increased as more and more people fought their way into the carriages. Most of them were bewildered by the sudden turn of events, asking questions which we could not answer for we knew no more than they. All sorts of rumours flew along the train. Some said that the Nazi troops had already crossed the frontier, others that the mobilization was purely a precautionary measure and that a treaty would be signed with Germany within the next twenty-four hours.

Every little country station had its group of recruits, stalwart young peasants bidding farewell to weeping wives and mothers, and at the big junctions we were held up for long waits in sidings while troop train after troop train flashed by on its way to the front. Where the main roads ran parallel with the railway line we saw more troops, columns of infantry on the march, detachments of cavalry, convoys of petrol lorries and ammunition wagons. Squadrons of aeroplanes roared over our heads and disappeared into the distance.

From many of the fields we passed the labourers had been called up before the harvest had been gathered and the corn was left half-cut, withering under the fierce sun. In others women and children were trying to get it in, loading their sheaves on to overflowing hand carts for most of the farm wagons had already been requisitioned. We saw long strings of them going towards Warsaw laden with provisions and fodder.

Everywhere there were signs of haste and emergency, of preparations still uncompleted, of a nation taken unawares. I remembered my husband's distrust of hurried mobilization and how he had always dreaded it for Poland, holding that in modern warfare the nation able to devote the time and the money to long and detailed preparation entered the field with an almost overwhelming advantage. Only a few years before he had written . . .

"The armed forces of all states remain during time of peace in an embryonic condition, more or less developed, never entirely completed. But from the moment the modern highly organized state proclaims mobilization it employs the whole technical, administrative and cultural services which exist in time of peace for non-military purposes. Therefore this immense technical machine—railroads, telephones—must interrupt its normal peacetime function and become for a while the monopoly of the army. The vast administrative organization built for the routine of peacetime—schools, factories, and various large establishments—must be taken over by the state for military purposes. Even the police must give up all their other functions in order to serve the cause of war.

"In a word the state must stop its whole peacetime activities until the army reaches the Front. Only in this way, by exploiting this technical machine, exploiting the legal obligations of the citizens, can the modern military force be mobilized. But it cannot be done in a hurry. It should take weeks, even months."

On arriving at Warsaw we drove straight to the small house where I have lived with my daughters since the death of my husband and which is situated within a stone's throw of the Belvedere Palace, our official residence during his years as Inspector and Minister of War. (But I must accustom myself to writing and thinking of this pleasant little house in the past tense for it has been completely demolished by a shell. Only the lovely old garden and the fruit trees are left standing to show that it was once a home.)

I lost no time in telephoning to the different Social Welfare organizations of which I was President. All of them were overwhelmed with work and in urgent need of helpers. The Communal Kitchens were especially over-taxed, for in addition to their normal peacetime function of feeding hundreds of old people, unemployed and children, they had to supply canteens for troops at all the principal stations. I made such arrangements as I could over the telephone and promised to be at my headquarters next day, and my elder daughter Wanda left to report for duty at the Red Cross.

The sun went down in a great globe of fire over Warsaw that evening. I walked through the gardens of the Belvedere Palace, empty now and rather desolate in its grandeur for it had been turned into a museum. I had never cared very much for its massive seventeenth-century architecture and I remembered that I had been full of misgivings when we had first gone to live there, and dreaded the receptions I should have to hold in its cold, formal salons. But our own rooms had been simple and comfortable, the long galleries had seemed less gloomy when my children played in them, and after a while it had become home.

I looked up at the room that had been my husband's cabinet de travail where he had so often sat working far into the night. Its lighted windows had always told me that he was awake. They were lighted now, bathed in a flood of gold, and for a moment I had the foolish fancy that he was still there, even though I knew that it was only the last shafts of the setting sun.

We awoke next morning in a city that had been transformed in the space of a few hours into an armed citadel. Anti-aircraft guns were set up in all the public parks, in private gardens; even the streets, hospitals and First Aid Posts were fully staffed, and while an endless chain of lorries carried troops to the Front the entire civilian population rallied to the task of defence. Those who had no definite duties volunteered for digging trenches. Elderly business men, students from the University, sturdy peasants and factory girls, society women who had never done a day's work in their lives, toiled side by side in the grilling heat, wielded spades and pickaxes till their hands were blistered and the sweat ran in rivulets down their faces. When one shift was exhausted another took its place and so they continued without interruption day and night. They worked silently and stoically and they worked well, for the deep earth trenches they dug proved to be the most effectual form of shelter in a bombardment such as we experienced and thousands of lives were saved by them.

The gay optimism of the past few weeks had given place to a fixed resolution, a great unity of purpose that spread throughout the city. Even the school-children marching through the streets on their way to dig trenches carried banners on which they had printed . . . "Death Rather Than Slavery to Germany." . . . Young as they were they understood the meaning of the words for they had played for as long as they could remember in a playground over whose gate was carved . . . "Laugh, children of Poland, laugh and be happy in that newborn freedom which your fathers never knew." But their banners were sadly prophetic for hundreds of them were killed by the German bombers.

At half-past six on the morning of September 1st we were awakened by the sirens. We dressed hurriedly and went to the nearest shelter, the trenches in the garden of the Belvedere, where we were joined by women and children from the neighbouring houses, gardeners and other employees of the museum and a few labourers who had been caught on their way to work. But although we waited for over an hour there was no sight nor sound of the raiders, and coming to the conclusion that the warning had been only a test we returned home. Just outside our door we met Marshal Rydz-Smigly's aide-de-camp.

"What was it?" I asked him . . . "A false alarm?"

"No," he answered heavily . . . "War." And told us that there had actually been a raid and that although our airmen had intercepted the enemy and driven them back from Warsaw several bombs had been dropped on the towns of Czestochowa and Lack.

After breakfast I went to the headquarters of the Welfare Organization where I found several helpers waiting for me. But we had only been there a few minutes when the sirens

warned us of another raid and we were forced to spend the rest
of the morning in the trenches. This time the enemy machines
succeeded in getting past our defences. The noise of the engines roaring through the clouds over our heads was punctuated by the ear-splitting crash of the anti-aircraft guns
firing from the corner of the square only a few yards away
from us. Then a volume of cheering from the crowds who,
ignoring the official instructions, persisted in remaining in
the street announced the arrival of our own fighters and the
enemy was driven off without having accomplished any serious
damage.

We left our shelter and dispersed for lunch, intending to
get through our arrears of work in the afternoon. But at half-
past two the bombers came over again, and again at four
o'clock. And after that again, and still again, always in waves
and in ever-increasing numbers. So like every one else in
Warsaw I had to reconcile myself to dividing my day between
frenzied activity in the short respite after the "All clear" had
sounded, when the whole city reverted to normal life and tried
to make up for the time that had been lost, and taking cover in
a variety of shelters. Sometimes it was in one of the public
trenches, sometimes the vestibule of a hotel or other big building. Frequently it was in the house of complete strangers who
extended their hospitality to me and to any other passers-by
who hurried in from the street as though it was the most
ordinary thing in the world. Once I remember taking refuge
in a teashop for nearly two hours during one of the worst
and most prolonged raids, and all that time the orchestra went
on playing through the terrific din and the people drank tea
and ate cakes as though they were unaware of anything happening outside.

The shortage of transport was one of the minor discomforts
to which we had to accustom ourselves. Every private car
which had not been commandeered was urgently needed for
the Red Cross or one of the other war organizations, taxis
were unobtainable because of the petrol shortage and the
majority of the motor buses were transporting troops. The
few which were still running and all the tramcars were so
crowded that it was practically impossible to get into them,

and after waiting an hour or more in vain one generally ended by walking to one's destination. As I had given over our own car to Wanda who was collecting supplies for the Red Cross I had to tramp for miles on that first evening of the war before I arrived home.

I had only been in the house a few minutes when the telephone rang. It was a call from the matron of the Home for crippled and tubercular children which I had founded in the suburb of Otwock, fifteen miles distant from Warsaw, and she had terrible news to give me.

The Nazi airmen, driven off Warsaw by our anti-aircraft fire and unwilling to return to their base without winning their spurs, had flown round the undefended suburbs and dropped several bombs at random. As they passed over the Home, flying so low that they only just cleared the housetops, the children who were out in the playing-field had stopped their game and waved up to them, not knowing that they were enemies. Their answer had been a bomb which had missed our house and fallen on the Children's Hospital next door, killing fifteen of the little patients and injuring many more.

This was one of the blackest incidents of the early days of the war but it was only the first of many, for the Nazi, true to the old German theory of "Frightfulness," began their campaign with the clear intention of breaking down the morale of the civilians, and ten mothers weeping over the mangled bodies of their children can do more towards accomplishing that end than the loss of an entire division in battle. So on the same principle the bombers visited Komarow, a peaceful little residential suburb of neat villas and well-kept gardens with a population composed of elderly retired people and the wives and children of Warsaw business men who were accustomed to spend week-ends there. It was completely defenceless, without even a public trench, for there had seemed no possibility of its ever being attacked. Yet on the second day of the war the Nazi airmen swooped down upon it like giant birds of prey. Unopposed they dropped twenty bombs on its neat little villas and machine-gunned women shopping and old men working in their gardens. By nightfall Komarow had become a place of mourning.

In the first week of the war the suburbs and small outlying towns suffered most severely, for the German bombers were repeatedly driven back from Warsaw by anti-aircraft fire and by our own fighters, though these latter were nearly always heavily outnumbered. Once I watched eight of our planes rout twenty-five of the enemy.

I was serving meals at one of the military depots a little distance from the Central Station when I heard the sirens. The raids had been almost incessant since early morning and as I could already hear the engines overhead I decided that it would be safer to stay where I was than to go out to the shelter. A moment later twenty-five aeroplanes came sweeping across the sky in close German formation, wing-tip to wing-tip, flying very high to keep out of the range of the guns. As they passed over the station they dived. The first bomb dropped . . . and missed its mark. Columns of dust and bricks flung high into the air showed that it had fallen on a house in the next street and a long tongue of flame shot skywards. The anti-aircraft guns boomed, puffs of smoke like white clouds rose into the blue sky and showers of shrapnel fell into the streets.

Then from across the city eight of our little fighter planes came roaring into action and engaged the enemy, driving a wedge through their close ranks. People ran out into the road forgetful of their own danger to watch the combat going on thousands of feet above them, as the opposing machines soared and dived in long graceful arcs, beautiful in movement as a flight of swans. Suddenly one of the bombers burst into flames and spun earthwards in a headlong dive and a moment later we saw trails of smoke coming from two others. Then the raiders wheeled round and with our fighters still in pursuit disappeared into the west.

There were many such successes in the early stages of the war before the German Air Force's overwhelming superiority in numbers broke down our resistance. Our pilots were as well-trained as the Nazis and were certainly not lacking in courage, but we had not enough machines for them to fly. Our anti-aircraft guns were of the best design and proved their worth by the heavy toll they took of enemy aircraft, but there were

too few of them. History has demonstrated again and again
that a nation's chances of victory in warfare depend not only
on her fighting men but on the money behind them, and of
money Poland had never had enough. From the earliest days
of our existence as an independent state we had been forced to
pinch and pare like a needy housewife and to practise petty
economies on a large scale. In opposition to Germany who
had for years devoted all her resources to rearmament and
whose exchequer was swollen by the confiscated funds of Austria and Czechoslovakia we were under a crippling handicap.

History will, I believe, find two main causes for our defeat.
Our poverty and the vast network of espionage with which
we were surrounded. It would be almost impossible to over-
estimate the importance of this factor.

In proportion to our population of thirty-five millions a
total number of 741,000 Germans residing in Poland did not
appear too serious to be reckoned with. But our real menace
came not so much from these acknowledged Germans as from
the hundreds of families avowedly Polish by naturalization
and by long residence but of German descent and wholly
German sympathies. Many of them had settled in Poland a
century, or even two centuries before, had intermarried with
Poles and had never even visited Germany. But so strong and
so persistent is Teutonic blood that when the crucial moment
came they betrayed without a qualm the land which had sheltered them and reverted to their far distant ancestry. This
was especially true of the younger generation, for the heart
of youth with its love for pageantry and its instinct for hero-
worship is fertile soil for the Nazi regime. So while the older
people among these German-Polish families would have been
content enough in the event of war to consider themselves as
Polish, or at least to remain passive in their pro-German sympathies, their sons were ardent Nazis filled with all the fire of
the Crusader, eager to be absorbed into the Reich. And in consequence there were bitter family quarrels and houses were
divided among themselves.

But from the ranks of these young Polish Nazis many of
Hitler's spies were drawn.

For some time before his death my husband had foreseen this danger of espionage, particularly where the army was concerned, for there were serving in it a number of officers and men drawn from these German minorities. He took the most stringent precautions to prevent information which could possibly be of use to an enemy from falling into their hands, and would never under any circumstances allow important documents and official correspondence to pass out of his own keeping even into the custody of his most trusted officers. When he was obliged to work late at night it was his custom to sleep on a camp bed in his office at the Inspectorate to avoid the necessity of bringing home his papers to the Belvedere, a distance of three minutes! The key of his bureau was always kept in his own pocket except when he was actually at work and then it lay on the desk before him within reach of his hand. But even so there was a steady leakage of official secrets, and at the time of his fatal illness he was engaged on plans for a comb-out of foreigners serving in the Polish forces. Unfortunately he did not live to complete them.

With the outbreak of war the potential danger of espionage developed into an acute menace, for the most vital secrets of our defences were betrayed to the Germans before the first shot was fired. The Nazi method has invariably been to first undermine the country which is to be attacked by propaganda and treachery from within, and Poland's mixed nationalities rendered her especially vulnerable to both these weapons. The Gestapo had its agents spread over the entire country in a vast organization which extended even to the humblest villages. These hundreds of spies, men and women in every walk of life, from professional men and even public officials of seemingly blameless loyalty, to workmen and labourers, had been maturing their plans for months in the separate localities to which they were assigned, and consequently from the very commencement of hostilities the whole espionage machine was functioning smoothly. Troop movements were reported, lines of communication cut and bridges blown up according to program. The exact position of each of our most carefully concealed air bases had been betrayed with the result that they were subjected to mass raids of German aircraft which destroyed most of the machines while they were on the ground.

Dozens of these spies were arrested in different parts of the country and brought before the tribunals. Usually they were people to whom no breath of suspicion had been attached. One of the principal organizations in Warsaw had its head-quarters in the house of a prominent business man whose family, though originally of German descent, had been resident in the city for nearly a century. An apparently simple old marble engraver who had practised his trade in a cottage outside the cemetery at Wilno for fifteen years was found on being put under arrest to have been the master spy controlling a score of Gestapo agents, both men and women, all of whom were engaged in furnishing information to the enemy.

The colonel of one of our cavalry regiments told me that whenever the division had taken up new positions at night spies in their own ranks had signalled their movements to enemy aircraft by means of flares. Two of his non-commissioned officers had actually been caught during a halt in the act of laying dynamite to destroy a bridge which the regiment would have to cross.

An officer on Marshal Rydz-Smigly's staff told me that a spy had caused disastrous confusion and delay during the most critical stage of the defence of Warsaw by posing as a Polish staff officer and diverting a whole trainload of ammunition which was on its way to the Front so that it ultimately reached German lines.

CHAPTER III

THE CITY of Warsaw has survived many wars. Time and again its name has been written in letters of flames across the pages of Poland's stormy history, and its people have a proud tradition of endurance. The old walls that had been pounded by the cannon of the Swedes in the 17th century stood firm under the assaults of Hitler's bombers. The streets that had become a shambles when the Russian General Suvaroff entered the city after the siege of 1794 and butchered twelve thousand of its citizens ran once again with blood a century and a half later, but the new generation of defenders resisted, even as their ancestors had resisted, to the end. So every day the toll of killed and injured increased as the bombs rained upon Warsaw.

Yet in spite of them the life of the city continued. Even when half the houses had been reduced to jagged stumps of bricks and mortar and smouldering wood business men still went to their offices, cinemas and cafés remained open and in hundreds of homes the ordinary routine went on. And every day Mr. S. Starzynski, the Mayor of Warsaw, broadcast his courageous message from the ruins of his city. For years he had devoted all his energies to its development, to beautifying its poorer quarters and abolishing its slums. Its destruction meant the destruction of his own life's work.

As the days passed the raids became more and more frequent until there were intervals of only an hour or even less between them. The only respite we could count on was between midnight and dawn. But very few people could afford to waste those four or five precious hours in sleep. Instead we worked frantically, making the most of every minute. The wounded were attended to, the dead buried, and ammunition factories were kept at full blast until the sirens sent every one hurrying to the shelters.

One of the bombs which caused the worst casualties fell

on the Eastern railway station. Our welfare organization
had a depot and kitchen there and I had intended to go on
duty that afternoon, but as I was leaving the house Wanda
asked me to wait for her. She and one of her friends were
also going to the station to deliver cigarettes and stores for
the Red Cross and she suggested that we might all drive
down together. The ten minutes' delay probably saved my
life for just as we were loading our packages into the car there
was another air raid warning, and we went over to the trenches
at the Belvedere, where we were obliged to remain nearly
two hours for the German planes kept returning to the attack
in relays.

While the raid was at its height there was a terrific explosion
and even from our shelter we could see clouds of dust and
great pieces of iron hurled into the air. The man standing next
to me tried to tell me something but I could not understand
him for the pandemonium of the anti-aircraft guns made speech
impossible.

At length, after what seemed interminable hours, the "All
clear" sounded. We went back to the house and began to
collect our stores again. The telephone rang and I went to
answer it. The call was from one of the helpers at our depot at the Eastern station. In a voice rendered absolutely ex-
pressionless by shock she asked me to come to the station
immediately and to bring a doctor if I could find one, and a
supply of morphia and dressings. A bomb had fallen on the
station. Sixteen of the women and girls on duty there had
been killed and the rest seriously injured. She and another
woman who had been cooking in an out-building at the back
were the only ones who had escaped. They had tried to telephone to several of the First Aid Posts but without success for
most of the important lines of communication had already been
cut by spies.

Wanda met me as I turned away from the telephone. I suppose she read disaster in my face for she asked only the one
word: "Where?" "On the Eastern station," I answered; "A direct hit. We have to find a doctor."

All the colour left her face, for among those on duty at
the depot had been several of our own friends, but she got

into the car without speaking and started up the engine. We passed through streets that were almost blocked by the wreckage of fallen buildings, strewn with tiles and bricks and broken glass and where the houses were still smouldering, filling the air with the acrid smoke of charred wood. Fire engines were drawn up in front of some of them and ambulance men were carrying out stretchers covered with white sheets, hiding that which had been the image of God defaced by the work of Man.

We drove past a block of offices, one of the finest modern buildings in Europe. A crowd of women and children were still sheltering there for it was considered to be the safest refuge in the city. But a few days later a 500 lb. bomb cut through its eight stories of granite and marble as easily as though it had been made of papier-mâché and levelled it to the earth. Nearly two hundred people were trapped in its cellars, but although firemen, aided by gangs of volunteers, worked desperately with cranes and crowbars trying to lift the vast mass of stone, not one was found alive.

We passed through one of the fashionable thoroughfares where shop fronts had been torn off and plate glass windows shattered. Furs and silk stockings and bales of stuff littered the pavement, and police stood guarding the wreckage of jewellers' shops. A picture dealer was wringing his hands over his scattered canvases. Women were stepping across the fallen doorpost of a cooked provisions store and waiting to be served. A café opposite had had one of its walls staved in but it had been patched up and a few old men were sitting at the tables drinking coffee and reading the newspapers. Farther on was a hotel with a hole in its side like a gaping wound through which broken furniture and tattered wallpaper protruded.

In some of the streets in the poor quarters of the town the bombs had dug great craters in the road and scarcely a house was left standing. The big block of workmen's model flats, of which we had been so proud that we always took visiting foreigners to see it, was razed to the earth. Whole families were patiently digging in the debris trying to rescue the few sticks and bits of furniture which were all that remained of their homes. An old woman was limping out of the bare husk of a house triumphantly waving an undamaged picture.

At last we found a doctor who was just returning home hollow-eyed and haggard after a long spell of duty at one of the hospitals. Although he had had no sleep for five nights he came with us immediately. But by the time we reached the station the ambulances had already been there and the injured had been removed to hospital, so there was nothing for us to do except to break the news to the relatives of those who had been killed. Among the dead were several little Girl Guides and the grief of the poor mothers was heartrending to witness.

In looking back I sometimes wonder how we lived through the nightmare of those days, yet at the time every one was calm. Even during the worst raids there was no sign of panic. I suppose that all of us discovered that there is a merciful limit to humanity's capacity both for suffering and for fear. You can be afraid up to a certain point. Once you have reached it peace descends upon you either because you draw upon some spiritual reserve of courage within yourself or because you become numbed into apathy and cease to react to emotion. So after the first hours of stunned horror you found that it was possible not only to endure, but even to accustom yourself to spending most of the day with death lurking in the clouds above you, herded in cellars and trenches that vibrated at each impact of falling masonry; to having your ears assailed waking and sleeping by a pandemonium of noise like all the forces of hell let loose; to seeing men and women mangled beyond recognition. You endured it not from any false heroics but simply because you had to. There was no escape from it. That realization and the work that had to be done by every one in the city kept our sanity.

To live under the present shadow of death is to understand the real meaning of life. In the first forty-eight hours of the war we shed our false values. Our needs were the primaeval needs of Man. Food, warmth and shelter. Political feuds and private quarrels were alike forgotten as people were drawn together by their common danger and sorrow. All that remained was our mutual responsibility in keeping going the daily life of the community. We shared whatever there was to share and our neighbour's trouble became our own. So when a house was wrecked every one in the vicinity ran out immediately the "All clear" had sounded to help its owner in salvaging what was left; people whose homes were still standing took in those who had not a roof over their heads; women huddled in the trenches in the chill dawn shared their fur coats with other women who had none; mothers whose babies had been killed in their cradles tried to dry their tears as they suckled the children of dead women. Every day the peasants left the comparative safety of their homes in the out-lying villages and ran the gauntlet of the raids to bring their loads of vegetables and provisions to the city. The trains continued to run though they were the special target of the bombers and the splintered wood hung in strips like ribbons from many of the wagons. Outside the principal stations great chunks of the railway lines were torn up by the bombs but gangs of platelayers went out to repair them, working day and night under a hail of machine-gun bullets from the Nazi planes. When one man was killed or wounded another came forward and took his place and the work went on without interruption until it was finished.

Centuries of warfare in which Poland has been the battle-ground of Europe have made us a constructive people, given us a heritage of tenacity and an instinct for repairing that which is broken. We have had so much practice. Our towns have been destroyed again and again in successive wars and patiently rebuilt as many times only to withstand the onslaught of another foe in another generation. But when the tumult of battle has passed there has always been some one to repair the havoc. So in Warsaw the smoke and dust of the bombs had hardly cleared away before there were people raking in the ruins, patching and mending houses that were like the jagged stumps of decayed teeth, making the semblance of a home though it might only be one room with a piece of tarpaulin stretched across it to hide the rent in the roof.

The actual measure of time ceased to be of much importance to us except where it marked the intervals between raids. One day was so like the next that I lost count of them until one morning I was awakened very early from the only sleep I had had for several nights by the insistent ringing of the telephone. The call was from one of our Generals, an old friend of my husband's, and he had rung up to beg me to leave Warsaw with my daughters immediately as the German Army was now only thirty kilometres from the city. I replied that we could not go on account of our work in the Red Cross but he explained that there would be no object in our staying as the Government had decided to evacuate the hospitals and all civilians who had not some urgent reason for remaining.

I woke my daughters and told them what I had heard and after discussing the position we agreed to go to our country house at Kamienny Dwor, which could easily be equipped as a hospital to accommodate some of the overflow of wounded evacuated from Warsaw. Then I called in my two servants and gave them the alternative of coming with us or returning to their homes. One of them, a peasant from Kamienny Dwor, chose to go back to her own village, the other crossed herself and said: "Whether I am killed by the Germans or not depends upon the will of God, but in this city I will remain, and I will look after the house if you will let me stay in it." And no argument could dissuade her.

We had arranged to go to Kamienny Dwor that afternoon but our plans were upset by the news that it was practically impossible to get there. For some unknown reason the Germans had chosen to make that peaceful and undefended part of the countryside a special object of attack. Their bombers had already wrecked several trains going there and made such havoc of the railway lines that further traffic was suspended for the time being.

We were discussing our best course when a distant relative of mine who was in Warsaw suggested that we should go to his home in East Poland. Several houses in the neighbourhood had already been requisitioned as Red Cross hospitals, his own among them, and helpers were urgently needed. This seemed an excellent plan for one of my nieces had a manor there and we could stay with her for the time being.

We started at seven the next morning, myself, my daughters, my sister and Anna, a young cousin who was expecting her first baby in a few weeks' time. She was very reluctant to leave Warsaw as her husband was serving in the army and she wanted to remain as near the Front as possible, but in the end we persuaded her to accompany us. We set out in two cars, taking with us only a small amount of personal luggage.

We had decided that it would be safer to drive to our destination than to go by train, for while the indiscriminate bombing of railroads had become an established fact there seemed no reason to suppose that the German pilots would waste their ammunition on what were obviously tourist cars filled with women. We were soon to discover our mistake for the drive which should normally have taken four hours took instead nineteen, and most of those hours were spent crouching in fields and in ditches, in barns and cowsheds by the roadside, anywhere that offered even a frail shelter.

We drove out of the city in a long file of cars, lorries and carts packed with women and children, with here and there a few old men and boys too young for military service. The pathetic, helpless procession of a civilian populace in flight, without the dignity of a retreating army. Sad-eyed mothers and crying babies huddled together with their homely belongings piled round them, sewing-machines, perambulators, pots and pans, crates of chickens.

We were a straggling, unwieldy caravan, and the going was slow. Towards the middle of the morning we realized that we were hungry. "We'll stop at the next village and get some milk," I said. But when we reached it there was no one to sell us any. We stopped outside farmhouses and cottages but not a soul was in sight. The market square and the little inn were deserted. Then we remembered that there had been no sign of life at the last village, nor at the one before it. The peasants with the age-old instinct of a primitive people had fled to the safety of the woods leaving everything behind them, the cows unmilked and the loaves burning in the oven.

We continued on our way wondering at their sudden flight,

but our questions were answered almost before we had voiced them. Out of the cornflower blue sky came the drone of engines and a German squadron swooped down upon us. I heard the sharp crackle of machine-gun fire followed by pitiful sobs and shrieks from the cars behind us. A second later and the planes were directly above us, flying only a few feet over our heads so that we could see every detail of their markings. The guns crackled again and again, and the driver of one of the cars just ahead of us threw up his hands and fell forward over the steering wheel. The car plunged forward violently and overturned into the ditch. A chauffeur behind sprang from his seat and ran to release the people trapped inside it, only to be shot down before he had even reached it. From somewhere in the rear a horse bolted and raced wildly down the road, missing our car by only a few inches. We could see pale terrified women clinging to the benches of the cart behind it. Then the aeroplanes were over us again and we caught glimpses of arrogant faces looking down at us, laughing at the confusion they had caused. I heard my chauffeur, an old soldier who had served with my husband, muttering through clenched teeth . . . "Mother of God, if only I had even a rifle!" When the planes veered sharply and began attacking the head of the line of cars he drew to the side of the road and opened the door. "Quick, Madame. Make for the fields and lie down in the ruts. It's your best chance." On our left was a field of potatoes. The high-growing green shoots would at least afford some sort of screen and there was a thicket at the far end. If we could reach it we would be fairly safe. At any rate nothing could be worse than sitting still in an open car sprayed by bullets. So I sprang out calling to the others to follow me and we leapt over the ditch and started to run across the field. The occupants of the other cars behind copied our example and soon the field was full of women and children running and stumbling among the rows of potatoes.

A girl in a silk dress caught one of her high-heeled shoes in a rut and fell over sobbing with a sprained ankle. Two sturdy peasant women grasped her under the arms, lifted her up and half carried her between them. An old man with a child staggered suddenly, sagged slowly to the ground and lay very still. A nun bent over him for a moment, then took the child from his arms and ran on with it.

Then once again we heard the roar of the returning squadron and a woman near me, winded and gasping, began to scream like a hare when the hounds are just behind it. I called to her to lie down but she took no notice so I caught hold of the two children she was dragging by the hand and pulled them down beside me. One of them, a little girl of three, laughed delightedly at this new version of "Hide and Seek" and attached herself to me for the rest of the day.

We lay flat on our faces among the potatoes for what seemed an eternity, though actually I suppose it was only ten minutes, while the airmen returned to the attack again and again, sweeping the field with their machine-guns. Then they seemed to tire of their sport and soared away into the distance.

We got back into the car and started on our journey again. We pushed forward for another ten miles and then the Nazi airmen returned to the chase and again we had to take cover, this time in a deep ditch at the side of the road. Fortunately it was dry for we had to lie for half an hour among the twigs and fallen leaves.

At the third raid we were more lucky for we were on the outskirts of a fair-sized town and the anti-aircraft guns were in action. We stopped outside one of the first houses and the owner very kindly beckoned us in and insisted on our remaining there until the "All clear" sounded. Then we went on again despite her offers of hospitality for we were anxious to arrive at our destination before nightfall, and though it was afternoon we had not covered even half the distance.

Our next shelter was a cowshed and the next after that a granary which we shared with some peasant women. One of them stood at the open door oblivious of her own danger, shaking her fists fiercely in the air and screaming curses at the pilots. An old woman with her told us that both her children had been killed by a bomb the day before.

There were three machines in that raid and the airmen contented themselves with wrecking the lovely old sixteenth-

century village church, setting fire to the houses and killing
and injuring ten people. Then they flew off in the direction
of Warsaw and left us to continue our journey. At the end
of another half hour's driving, which was necessarily slow
because of the stream of cars on the road, we heard the roar
of aeroplanes once again and on rounding a bend we saw great
clouds of smoke and flame ascending. An incendiary bomb
had set fire to an entire village of wooden houses and the
raiders were still circling round machine-gunning the fleeing
inhabitants.

To our right was a dark belt of green and we saw running
figures making for its shelter across the fields, so we followed
their example and a few minutes later found ourselves in the
peace and silence of a pine forest. Here at least was sanctuary.
The tall tops of the fir trees screened us more effectively than
any man-made shelter, and we sank down on the ground too
exhausted to go any further or even to talk.

I had closed my eyes but the snapping of a twig made me
open them again. A little boy was standing observing us with
round-eyed wonder. Presently he gave a shrill call and two
women came up and scrutinized us in their turn. Evidently
the result of their examination did not satisfy them, for suspicion was written on their faces and although we could not
hear what they were saying we caught a murmur of German
"spies."

Then one of them disappeared to return with one of the
forest keepers who asked us for our papers. I explained that
we had left them in the car. Where was the car? On the road
behind us. At this there was shaking of heads and obvious
disbelief. My suggestion that one of us should go back and
fetch the papers not only met with no approval, but was
obviously considered a ruse to gain time . . . perhaps to bring
up reinforcements.

I was quite prepared to be put under arrest, when to my
relief an officer arrived upon the scene and immediately
recognized me and apologized. Then he explained that there
had been so many spies in the neighbourhood that the small
landowners and peasants had organized themselves into
bands in order to round them up. They had actually caught

a number, several of whom had been dropped by parachute from German planes, while others had been found in the very act of signalling the Nazi airmen. Consequently all travellers who could not produce proof of their identity were being detained and handed over to the local police. He advised us on no account to leave our papers behind us again as the forest was full of these armed bands of peasants and we would in all probability be stopped several times before we arrived at our destination.

By that time dusk had fallen and we decided to continue on our way for the road now lay through deep forests which the raiders could not penetrate. The tranquil silence of those long shadowy avenues of trees with only an occasional slumbering village to mark the presence of humanity was indescribably restful after the turmoil of that day.

It was 2 A.M. when we arrived at my niece's house, tired and dishevelled and very glad to go to bed.

CHAPTER IV

THE FIRST glimmer of dawn was beginning to lighten the sky when I went up to bed. I slept in a room that was full of the fresh fragrance of tobacco flowers and verbena from the garden below and my lullaby was the gentle murmur of the river and the soft rustling of branches in the wind. In that quiet house I could almost imagine that the last few days had been only a terrible dream. Yet war had descended even on that peaceful countryside. My niece had warned me that I would be awakened by the German bombers flying over the house on their way to attack the town thirty miles north. There were three raids every day, timed with clockwork regularity, at seven in the morning, midday, and five in the afternoon. Up to the present no bombs had been dropped on the village, but its immunity seemed to have been more a question of luck than anything else, for the sleepy little hamlet on the opposite bank of the river had been reduced to ashes only two days before by a squadron returning to its base. But I was too tired to be disturbed even by the prospect of a raid, and only pulled the blankets over my head when I heard the roar of engines.

My niece's house, which was one of those enormous patriarchal homes of the old Polish country families, was full of women, all of whom were engaged in some form of war work, either in the Red Cross or on the land for nearly every able-bodied man in the district had been called up. So there was consternation in this feminine community when some village women returning late from the fields caught a spy in the act of laying dynamite on the railway bridge which spanned the river and which was of considerable importance since the line was used for the transport of troops and ammunition to the Western Front. The man, who was dressed in the habit of a monk, was in possession of a revolver, but the strong peasant girls

42

threw themselves on him before he had time to use it, and after disarming him bound him with a length of rope and led him into the village to be delivered over to the old local policeman. When he was taken before the authorities in the neighbouring town he was found to be a Nazi who had worked in a factory there for some years. Sewn into the folds of his habit was a chart of the district on which all the important points of communication had been marked.

In the meantime a deputation from the village came up to my niece's house to report the attempt on the bridge and ask for advice. It was obviously no longer safe to leave it unguarded and as it was just at the foot of our garden we undertook to patrol it until the military authorities could be notified. So with the aid of two boys, we collected every available gun in the village and formed ourselves into a sentry party. Then we divided our numbers so that two of us were always on duty night and day.

At about six o'clock on the second evening of our vigil I handed over my rifle to the young cousin who came to relieve me and joined my niece in the garden. It was one of those golden, mellow days of September and the countryside was wrapped in the calm of the Sabbath. Groups of women in their best dresses stood gossiping at the cottage doors, a few old men were fishing on the river bank, and from the meadow adjoining our garden came the laughter of village children rounding up the cows before driving them home.

I was half reading, half dozing when suddenly I heard what sounded like a tremendous peal of thunder echoing from the other side of the valley. Yet there was not a cloud in the sky nor any sign of a storm. I looked over questioningly at my niece. She too had turned in the direction of the sound and her face was pale and set as she answered . . . "The Germans are bombing the next village." As she spoke there was another explosion and after that several more.

All that day the squadrons had not once flown over us. We had waited in suspense divided between the conviction that we should hear them sooner or later and the faint hope that they might have changed their route. Evidently they had, but our hearts sank as we listened to the crash of the bombs, thinking

of the pretty village only three miles away and the fate that
had befallen it.

The last of the explosions had been succeeded by a fairly
long period of silence when all at once we heard the drone of
engines right overhead and nine machines came sweeping down
upon us. As usual they were flying very low. We had barely
time to spring out of our chairs and throw ourselves flat on the
ground when the first bomb fell sending up clouds of dust and
just missing one wing of the house. At the other side of the
lawn was a thick clump of bushes, a poor enough shelter but
better than nothing, and we ran for it. We reached it but
with not a fraction of a minute to spare before the planes
were over us again. We heard the spatter of machine-gun
bullets and the snapping of branches only a few feet away
from us. Seven or eight times they skimmed past us shooting
into the trees, missing us by what seemed a miracle. Then the
airmen left us to circle low over the meadow. We could only
look on helpless and sick with horror while they trained their
machine-guns on the children there who were too paralysed
with fright even to throw themselves down. Several of them
were killed before the bombers swept onwards to carry death
and destruction to the village. After they had set fire to the
fifteenth-century wooden church and the little houses clustering round it, and buried the old miller and his wife beneath the
wreckage of their water mill, they departed on their way
leaving behind them silence broken only by the weeping of
women.

I was preparing to go to bed that night when my niece came
to my room and begged me to leave her house since it could
no longer be considered even tolerably safe. The German pilots
were never satisfied with a single raid, she reminded me. Even
the humblest village, unless it had been completely destroyed,
usually received its second baptism of fire. In all probability
they would return to-morrow.

If I had been the only one concerned I might have answered
that I had been used to taking risks all my life, and that it
was rather late in the day to change my way of living, but
there remained the question of Anna whose child might be
born at any time and who ought to have more skilled attention

than the ministrations of the old peasant woman who had
assisted at the births of the entire villages for the past fifty
years. So we decided to go on to Wilno and, since night was
the safest time to travel, to start immediately. After an un-
eventful drive we arrived just in time to see the sun rise over
the towers and steeples of the beautiful old University city.

At Wilno the war seemed so remote that it would have
been almost possible to forget it. The colleges were being
aired and repainted in preparation for the autumn term. Every-
one we met talked of the usual topics of local interest, the
new appointments at the University, the crops, the prospect
of increased taxation. We heard that the German airmen had
flown over the city in the first days of the war and had dropped
one or two bombs but only on the aerodrome, and since then
all our machines had been removed. There had been no repetition of the raids and by the time we arrived in the city life
had reverted to its normal leisurely tempo. Our only echo
from the war zone reached us spasmodically in news brought
by men passing through on their way from one part of the
Front to another.

One afternoon I went to visit a friend, the wife of a colonel
in an infantry regiment, and found her in great distress. She
had had no news of her husband since the outbreak of war, until
that morning when a captain in his regiment had returned to
Wilno. He had told her that the battalion had been practically
annihilated in an engagement with the enemy tanks and that he
feared the Colonel and most of the other officers had been killed.

While I was trying to comfort her we heard a car draw up
outside the house and instinctively glanced out of the window.
With an exclamation . . . "It's my husband's chauffeur . . ."
My friend ran to the front door. I followed her. Outside
stood the battered wreck of what had once been a big limousine.
Not a vestige of paint remained upon it and only the bare
skeleton of a body. The mudguards had been torn right off,
there were great dents in the sides and strips of jagged wood
hung crazily from apertures that had evidently been windows.
Never had I seen or even imagined a car in such a sorry state.
Yet the engine was still chugging valiantly. A stolid young
soldier got out and saluted us. There were rents in his

overcoat and his face was pale and streaked with grime but he handed over a large parcel as casually as though he had just returned from an errand in the town.

"I came to fetch some clean linen for the Colonel, Madame" . . . he said . . . "This is dirty, so I brought it home to be washed."

After he had had a meal he told us his story. The Colonel had not been killed but had joined another battalion. Before going up the line with it he had told his chauffeur that he would be unable to take the car, and advised him to abandon it. This the man, who had been his personal chauffeur before the war, was most unwilling to do and had begged to be allowed to drive the car home. The Colonel had warned him that it would be practically impossible since he would have to cut through the enemy lines, but finally he had consented to his making the attempt. Incredible as it seemed he had actually got through, forced his way between the German lines at top speed, under heavy fire from the tanks. The car was literally riddled with bullets but by some miracle he had escaped without a wound. He seemed quite surprised when we praised him for his courage . . . "But you would not have had me leave the car, Madame?" he said . . . "I had to bring it home safely."

It appeared to give him immense satisfaction when that poor ghost of a car was restored to its own garage, and after collecting another parcel of clothes for the Colonel he went to join a train leaving for the Front.

Our life in Wilno during that first three days had the calm of an oasis after our experiences in Warsaw and at my niece's house. Although the University was of course closed for the vacation the Principal had returned and placed at our disposal one of the professor's houses within the precincts of the old building. To me Wilno will always be especially dear, not only for the charm and beauty of the mediæval city but because of its associations with my husband. He loved every stone of it. . . .

"One of the most lovely things in my life had been Wilno, my native city" . . . he wrote. . . . "How often when I was in prison I thought of Wilno and longed for Wilno, that dear city, full of so many memories. All that is beautiful in my life has been touched by Wilno: there I heard the first words of love, the first words of wisdom; all my childhood and my boyhood were rounded by these hills."

When he restored the old Polish University which had been suppressed by the Russians he realized the dream of his lifetime. His entire income as Marshal was devoted to its endowment; he used to deny himself many small luxuries to augment it. And I too grew to see Wilno through his eyes.

Generations of scholars had left the imprint of their own tranquillity of mind on our simply furnished little rooms, and as we had many friends in the city the time passed quickly. But those were the last days of peace that Wilno was to know.

At ten o'clock on the Saturday morning we heard the wail of the sirens and a few seconds later the Nazi airmen came swooping over the city. In the space of less than five minutes they wrecked the railway station, and set fire to several houses. Then like a flight of birds they were gone. But no sooner had the startled populace left their shelters and begun to attend to the injured and clear away the wreckage than they were back again, and this time, emboldened by our obvious lack of defences, they had their will of the city, flying low and sweeping the streets with their machine-guns. They shot the mourners in a funeral procession and the women waiting in a queue outside a baker's shop. They shot old men sitting in the garden of an almshouse and a group of boys playing football in a field by the river. They had time to shoot a great many people in the five hours during which they kept returning again and again to Wilno with intervals of only a few minutes between each raid. It was after three o'clock in the afternoon when at length we heard the "All clear." . . .

I went out almost immediately for I was due to go on duty at the Red Cross and I knew that I should have to walk there. Getting a taxi would be out of the question. Wherever I went I saw the terrible harvest of the raid, for although every ambulance in the city was out in the streets there had not been time to take all the dead and injured to hospital.

Two Red Cross men were carrying a stretcher out of a garden. On it lay a little girl, lovely in death as one of Della Robbia's angels. She had been killed by a machine-gun bullet but her face was smiling and untroubled and in her arms she still clasped a doll. A soldier helped to lift her into the ambulance. As it drove away he stooped to pick up something in the gutter. He held it out in the palm of his rough hand, and I saw that his eyes were full of tears. It was a doll's shoe.

"I've got children of my own," he said huskily, "but I'm glad I'm going back to the Front to-day. I've been in the Army since I was a boy and I've seen plenty of war. But this is different. I reckon you would never get accustomed to it."

As I walked on I thought of his words. Surely it would only be wiping out centuries of evolution that men and women could ever accustom themselves to this wholesale murder of the weak and helpless since it represented the triumph of every evil instinct which Humanity has taught itself to conquer!

A little farther on I came upon a knot of peasant women gathered round a proclamation which had been pasted on a door. I stopped to read it. It was a crudely-worded boast that as the Virgin of Czestochowa had already favoured Hitler, so also the Virgin of Wilno would bless his cause and that the German troops would be in Wilno in time for Mass at noon on the following day.

I explained to the women that it was Nazi propaganda, for in their ignorance they were greatly distressed. The Virgin of Wilno is known and venerated throughout Poland, and this cynical exploiting of the faith of a simple and devout people was typical of the Nazi mentality.

The next day, the fateful Sunday of September the seventeenth, passed in an atmosphere of almost unbearable suspense. We were prepared for more air raids, but they did not come. And from morning until evening we waited in vain for any news from outside the city. All communications had been cut without our knowing it. Only at night we heard the truth, and then we could not bring ourselves to realize it. The Russians had crossed the frontier.

For the first twenty-four hours the wildest rumours and conjectures flew about for many believed with tragic optimism that a secret military treaty had been signed with Russia and that Stalin's troops had entered Poland as our allies and were on their way to the Western Front. It was even said that the tanks preceding them were supplies sent by Great Britain and France who were delivering them to us over the Russian frontier. This unfortunate theory originated at the very frontier and was responsible for the fact that the Soviet Army met with no resistance of any sort. All telephone lines to the Polish headquarters having been already cut by spies, the officers responsible for guarding the frontier in the ordinary way, none of whom were of very high rank, were afraid to take the initiative in view of the mysterious rumours of Russian aid which had been carefully circulated among them. Confused and bewildered by the sudden turn of events they ordered their own troops not to fire on the Soviets with the result that the invaders found all barriers removed and no one to challenge them except a few peasants who hailed them as their defenders.

It was only on the Monday that officials in Wilno took command of the situation, rallied the dazed frontier regiments and proclaimed the Soviets as enemies, but by then valuable time had been lost. Polish troops rushed to this new Front, wearied as they were with repelling the German advance, fought with desperate courage, but they were hopelessly outmatched both in numbers and in mechanism, and the Russians continued their advances, sweeping all before them.

With the Soviets alone we could have reckoned. We had beaten them before and would have done so again. Against Germany alone we could, I believe, have held our own until our Allies were able to give us tangible aid. But in the face of that ruthless combination we were powerless. Our defeat was inevitable.

.   .   .   .   .

The guns of Stalin's advancing Army were thundering in the distance on that September evening two days later when we

left Poland and crossed the frontier into Lithuania. I had insisted on remaining in Wilno until the last moment, and even
when the car stood waiting for us at the door I was tempted
to send it away. But the Governor of the city had urged me
to go, for, as he said, the wife and daughters of Joseph Pilsudski
could hope for no mercy at the hands of the Soviets. Two of
my husband's brothers had already been arrested. I had spent
many months in a Russian prison and I was not going to let my
daughters risk the same experience. So we obtained visas and
packed just such few necessities as we would require on the
journey, for the Governor had warned us to travel with the
minimum amount of luggage. But when I wanted Anna to
come with us she refused.

"I cannot go. I must stay in Wilno. Perhaps I shall be able
to leave later." "But the Russians will be in the city in a few
hours" . . . I said. "I know," she answered quietly . . . "but
at least there are doctors and hospitals here, and if I come with
you where will my child be born?"

I thought that the question must surely be as old as the human race itself, for she was the eternal mother, caring nothing
for her own danger but only for the giving of life. Men might
make wars and sweep away frontiers, I thought; nations might
rise and fall; the world might be shaken to its foundations.
Yet as long as humanity survived women would continue to
ask the same question and to safeguard the future of those
yet unborn, even in the midst of death and destruction. But
I realized, too, that she was wise in her decision. She would be
safer in Wilno than as a refugee in flight across Europe, for
we had no definite plans and did not even know to what country we were going. So we left her there in the city and my sister
remained with her.

The evening shadows were beginning to close in when we
crossed the frontier into the friendly Lithuanian territory.
As I looked back for the last time on the rolling plains and dark
forests of Poland I thought that the past twenty years must
surely have been only a dream of freedom. The land that we
had so hardly regained was lost to us once more, the long
and bitter fight had been in vain. All that we had built up
in those slow, patient years of toil and hope and planning

had been destroyed. We had thrown off our fetters for a brief while but only to be bound anew.

The roads into Lithuania were black with retreating troops. We passed whole regiments of infantry trudging along through the dust, almost stumbling with fatigue, cavalry on weary, sweating horses, hundreds of wounded evacuated from the hospitals in ambulances and lorries, even on farm wagons. And then came a crowd of refugees, wives and children of Wilno business men, peasants in market carts, factory workers on foot. The first inn across the frontier was so full that we could hardly get inside it. Every room had been taken, people were sleeping in bathrooms, in storerooms and pantries, even on the stairs. Whole families were camping out in the courtyard with their possessions piled round them. They were dazed and bewildered by the unexpected turn of events and by the complete absence of news (for the brave Wilno and Baranowicze radio had at last been silenced); many of them did not know whether they were fleeing from the Germans or the Russians.

We were reconciling ourselves to the prospect of spending the night in the car when the landlady of the inn, who was a Polish woman, very kindly gave up her own room to us. It was not much bigger than a cupboard, but she made up two small beds and on these the three of us slept.

While we were waiting for it to be got ready some of the people in the courtyard who had heard my name drew near to talk to me, simple working men who wept openly when they spoke of my husband. . . . "Ah, Madame, if our Marshal had been alive this would never have happened. All would have been well!" Their childlike confidence in him was profoundly touching. He had so often called them "my children."

I was turning away to hide my own tears when an old man came and kissed my hand . . . "I was one of the first to serve under the Marshal" . . . he said proudly . . . "I was with him when he formed his first troop and I followed him all through the Russian campaign . . . Poland was victorious then, Madame, and the day will come when she will be victorious again. Even though I may not live to see it these will" . . .

and he laid his hand on the shoulders of the child who stood beside him.

His faith comforted me. I remembered that my husband had so often said . . . "To be vanquished and yet not surrender, that is victory. . . ."

.   .   .   .   .

The next morning we continued our journey through Lithuania where we found a state of feverish unrest. The Government, uncertain of Russia's intentions, had ordered immediate mobilization and the city was full of troops, both Lithuanian and those of our own retreating army who were endeavouring to reorganize their ranks. Streams of refugees pouring over the Polish frontier besieged the foreign legations and consulates in Kovno endeavouring to get news of their relatives. Many of them had spent the night in the parks and squares, even slept under archways and on doorsteps. Red Cross workers went round among them distributing soup and bread. Every hour the crowds and confusion seemed to increase and as we could achieve nothing by remaining there we decided to go on to Riga.

But in Riga, too, there was no hope of any permanent sanctuary for the Estonian Government had been thrown into apprehension by Stalin's demands, and the decision between peace and war hung in the balance. The Polish Minister there advised us to go straight to Stockholm as soon as possible and to travel by air. There was, he explained, an air service to Sweden which had not yet been cancelled but it was extremely difficult to get places. He would apply for them immediately for us.

Half an hour later we received the welcome news that there had been a last moment cancellation and three seats were available in an aeroplane which was leaving for Stockholm in less than an hour!

We had so little luggage with us that packing was only the work of a few minutes and we arrived at the aerodrome with plenty of time to spare. But when I went into the office to book our seats and register I discovered to my dismay that

the machine belonged to a Swedish-Soviet line and that the
pilot was not Swedish as we had been given to understand, but
a stalwart young Russian. If he guessed our identity he would
most probably consider it worth while to take the aeroplane
out of its course and land us on Soviet territory! However, it
was too late to draw back and I consoled myself with the re-
flection that as we were certainly not safe in Estonia, which
was faced with war or vassalage to Stalin, we were justified
in taking the risk. But I knew no peace of mind until we had
actually landed at the aerodrome in Stockholm.

The British Minister in Stockholm showed us the greatest
kindness from the moment of our arrival and made arrangements for us to travel to England in a special aeroplane. Only
the previous day a machine flying on the regular air service
had been chased and fired at by German airmen and a passen-
ger had been killed. Even as it was our journey was not without adventure for after we landed our pilot told me that at one
stage he had been pursued by a Nazi plane and had only managed to evade it by climbing into the clouds.

So at length on a calm and lovely morning I looked out
of the cabin window and saw far below me the gentle slopes
of the English Downs. They were rather like the hills of that
other land which I had left, I thought, that land which held
the memory of everything that was most dear in my life. For
the first time since leaving Warsaw I had leisure to think of
the future, to realize that I was an exile, without a home or
country and that the road ahead was dark and insecure. But
then I remembered that I had never set much value on security, perhaps because I had never known it in those years
when my husband and I journeyed from place to place, wan-
derers and fugitives, uncertain even of what the next day might
hold for us.

And so I stepped out on to the soil of that England of which
he had so often spoken, the country which had given him
shelter, and which had always represented to him freedom, and
courage came back to me.

PART TWO

★

LOOKING BACK

CHAPTER V

"WHEN ONE is born a Pole one must of necessity be born a patriot." My grandmother said that so often that the words imprinted themselves on my childish memory long before I understood their meaning. Not that I gave them any serious consideration in those days for I was still at that happy age which is concerned only with concrete facts. They slipped somewhere into the background of my consciousness to join an array of other incomprehensible things which had been vaguely wondered at and stored away. There was, for instance, the problem of why I had to hide my Polish lesson books and only bring them out in secret instead of going to school like other children. And why I might not speak to the little girl who lived in the house at the opposite side of the square even though I met her every Sunday walking between her parents in the Public Gardens. She was a pretty little girl with flaxen hair like my doll and we always smiled at one another, but when I told my aunt that I should like to play with her she said, "No" . . . very sharply and hurried me along.

"But why not?" I persisted, tugging at her hand.

"Because she is Russian and you are Polish. Now do not ask any more questions."

She was usually so gentle and indulgent that I was surprised into silence. But after a while I began to establish a link between these incomprehensible things.

I was born in that part of Poland which was under Russian rule, in Suvalki, a quiet little provincial town, undistinguished by history, consisting principally of one long street, pitted by deep ruts which were the despair of the Mayor because money for repairing them was always promised and was never forthcoming, and bordered by beech trees screening the neat rows of low-built white houses.

The town was one of the Russian Government centres and pride of place was given to the barracks occupied by two Russian Cavalry regiments and to the group of villas clustering round it which housed the officers' wives and families, and various Government officials. Dominating the whole was the Russian Church surmounted by its large cross of crystal, which appealed to my childish eyes as an object of great beauty as it sparkled in the sunlight.

Except for strictly official matters there was no contact between the Russian and the Polish communities. The Russians had their own Casino, held their own dances and concerts, and amused themselves in their own fashion, and we did the same. Even on spiritual ground there was no meeting, for while we were Catholics they were of the Greek Orthodox faith and therefore their religious festivals were held at different times from ours. The few yards which separated us might have stretched over a bottomless chasm, which indeed they did. A chasm wherein was buried the accumulated grief and bitterness of centuries of oppression.

But these distinctions did not shadow the happiness of my childhood for I accepted them as a mysterious but evidently essential part of my world.

My parents are enshrined in memory as dim figures for they died within a few months of one another when I was ten years old. My father was a dreamer, unpractical and artistic. He was passionately fond of music and his image evokes long slender fingers wandering over the yellow keys of the old piano in the salon. My mother I remember most vividly in a grey silk dress seated before the big mirror in her bedroom, trying on a new hat which was covered with flowers, while I stood behind her lost in admiration. She was a beautiful woman, but her health and vitality were sapped by the incessant routine of child-bearing. When she died, still under thirty, she had brought into the world twelve children of whom only five survived, myself, three sisters and a brother. I was the second from the eldest, was christened Alexandra and always called Ola.

We lived, the whole family of us, after the good old Polish patriarchal fashion, at my grandmother's house which was dominated by her forceful personality and iron will. She was a despot whose rule had been undisputed since the death of her husband many years before. None of us dreamt of opposing her, not even my father who used to take refuge in silence when worsted in an argument with her—which was usually the case. To my mother she was kind and indulgent because she was scarcely ever well, was easily reduced to tears, and it was not good for her to be upset. Aunt Maria, the unmarried daughter, who completed the generation of our elders, had long before been crushed into colourless submission. She was a gentle spinster, domesticated and affectionate, with a soft voice, kind mild eyes like a Madonna, and great braids of hair which she wore coiled round her head. It was typical of her that Grandmother had chosen her style of coiffure for her when she was sixteen and that even at sixty she had not changed it. She was one of those women born for motherhood and denied it by circumstance. As it was she lavished all her maternal instinct on us children, nursed us through our illnesses, mended our clothes, taught us our first prayers and mitigated the severity of our punishments. I believe that in all her life the only occasions on which she ever disobeyed her mother were when she used to steal secretly upstairs with a well-filled plate to some culprit sent supperless to bed, and I realize now what a spiritual conflict that must have represented for she was conscientious and truthful to the last degree. I was far more attached to her than to either of my parents perhaps because she nursed me devotedly night and day through a very serious illness when I was three years old. After the doctors who were attending me had given up all hope and predicted that I could not even live through the night, she remembered an old peasant remedy and decided to try it as a last resort. So she wrapped my entire body, heated with 104 degrees of fever, in ice-cold compresses. Drastic as it was it apparently cured me, for by the next morning my temperature had dropped, and I was sleeping naturally.

Actually that illness is my earliest recollection, chiefly, I think, because it was associated with the wearing of my hated blue dresses. While I lay between life and death my

parents prayed to the famous Virgin of Czestochowa and
dedicated me to her so that for three years after my recovery
I was never dressed in anything but that one shade of blue. It
made me conspicuous among other children who teased me so
mercilessly that I shed tears of anger and humiliation in secret,
and grew to loathe the colour to such an extent that when
once I was released from my obligation I would never wear it
again. I still think it was a severe strain to put upon the faith of
a child, and one calculated to set up a violent anti-religious
reaction. Yet in those days I prayed with a fervour and a certainty of belief that I often longed to recapture in later years
of storm and conflict.

Although Suvalki was in itself an ordinary little provincial
town the surrounding country had a wild and majestic beauty.
Gently-swelling hills sparsely dotted with farms and cottages
sloped down to dense forests of beeches, oaks and pines stretching for miles and framing great lakes, deep and silent and so
lonely that the footprints of an occasional fisherman were the
only signs of human life.

The largest of these lakes was Wigry where we used to
go for excursions on Sunday afternoons, packed tightly into
a big hired wagonette, drawn by two horses and driven by a
garrulous old coachman. When we reached the lake a primitive
ferry took us across to the opposite shore where there was a
bird sanctuary on the edge of the forest. Every year at the
migrating season thousands of birds would assemble there to
break their flight from the cold of the plains to the sunny
lands of the South, and the whole forest echoed to their song.
Some of them were so tame that they would approach quite
close for they had no fear either of us or the monks of the
Camaldoleze Monastery on the shores of the lake, which was
famed for the music of its bells. The sound of the chimes
ringing across the water at the hour of Vespers is one of the
loveliest memories of my childhood. But during the Great
War the Russian troops descended on Wigry, took possession
of the Monastery and disbanded the monks. They left behind
them silence, for the bells were sent to Moscow to be melted
down, and the noise of the Russian guns scared away the
birds so that they would never come back in spite of the

efforts made to re-establish the sanctuary. Warned by some strange instinct which must have persisted through generations of their short lives they deserted the forest.

After sunset when the shadows lengthened and the first pale stars came out over the tops of the fir trees the shores of Lake Wigry grew eerie and desolate with their long alleys of darkening forest and their gaunt roots of trees torn up and twisted into fantastic shapes by the storms of many years. Local superstitions had given the place an evil repute and woven strange legends around it. Rosalia, our housemaid, used to regale us with them on winter evenings. . . . Her favourite was the story of the Camaldoleze monk who made a bargain with the Devil.

Long ago, said Rosalia, there were fish in Lake Wigry which surpassed in delicacy and flavour any other in Poland, and which were much appreciated by the good monks on fast days. Imagine then their disappointment when suddenly and for no apparent reason the supply failed. Hour after hour, day after day, the brethren fished the waters patiently to be rewarded with not one single bite. At length they abandoned the attempt, all but one young brother more persevering than the rest. One evening he took his line to the shore and became so absorbed in his efforts that he did not realize that the sun had set and the moon had risen over the lake. The sound of a cough behind him made him turn . . . and there stood the Devil.

The monk knew the correct procedure on being confronted with the Devil, explained Rosalia, and immediately recited the prescribed prayers. The Evil One politely waited for him to finish but when he had done so neither disappeared in a circle of flames nor showed any sign of wishing to harm him. Instead he remarked conversationally that he had heard of the shortage of fish and regretted that the brethren had been inconvenienced by it. He knew a means, he added, by which he could replenish the Lake immediately. The Camaldoleze, delighted, besought him to do so. The Devil consented—but only at a price. The monk must give him his soul in exchange.

The poor Camaldoleze was sorely tempted. He pictured the joy of the community when their favourite dish was restored to them. But on the other hand the bargain was a terrible one. At length he decided on a compromise. He told the Devil that he would agree to his terms but on one condition only. The fish must be in his possession before midnight. They looked at the Monastery clock which was illuminated by the moon. It was just ten o'clock. The Devil hesitated. Two hours was a short time—but the soul of the holy Camaldoleze was a prize worth having. He accepted the condition and flew off.

The monk, left alone, bitterly repented his bargain. Too late he realized the terrible consequences of what he had done and began to pray. So full of remorse was he that he scarcely noticed how time was passing until in despair he glanced up at the Monastery clock. The hands pointed to three minutes before midnight. Suddenly inspiration came to him and he ran up the steep stairs to the clock tower. As he reached the top he saw by the light of the moon the Devil already flying over the farther shore of the Lake with the fish under his arm. The monk did not wait another second but moved the hands of the clock to midnight. Immediately the twelve strokes rang out over the water. The Devil, half-way across the Lake heard, gave a start, and in baffled rage and disappointment dropped the fish into the Lake. Then gnashing his teeth he turned and flew away never to return. But ever after the Monastery table was well supplied with fish.

That was the story that Rosalia used to tell us on winter evenings in the kitchen while we sat in a circle on our little wooden stools round the glowing stove and watched her plucking the down that had been stored all summer for filling pillows and eiderdowns. I can see her now in her blue check apron and peasant blouse, her wide lap full of the snowy goose feathers, her strong brown fingers never stopping in their task of stripping the down from the quills as she talked. I used to think that she must look like Mother Holle—which was another of her fairy stories. She had an endless repertoire which we never tired of hearing, and a sense of the dramatic which kept us spell-bound. We loved those long evenings in the warm kitchen with its savoury odours of new-baked bread, roasting apples, spices and smoking hams, and, as an added treat, there would be plates of faworki, the crisp little

cakes of sweet batter fried in lard which Anusia the cook would
bring us still hot from the stove. We would sit there, warm
and drowsy and replete until Rosalia's voice faded into a
restful drone and our heads would begin to droop, and one by
one we would be taken off to bed.

Anusia was a wonderful cook. Her stuffed cabbages and
spiced meat pies were held to be unequalled in Suvalki, and
the cool larder opening off the kitchen was always full of
her handiwork. Strings of home-made sausages and enormous
hams smoked to perfection over a charcoal burner hung from
the ceiling, pots of jam and apple cheeses were arranged in
neat rows in the cupboards, sloe wine and peach and cherry
brandy were stored in stone jars on the floor. She was a
peasant from the hills and not even Aunt Maria's lectures
could induce her to discard some of the customs of her native
village. She could never, for instance, be induced to sleep in
her bed which stood in the warmest corner of the kitchen behind the stove.

This bed was an object of our admiration for it was piled
almost to the ceiling with embroidered cushions of brilliant
colours and designs made and stuffed by Anusia's fingers, and
the sheets were hand-woven and adorned with the finest drawn
threadwork. But its purpose was purely ornamental for Anusia
had never been known to lie upon it. Instead she slept on
the hard kitchen settle with one plain pillow beneath her head
and a couple of old blankets as covering. The bed was being preserved with all its splendours intact against the two
great occasions in a peasant's life, the marriage night and the
lying-in-state. As Anusia was well past fifty I feared that it
would be occupied only once, but this possibility never seemed
to depress her. She was constantly making new cushions to
embellish it.

Another of her customs which sorely tried Aunt Maria was
that she would only wash her face once a week, before going
to Vespers on Sunday afternoon. No matter how grimy it
might become during the middle of the week she would never
do more than wipe it with a cotton handkerchief, for she had
the peasant's deep-rooted belief that washing takes the health
out of the skin.

But on Sundays immediately she had washed the dishes
after dinner she would retire to the scullery to emerge later
rosy and shining like an apple and redolent of soap and lav-
ender. Then she would open the stout wooden chest by her
bed and take out the gala costume of her native district,
voluminous skirt nearly covered with gold braid and bands of
ribbon of every colour, black velvet bodice embroidered to
match, and a crown of flowers for her hair. Arrayed in its
glories she would depart to Vespers followed by our admiring
eyes.

In contrast to the homely comforts of the kitchen were
evenings in the salon with its stiff mahogany furniture and its
Biblical engravings. Perched primly upright on our hard chairs
we would read or prepare our lessons under the observant eyes
of Grandmother who sat opposite us in her big armchair, the oil
lamp on its special table beside her, her crocheting in her hands.
No matter how restless we might feel inwardly we were too
much in awe of her to fidget, and an hour or more would pass
without any sound to break the silence except the chiming
of the alabaster clock, and the hissing of the samovar over its
charcoal burner. Then Aunt Maria would make a welcome
appearance with biscuits and jam and pour out steaming glasses
of tea for us all.

Grandmother would never take more than half a glass
at a time but she drank tea almost continuously, twenty or
thirty glasses in a day. When I try to picture her I always see
her small hands which were beautiful even in old age, manipulating the silver filigree samovar or else tending her flowers.
She took great delight in her garden and there was scarcely a
week in the year when it was not full of flowers. Even in the
depth of winter she had myrtles and dwarf maples, and sweet-
scented musk and heliotrope growing in pots in the window-
boxes. She had far more knowledge of them than the old
gardener who came for the rough work, for she seemed to
have a curious affinity with flowers. During the two months
of her last illness they drooped and withered in spite of the
conscientious care expended on them by Aunt Maria, and when
she died there was not one left to put on her coffin.

She was a woman of great strength of character, in many

respects far ahead of her generation, broad-minded, intelligent, very well-read. Since the death of her husband she had managed her big country estate without even the aid of a bailiff, governing the peasants with a firm hand, arbitrating in their disputes among themselves, giving them shrewd advice when they came to her with their problems and medicine when they were ill.

Her patriotism was the mainspring of her life. All the fierce ardour of her nature was dedicated to the fight for liberty. Her home, her children, her material interests counted as nothing beside it. So great was the force of her personality that although she was a woman and a widow and lived in an age when women were of little or no account politically, she was one of the acknowledged leaders in the undercurrent of intrigue, and had played an active part in the Insurrection of 1863, holding secret meetings in her house and hiding stores of arms and ammunition regardless of the risk she ran. She was utterly fearless, contemptuous even of danger and no sacrifice would have been too heavy for her. She would have faced exile to Siberia or even death with the exaltation of a martyr for she came of a line of patriots who handed down the ideal of liberty as a sacred trust, rekindling in each new generation the flame of rebellion no matter how many times it might be extinguished.

The failure of the Insurrection had been the bitterest disappointment of her life. Ever after she dressed in deepest black, relieved only by a narrow white edging of lace at the neck and wrists, and on her finger she wore a mourning ring, a tablet of onyx in which was set a cross of pearls. I must have been about seven years old when I asked her about it, one evening when we were alone in the salon together. I was holding a skein of wool for her to wind and I watched the lamplight playing on the pearls as her hands moved in and out.

"It is a ring worn in memory of those who died" . . . she said in answer to my question, and took it off and showed me the date engraved inside. I spelt it out slowly. 1863.

"Oh, Grandmother, let me try it on" . . . I begged her. She shook her head. "You can only wear that ring if you are a patriot, Ola." Then I asked the question that had been at the back of my mind for so long. "What is a patriot then?" She paused a moment before answering and her deep blue eyes shone as though with the light of some inner fire.

"One who puts the love of Poland before all else in the world and who is willing to sacrifice everything, even his life if it is needed, in fighting for her freedom."

"I will fight for Poland, Grandmother," I said, only half understanding, but wanting very much to wear the ring. She was silent for a moment and her eyes searched my face.

"I believe you will" . . . she said at last . . . "Ola, my child, promise me that you will!"

"I promise, Grandmother" . . . I repeated solemnly, awed by the intensity of feeling in her voice. She drew me to her with one of her rare gestures of tenderness and kissed me and put the ring on my finger, holding it firmly for it was much too big for me. Then she restored it to her own hand and the spell was broken.

"Now run away, Ola, and play with your sisters" . . . she said in her ordinary brisk voice . . . "Do not speak of this to any one, but do not forget."

I went off very proud at sharing a secret with Grandmother, and I did not forget, for that evening is still the most vivid memory of my childhood. The promise I had given meant nothing to me then, yet without realizing it I, too, had been consecrated to the cause for which thousands had died or gone into exile.

CHAPTER VI

THE POLAND of my youth was the most unhappy country in Europe, a country once proud and free that had been humbled into the dust. A country of shadows, haunted by memories of a greatness that had fled like a dream in the night. A country whose people had been slowly crushed into the semblance of submission, who had learnt to endure sorrow and humiliation in silence.

Just as the lives of men and women are usually made or marred by their early environment, so Poland's tragedy began with her setting in the map of Europe. For she was not only the buffer between the civilization and culture of the West and the barbarity of the East, but the battleground of all the nations. In every generation there was an enemy to menace one or other of her frontiers. The fierce Tartars swept down upon her cities burning and pillaging and killing. The Cossack tribes revolted against her and harried the Ukraine. The Turks threatened her existence until her warrior king, John Sobieski, routed them in a great battle on the plains of Vienna in 1683, drove them out of Hungary and established the triumph of the Cross over the Crescent. There were wars with the Muscovites and wars with the Swedes which left scant breathing space. But the most prolonged of all these wars was the conflict with the Teutonic Knights, that centuries-old conflict which only entered another phase when Hitler's troops marched into Poland last year.

So little has the German mentality changed that there is an almost complete parallel between that arrogant and cruel Order which terrorized half Europe in the Middle Ages and the Nazis of to-day. The ruthless ambition and greed for domination which caused the Knights to drop all pretence of spiritual calling in the pursuit of material conquests inspires the Nazi program of annexation. The cynical hypocrisy which enforced Christianity at the point of the sword and by barbarities

67

which outmatched those of the heathen races on whom they were practised finds its echo in Hitler's persecution of the Jews and the Catholic Church. The methods used in quelling the conquered nations are identical, despite the passage of more than five hundred years. Even the "Fifth Column" of the Gestapo did not originate in modern Germany for it was invariably the habit of the Knights to undermine the countries which they proposed to attack by intrigue and propaganda from within. And in the code of the Teutonic Order were many points in common with that of the modern Reich, down to the glorification of Teutonic blood and mass obedience to the chosen leader.

Between Poland and this powerful Germanic Order there began at the close of the fourteenth century the contest which was to endure until to-day, which was to change many times in character but never in motive. The struggle for access to the Baltic.

The Order, which was founded by the Pope in 1191 for the protection of pilgrims on their way to the Holy Land, and which originally numbered forty Knights, each of whom had to take an oath on entrance testifying to the purity of his German blood, was actually invited by the Poles to settle in their territory to carry out missionary work among the heathen Prussian tribes there. The Knights, who had already been expelled from Hungary because of their intrigues, were glad to avail themselves of the offer, but no sooner had they gained in power and numbers than they proceeded to exterminate the unfortunate Prussians with fire and sword, seize their territory and then turn against Lithuania and Poland.

These two countries menaced by the common enemy formed an alliance, and the beautiful young Polish Queen Jadwiga was married to the Lithuanian Grand Duke Jagiello, a prince who was not only the military genius of his time but who, under the influence of the cultured Polish nobles, developed outstanding qualities of statesmanship.

The new alliance was formidable enough to hold the Knights in check for some years, during which time they pursued a campaign of terror among the smaller neighbouring states, but in 1410, enriched by plunder and enormously strengthened in numbers, they issued a direct challenge to Poland and Lithuania. The allied armies under the leadership of Jagiello, and supported by small numbers of auxiliaries from Bohemia and Ruthenia, who rallied to their standard from fear of their enemy, met the redoubtable Knights of the Teutonic Order at Grünwald near Tannenberg and inflicted a crushing defeat on them. Unfortunately, the Poles, magnanimous in victory, showed a clemency which was to prove disastrous to them centuries later, for they did not expel the Order.

The respite was of short duration, for the Knights, smarting under their reverse, launched guerilla campaigns against the Poles, culminating during the reign of Casimir IV in a war which dragged on for fourteen years. But the Order had deteriorated both in military prowess and in leadership, and once more the Poles were victorious, pressing home their advantage until their adversaries were forced to sue for peace. By the resultant Treaty of Thorn Poland gained access to the Baltic and possession of the territory west of the Vistula with the city of Danzig, while the Knights were relegated to the occupation of the territory east of the Vistula, known later as Prussia. This they held as vassals of the Crown of Poland, and in token thereof the Grand Master of the Order bound himself to perform the requisite acts of homage. The repercussions of that pact, which was signed in 1466, were to continue through the centuries, for out of that fiefdom, held by a lawless and brigand Order, was born the Kingdom of Prussia. The last Grand Master of the Teutonic Knights, Albrecht von Hohenzollern, Duke of Brandenburg, broke up the Order when he adopted the Lutheran faith in 1525, and with the consent of Sigismund I of Poland founded the hereditary Dukedom of Prussia. He went to Cracow dutifully and in gratitude to confirm his new title and to put his hands between the hands of the Polish King and swear fealty to his liege lord. The citizens of the ancient capital who watched the Black Eagle lowered in homage to the White did not know that they had seen the turning of a new page in history, a page that would be stained with the blood of future generations. For Albrecht's successor was crowned King of Prussia. The foundations of the German Empire had been laid.

But as the star of Germany rose in the ascendancy so that of Poland began to wane. The weakness of her political construction, which was neither that of an hereditary monarchy nor of a republic, but lent itself to the abuses of both; the system of electing her kings from candidates who were usually foreigners, rendered her vulnerable to the alien influences which brought about her ruin. In 1764 the last of her kings ascended the Throne, that weak, ineffectual but none the less tragic figure, Stanislas Augustus, whose evil genius was Catherine of Russia. Long before it had been foretold that a woman would bring sorrow and desolation to Poland, and the prophecy was fulfilled, for the Empress, who was as cold-hearted and unscrupulous as she was beautiful, completely subjugated the handsome, accomplished young Polish noble, who first visited her court in the train of the British Ambassador and after her intrigues had secured his election to the Throne used him ruthlessly as a pawn in the intricate game of European politics. Expert as she was in psychology, she was able to keep him enslaved both by his passion for her and by the attractions of her Court, whose extravagances and barbaric splendour appealed to his sensuous, pleasure-loving temperament. And so after years in which the tentacles of Russian influence stretched ever more tightly over Poland, her martyrdom was sealed with the First Treaty of Partition, a scheme evolved by the fertile brains of the Empress Catherine and Frederick the Great of Prussia, and entered into, albeit with some reluctance, by Maria Theresa of Austria. When they had made an end of arguing and explaining and wrangling like dogs over a bone, Prussia took all West Prussia, except the cities of Thorn and Danzig, Russia three provinces, and Austria parts of Galicia, Podola and Little Poland. They reached agreement among themselves in 1772, but they gave no notice of their intentions until September, when with a technique strangely resembling that of Hitler and Stalin they announced that they proposed to enforce on Poland "claims as ancient as they were legitimate." As a further excuse, they added that since a state of anarchy existed in Poland threatening an entire dissolution of that kingdom they were constrained to take these steps to preserve the peace of their own borders.

The Poles, confronted with this manifesto, were stunned. The unhappy Stanislas, awaking too late to realities, protested to the imperious Catherine and got the callous reply that he ought to consider the Partition preferable to the loss of the entire country, which was the only other alternative.

In despair he threatened to abdicate, appealed to the British Minister in Warsaw. But England had her own troubles at the moment, and the rest of Europe turned a deaf ear to his plea. With the troops of the three partitioning powers already in provisional occupation of his territories he could only sign the Act of Partition which sold his people into slavery.

The next twenty years saw a period of evolution in Europe. Everywhere the old order was changing. Frederick the Great of Prussia and Maria Theresa of Austria, bulwarks of absolute monarchy, died. A breath of independence was wafted over the nations, raised the whirlwind of Revolution in France. And in the stricken and dismembered Poland there came into being a constitutional reform far ahead of its time. The King shook off the leading-strings of St. Petersburg and became for the first time the real leader of his people. A committee of patriots drew up the New Constitution of May 3rd, 1791, abolishing the old elective system of monarchy with all its attendant evils, increasing the Army, granting reform to the peasants and privileges to the middle and lower classes. It was a triumph of liberal progress, inspired by freedom of mind in a shackled people.

It only accelerated the inevitable disaster. Catherine of Russia saw in it a menace to her own authority. Her agents had not failed to report on the new and independent spirit which was gaining ground among the Polish peasants. She could not afford to have it spread to the wretched serfs of Russia, and before there was any chance of it doing so it must be nipped in the bud.

She appealed to the cupidity of Frederick William of Prussia who had succeeded his uncle, Frederick the Great, suggested a further share-out of Poland. Between them they drew up the Second Partition in 1793. After months of haggling and barter in which each strove to outwit the other and get possession of the choicest spoils, they arrived at a compromise by which Russia gained the Palatinates of Kieff, Minsk, Braclaw, and most of Volhynia, while Prussia got possession of the long-coveted prize of Danzig and Thorn and the provinces of Posen, Kalisz and Plock. A further carve-up was inevitable with Austria, too, clamouring for her share, and the dismembered country was not even left time in which to heal her wounds and reorganize her dismayed population. With the Third Partition, which was signed two years later, her martyrdom was accomplished. Her remaining territories were parcelled out between Russia, Prussia and Austria. Her name as an independent state disappeared from among the nations. Her king, Stanislas Augustus, was forced to abdicate. A broken and humiliated old man, cursed by his own subjects and despised by the rest of Europe, he was still drawn as though by an irresistible magnet to the Court which had been his ruin. He retired to St. Petersburg to live out the rest of his days. There he had his last interview with Catherine a few weeks before her death.

He did not long survive her. He ended his days in St. Petersburg, and the men and women who had been his subjects forgave him in death for his betrayal of them and mourned him sincerely because he was the last link with all that had been swept away.

But fetters cannot kill the spirit of freedom in a people although they may cripple it, and out of the gloom and despair that settled over Poland there emerged again and again leaders and patriots who blazoned their names in chapters as glorious as they were tragic, who fought against overwhelming odds, were defeated and died, having failed in their object. Yet they left behind them a memory to inspire those who came after, a trail to be followed no matter how great the sacrifice. And of these men one was Kosciuszko, the first patriot to raise the standard of war against the partitioning powers. The rebellion which he led in 1794 is one of the epics of Polish history.

Thaddeus Kosciuszko was a Lithuanian of noble birth who had spent many years in America, fought with Washington in the War of Independence, and acted as aide-de-camp to La Fayette, showing such gallantry and resource that he was promoted to the rank of Brigadier-General. His contact with the New World had given him experience of military technique acquired under the greatest generals of his day, a standard of efficiency in advance of that of his contemporaries, and a broad and human outlook.

From the beginning he constituted himself the leader of the common people, the first Polish noble to break through the age-old caste traditions. He had learnt that courage in the field is not dependent on birth or tradition. He had seen men drawn from the dregs of the American populace, the sweepings of the camps, ragged and drunken, fighting like Spartans under the banner of Washington, standing firm under the onslaughts of the picked British troops. He looked for that same valour and endurance in the humble peasants of his own land. And found it. He was the first leader to treat them as anything other than slaves of the soil, to appeal directly to them as sons of their country, capable of defending it against the invaders. He went about among them, roused their patriotism, called upon that love of the land that is innate in every peasant, showed his confidence in them. And in return they followed him to a man, gave him a devotion almost amounting to worship, and an unswerving loyalty that was consummated in death for thousands of them. At his bidding they left their farms and marched out to encounter the Russian troops at Raclawiezc. Armed only with their scythes and hunting-knives, they stood unflinching under cavalry charges in which they were mown down like grass. They flung themselves on the Russian cannon and captured them, over mounds of their own dead. They drove the enemy from the field with heavy losses.

The flame of revolt flared through the country. A brigade of Polish cavalry swept down upon Cracow and routed the Russian garrison. The artisans of Warsaw formed themselves into battalions and drove the Russians from the city. There were risings in Lithuania.

But the peasant troops for all their courage were no match for the joint armies of Russia and Prussia which advanced upon them in overwhelming numbers over the plains of the Bug, and at Maciejowice two-thirds of them were annihilated, while Kosciuszko himself was wounded and taken prisoner.

The victorious Russians marched upon Warsaw which was being held by a small number of Polish troops reinforced by citizens, numbering some eleven thousand in all. After two days of desperate fighting the city was forced to surrender. Its capitulation was followed by one of the most cruel massacres in history, for the Russian soldiers roamed the streets butchering men, women and children, till the very gutters ran red. In the space of a few hours twelve thousand people were put to the sword or thrown into the river.

The revolt was broken. The star of Poland had shone once more for so brief a moment, only to set in blood.

Yet time and again the dream of freedom hovered over the country. Once when its destiny was linked with that of Napoleon. The obscure young officer who had risen to power through the storm of the French Revolution, the leader of a people which had thrown off its chains, caught the imagination of the youth of Poland. Thousands of recruits from all classes flocked to his standard. The Polish Legion of the Grande Armée was formed on foreign soil, just as it has been formed to-day. It fought with rising enthusiasm through every campaign against the partitioning powers. With the defeat of Prussia a new era seemed to be dawning, and when Napoleon entered Warsaw in triumph after the battle of Poltusk he was hailed as a deliverer. But true to his policy of egoism gave little but compliments and vague promises. He was more concerned over his war with Russia than over the freedom of the Poles. He defeated the Russians at Friedland, founded the Grand Duchy of Warsaw with a great show of liberality, and then applied himself to dealing with Austria.

During the five years that followed, the Poles bore their disappointment as philosophically as they might. They had given their loyalty to Napoleon and they would not retract it. When he embarked upon his final and disastrous war with Russia, their hopes were rekindled, for finding them necessary to his plans he guaranteed them, in return for their support, the full restoration of their ancient territories and rights. Once again they believed him. The French Ambassador, at a meeting of the Diet of Warsaw, delivered many flowery promises, and amid scenes of frenzied enthusiasm a Polish army of eighty thousand assembled and marched with the French on Moscow.

Not more than three thousand of them returned. The Russians, following up their triumph, captured Warsaw, abolished the Grand Duchy, and took possession of all the territories from which they had been driven. But ideals die hard, and so at Waterloo there was still the remnant of a Polish Legion fighting in the cause of the Emperor who had betrayed their trust.

After the fall of Napoleon Poland was once again partitioned by the Congress of Vienna. Austria was given Galicia, with the exception of the province of Cracow, which was established as an independent republic; Prussia regained Danzig, Thorn and the province of Posen, while Russia took the largest share, the Grand Duchy of Warsaw, which she undertook to maintain as a separate kingdom with the Czar as king. Once again a faint ray of hope illumined the darkness, for the young Czar Alexander I was impulsive, easily moved to sympathy and full of liberal intentions which he had not the tenacity of purpose to carry out. In the first flush of enthusiasm he championed the Polish cause at the Congress of Vienna valiantly and with apparent sincerity and therefore when he entered Warsaw in 1815 as its new ruler, he was acclaimed by the people. They had been accustomed in the past to receiving a foreigner as their king, and this one was a figure of chivalry. He had promised them complete liberty, a constitution of their own and the perpetuation of the Polish nationality and language. In spite of the sufferings that Russia had inflicted on them in the past they were prepared to accept him and even to give him loyalty.

He kept his promises to them with a Constitution that was fair and liberal, but with characteristic carelessness he did not take the trouble to see that it was properly drawn up, and therefore it contained a number of clauses open to misinterpretation which were exploited by his successor. The choice of the Grand Duke Constantine, a moral degenerate and a despot with all the failings of the house of Romanoff and none of its virtues, as Commander-in-Chief of the Polish Army was another blunder, for under his unjust and tyrannical regime

there was constant friction. Even so, however, there were ten
years of peace and comparative prosperity until in 1825 Alexander died, still full of promises to his Polish subjects, promises
which he was never to redeem.

His brother Nicholas I who succeeded him was a man of
very different calibre, ruthless, harsh and unbending, whose
only argument was force. From the beginning he regarded the
Poles as potential rebels to be terrorized into submission. His
agents roamed the country, ordering arrests of "suspects"
whenever it pleased them, generally without the faintest justification, often because of some private grudge. For five years
exasperation rose steadily, reached boiling-point with the Insurrection of 1830.

It was a tragic, abortive affair, doomed to failure from
the outbreak though it lasted for nearly a year in spite of
desperate odds and the immense superiority in numbers of
the Russian army which was sent to quell it. When at length
the last lingering spark was extinguished it was punished
with a savage ferocity intended to serve as a warning not
only to Poland but to the Russians themselves, lest they, too,
should cherish any false illusions. So in many a village the
baying of the imperial bloodhounds was heard at night as they
tracked their quarry to the woods. Hundreds of men were
dragged out of their houses and shot or hanged, thousands
were sent to the salt mines of Siberia. Their estates were confiscated and sold by auction, knocked down to Russian bidders
for a fraction of their value. Their wives and families were
expatriated to remote districts of Russia and left there to
starve.

All the semblance of freedom that even the perfidious Alexander had respected was swept away. His Constitution was
annulled. The Polish Army was abolished, its forces were incorporated with the Imperial Army. The national flag was
no longer permitted to be displayed. Russian was made the
compulsory language. Russians filled all the posts in the Government, swaggered about the cities, forced the shopkeepers
to sell to them at their own price.

Poland could only endure in silence as she had learnt to
endure in years of misery. Her men were flung into cages like

wild beasts, manacled and chained together and herded into columns to be marched to the Siberian mines. Her women wept at her wayside shrines on their way to toil in the fields for the Russians who had taken possession of their lands. Her children grew up to manhood before ever they had been young. Out of the mute suffering of millions was born the music of Chopin, the poetry of Slowacki and Mickiewicz.

Thirty years passed. Another generation grew up, burning with resentment at the wrongs inflicted upon it, longing to throw off its fetters. A generation not yet crushed by failure and who had not known the bitterness of defeat. So in hundreds of homes, in manor houses and in students' lodgings, in city slums and in lonely peasant huts the fierce patriotism that had so long been cherished in secret burst into a flame that spread throughout the land. The Insurrection of 1863.

It was not a well-planned and carefully organized revolt. It broke out here and there with no definite program. But it came from the very soul of Poland, the spirit of freedom crucified but living still.

It was the revolt of youth. In towns and villages and in isolated farms young men and women, undeterred by memories of the retribution that had fallen on their fathers, banded themselves together in one common impulse to liberate their country. Those who had money to give gave it, the landowners mortgaged their farms, the poor parted with their savings. Boys still in their teens started drilling by moonlight in deserted woods and meadows, women and girls collected stores and acted as messengers between the different centres. A number of young men, many of them the sons of the greatest families in Poland, went to the Military Academy at Cuneo to study tactics in preparation for taking command. Others were sent to Paris to buy rifles and ammunition, but the French authorities, distrusting their activities, had them arrested, and only released them after lengthy investigations. Representatives who went to England were more successful, for they succeeded in rousing the sympathies of the liberal-minded North-country arms manufacturers who gave them credit, and guns were smuggled into Poland in small quantities at a time.

But long before the plan had time to ripen the Czar's agents noted the signs of growing restlessness, made their reports to St. Petersburg.

Russia had only one way of dealing with discontent. Poles who were chafing under the yoke must be made to feel the goad. A measure was brought in conscripting all men of military age in Poland. In order to make the lesson still more effective, no warning was given. Thousands of young men were seized at work or in their homes at night, packed off to Russian barracks in Siberia or the Caucasus without even time to bid farewell to their families.

It was the one spark needed to precipitate the conflagration. The half-matured plans were hurriedly put into action. The call to arms echoed over the whole country. The Cadets came back from Cuneo, put themselves at the heads of hastily formed units. Polish flags were taken out of their hiding-places and proudly displayed, forbidden songs were sung once more. Every valley rang with the tramp of marching men. The proportion of rifles was pitifully inadequate, but there was no time to wait for more. Those who had fowling-pieces carried them, those who had not brought their scythes and reaping hooks which were made to serve as lances after the blades had been beaten out straight. The fires in many a village smithy were kept roaring all night, for the work could only be done in secret. In the churches the priests preached the crusade for freedom, came out of their pulpits and marched with the recruits into battle, gave them absolution as they lay dying in hundreds.

It was a lost cause and a doomed army. An army without money and without equipment, with no military experts to plan its campaign, with no assets except its own unquenchable courage. Yet for nearly two years its unskilled troops waged a desperate fight against all the resources of the Russian Government. They fought in battalions, and they fought in scattered bands in the woods and the fields. Their scanty supplies of food and clothing gave out, but still they fought on, half-starved, barefooted and in rags. Armed with their reaping-hooks and shotguns, they faced the Russian Artillery brigades. The Czar sent regiment after regiment to quell them, blood was poured out like water, but still the revolt continued to spread.

No sooner was it suppressed in one district than it broke out in another. It was the strength of an ideal pitted against material force.

Behind that army, composed of the flower of its youth, the nation waited and prayed and made sacrifices. The rich almost beggared themselves to buy ammunition, the peasants gave the produce of their farms down to the last bushel of grain, the owners of country houses turned them into hospitals and nursed the wounded, unmindful of the death penalty for harbouring rebels. "It was a sublime effort" . . . wrote Joseph Pilsudski in describing it years afterwards . . . "an effort in which every one in the land, old and young, man, woman and child, shared. A unity of purpose so beautiful and so great that the vast military force of Russia with all the weight of its Government machinery behind it, could not destroy it. The strength and power of that resistance lay not in the guns that were carried through woods and marshes, but in the sublime self-sacrifices of the whole civilian community which sent forth that army and protected it, in the spiritual height to which the nation was able to attain. It was defeated, but that defeat is one of the most beautiful leaves in Poland's crown of laurels."

The Czar's vengeance on the vanquished was swift and barbaric. He proceeded to administer a lesson to Poland which shocked the whole of Europe. In England the House of Commons debated the question of active interference and expressed the view that the treatment of the Poles by all three partitioning powers was a flagrant violation of the Treaty of Vienna. As a result the Government, which was then under Lord Palmerston, addressed a strong remonstrance to Russia, asking for a full amnesty for all concerned in the Insurrection and suggesting various reforms in the policy which had been adopted towards Poland.

The answer was disarming in its hypocrisy. The Czar affirmed his earnest intention "to provide for the welfare of his subjects of all races and of every religious conviction as an obligation which he had accepted before God, his conscience and his people."

Palmerston, however deep his sympathy with Poland, would not contemplate a war with Russia on her behalf, and therefore there was nothing further to be done. So the civilized world averted its face while thirty thousand Poles were shot or flogged to death by Russian knouts, and another hundred and fifty thousand were exiled. Once more the long processions wound northwards to Siberia. The more fortunate fell by the roadside and died still in their chains. The rest went on to the doom that was worse than death. The flame that had burnt so ardently was quenched in blood and tears.

I was born more than twenty years afterwards but I can remember how the women used to sit around the fires at night and talk in hushed voices of the things they had seen in those days, and the almost incredulous joy in the village which greeted the return of an exiled son or husband, for of the many who went to Siberia few ever came back.

My grandmother's two brothers were among those who paid a heavy price for their part in the Insurrection. The elder ended his days in the prison of the Katorga, in solitary confinement in an eight foot cell, with iron fetters on his wrists and ankles and a fifteen pound weight hanging between his knees lest he should try to escape. The younger came back after twenty years of exile in Siberia to sit huddled over the stove for the rest of his life, crippled with rheumatism, scarred with the marks of the knout, but undefeated. His eyes had still the fire of youth in a sunken face. When he talked it was with the words and thoughts of the eighteen-year-old boy he had been when he was arrested. Child though I was I was struck by the incongruity of a prematurely aged body and a mind eternally young. Later I saw it many times, always in men who had returned from Siberia. In the silence and loneliness of exile, life had stood still for them. The passing of the years had left no impression upon them because time had ceased to exist.

I was very fond of this Great Uncle Ludwig, perhaps because he always treated me as an equal and never as a child. In the long winter evenings I used to draw my chair up to his (after I had first tiptoed to the door to make sure the servants were not spying on us, for I knew our danger even in those days) and listen to his stories of the Insurrection and of the men who had led it. And as he talked there awoke in my heart the first feeling of love for my country and the desire to free her.

CHAPTER VII

As the child of a patriot family I grew up in an atmosphere of secret rebellion. The survivors of the last Insurrection, who had offered up their youth so gladly at the altar of freedom, were grey-haired men and women, outwardly resigned to their lot, even as my grandmother appeared to be. But the flame of resistance burnt within them as steadfastly as ever. They had fought their battle and lost, as their fathers had done before them, but they could still pass on the trust to their sons and daughters. So the undercurrent of revolt was always there. It was on the lips of confident youth, in the haunted eyes of men who came back broken from Siberia. It beat in the hearts of the old, it breathed in the very air. It was always there because never for a moment in our daily lives were we allowed to forget the Russian yoke.

The Governors and officials appointed by St. Petersburg availed themselves of their opportunities to exercise as many petty tyrannies as they chose. There were, of course, exceptions among these men, but the majority of them were without tact or judgment, owing their positions to the widespread system of intrigue and bribery which was one of the contributing causes of the Russian Revolution. Imoretinski, one of their own compatriots, wrote of them. . . .

> "From the very start of his appointment in Poland the Russian Government employee, ill-bred, semi-educated and injudicious, sees in every Pole a man who has been conquered, his country's enemy and his own. He sees himself as the conqueror, and, acting on the proverb that 'the conquered are outside the law,' he considers himself accountable to no one for his treatment of them, and is troubled neither by public opinion nor his own conscience."

These men were the arbiters of our destiny and conditions varied in the different districts according to their individual dispositions. Some were harsh and overbearing, others drunken bullies who paid their gambling debts with money extorted from the Jews and wealthy tradesmen as the price of their protection.

The landowners, like my grandmother, were taxed out of existence to provide money which was squandered on the extravagances of the Imperial Court, their sons were barred from a military career unless they chose to serve in one of the Russian regiments, and handicapped by their nationality in the choice of a profession. We were not even permitted to speak our own language or to receive any education except at approved Russian schools. Practically all our literature was banned, for our poets had sung of freedom, and heavy penalties were imposed on those found in possession of their works. Our history too was a sealed book. The victories of John Sobieski and Stefan Batory, whose fame had rung through Europe, had been blotted out. We had to learn instead the names and dates of every Grand Duke in the Russian hierarchy. Only in our own homes did we dare to speak of the forbidden past and read behind locked doors books printed in England or Switzerland and smuggled into the country.

My education and that of my brother and sisters was something of a problem, for my grandmother refused to let us attend a Russian school and heavy penalties were enforced both on those who "practised illegal education" and on those who permitted their children to receive it. Finally a friend came to the rescue and offered to set apart one of the rooms in his house as a schoolroom for us and his own nieces, and several other children in the neighbourhood. A teacher was found, a widow of fifty who was an ardent patriot. Apart from the fact that she ran the risk of imprisonment for educating us, her post was no sinecure for there were eighteen of us and as our ages ranged from three to fifteen the planning of the time-table needed considerable ingenuity. However, she rose to the occasion and not only succeeded in teaching us the usual subjects but in making us enjoy them. I can still remember the thrill of adventure in hurrying off to school with my lesson books hidden under my coat or disguised in parcels, after being warned by Aunt Maria of the danger of telling any one where I was going. But after some years of coping valiantly with her unequal task, our patriotic little teacher was taken ill and as there was no one to replace her Grandmother was faced with the alternative of either sending me to the Russian Gymnase at Suvalki or discontinuing my education altogether.

The question of educating their children was one of the many difficulties which beset the Poles under Russian rule. After the Insurrection of 1863, all Polish schools were declared illegal and so rigorously abolished that, incredible as it seems, there were actually fewer schools in existence in Poland at the close of the nineteenth century than there had been in the Middle Ages. In accordance with their system of keeping the Polish peasants and working classes on a level with their own in Russia, the Government made no provisions whatever for their education. It was practically impossible to find one who could even read or write. For the children of middle-class families there was only the Gymnase, that is to say, a secondary school run by the Russian Government and divided into two sections, for boys and girls.

After a long struggle with her patriotism, Grandmother bowed to the inevitable. My elder sister was old enough to leave school altogether; the ones below me were young enough to stay at home and take a few lessons with Aunt Maria. But I, at eleven years old, needed disciplined class-work, for owing to the rather erratic education I had so far received I was too far advanced in some subjects and too backward in others. So she decided to send me to the Gymnase, but, characteristically, made up her mind so suddenly that I was left with only two months in which to learn sufficient Russian to get through the entrance examination at the beginning of the term. Since not a word of Russian had ever been spoken in our house I was at a serious disadvantage and a special teacher had to be engaged to give me daily lessons. Even now I think of those weeks with resentment, for while the rest of the family went to the country for the summer holidays, I was forced to stay in Suvalki, grappling with Russian irregular verbs. But I managed to scrape through the examination in time for the autumn term.

The Gymnase in Poland gave, at least where girls were concerned, an education very much inferior to those of corresponding schools in Russia. At the same time it was Russianized to the last degree. Although three-quarters of the pupils were Polish there was not a single Polish teacher on the staff, with the exception of the priest, and even he owed his appointment to the fact that it would have been out of the question for a Russian priest of the Greek Orthodox faith to give lessons in the Roman Catholic doctrine. The Scripture classes were the only ones in which a word of Polish was ever uttered. All other lessons were given in Russian, even those on our own Polish language, which we had to learn from Russian textbooks, like French or any other foreign language. If during recess we forgot in talking to one another and lapsed into Polish in the hearing of any of the teachers we were immediately punished by being kept in.

Never a day passed in which we did not have to hear scorn being heaped upon our nation. The teachers, to show their own loyalty, vied with one another in trying to instil into us the sense of our inferiority and the might of Russia. History lessons afforded a special opportunity for this, and we used to sit through them listening to taunts and false propaganda, seething with rage which we dared not show while the few Russian girls in our midst sat smilingly conscious of their own superiority. The atmosphere was tense with hatred and the seeds thus sown bore bitter fruit in after years.

This anti-Polish campaign was so ridiculously exaggerated that it extended even to the most trivial things. We were, for instance, ordered to wear our hair after the Russian fashion, combed smoothly back from the forehead, plaited, and arranged in a coil at the nape of the neck. Once I had the temerity to wind my long plaits round my head to frame my face. The result was a storm lasting for days, not because I had disobeyed a rule but because I had adopted the traditional Polish coiffure. I was called out before the whole class, made to stand on the teacher's platform, take down my hair and rearrange it. Then I was solemnly reported to the Governor of the Gymnase for "rebellious tendencies" and kept in after school for the remainder of the week while the other girls were

not allowed to speak to me during recess. It was my first gesture of patriotism, and I got a stubborn satisfaction out of it
though I never had the courage to repeat the experiment.

Since persecution only serves to strengthen a cause, this
amazingly shortsighted Russian propaganda not only failed in
its object but had a completely reverse effect. The Gymnase
might ban our Polish history and literature, but it could not
prevent our reading them in our own homes. Its determination
to stamp out our language made us all the more fiercely resolved to keep it alive, and we not only met to study it in
secret after school hours, but each of us undertook to teach
at least one child of the working-class to read and write it
so that it should be preserved among them too. These children
used to join us in the evenings and on Sunday afternoons and
share in all our illegal studies, and neither they nor their parents ever betrayed us in spite of their great poverty and the
substantial rewards offered by the Russian Government to
any one furnishing such information. The forbidden books of
history and poetry were supplied to us by a young lawyer who
kept in secret a whole library of books smuggled in from Switzerland which he lent to patriotic families, regardless of the risk
which he incurred, for the penalties for being found in possession of banned literature were very heavy. I can still remember
the scandal at the Gymnase when it was discovered that a
fifteen-year-old student in the boys' section had a copy of the
patriotic poems of Slowacki hidden in his desk. The head-
master notified the Russian police with the result that he was
immediately put under arrest. Fortunately he escaped from
prison while awaiting trial, crossed the frontier, and with the
help of friends succeeded in getting to America.

Those years in Suvalki were happy, indeed some of the
happiest in my life, for the sombre background of patriotism and the sorrow of an elder generation were lightened by
our youth and gaiety. The stately old house that had hidden
rebels and harboured fierce resentment and passionate hate
used to ring with laughter in the evenings when we danced
the mazurka and the oberek in the salon. I loved dancing for
I was tall and slim and very supple in those days, full of
a tireless energy and a vitality that would not let my body

droop and be discouraged no matter how sad I might be in spirit. On Sunday afternoons we used to go out to the forest, a big party of young people packed tightly in wagonettes, and dance on the sward under the pine trees till the sun went down and the last rays of daylight faded into the purple of the distant hills. Then we would throw ourselves down on the ground panting and laughing while some of us gathered sticks and made a fire and others set out the supper. When it was ready it would have the faint tang of the smoking wood and fir cones, but to us with appetites sharpened by air and exercise it seemed delicious.

There were winter days when we skated on the frozen pond in the garden and tried to arrive at complicated figures and waltz on our skates: and summer holidays when we roamed over the plains and picked the masses of blue and yellow irises on the banks of the river. We were all very young, very enthusiastic, very sure of ourselves and of life, and full of plans for changing the whole universe. We discussed a great many things which we understood only vaguely, or not at all, and held many theories which we had to discard later. They were as much a part of the process of springtime as the catkins we gathered every year.

I was seventeen when I left the Gymnase and by that time the seeds planted in my childhood had taken root. I had only one aim in life. To fight for Poland's freedom. The love of country is natural to every child, but the awakening to it usually comes in some moment of pride and splendour, with the waving of flags and the strains of national music. But for me and for all the children of Poland it was different. There was no glory attached to our patriotism, only an undying loyalty to a lost cause, and a flag that had been torn down and trampled in the mud. It was a sad and sober emotion. It meant secret meetings and fugitive flights in the night, and sooner or later, retribution. Its martyrs were uncrowned and unexalted, shot down like dogs in the street or bundled off to the silence of Siberia. A hard road without splendour or romance to glorify it, but we had to follow it.

So the main essential in choosing a career was to find one which would bring me into contact with the people whom I

wanted to influence. There I was guided by remembering
Uncle Ludwig's stories of the Insurrection of 1863. He had
often impressed upon me the main flaw in its organization—
the lack of co-operation between the upper classes and the
peasantry.

Now the Polish peasants, notwithstanding the misery of
their lot, have always been by nature a far freer people than
the serfs of Russia, perhaps because they were not originally
enslaved to the same extent. In the Middle Ages when the
Russian Boyards wielded the power of life and death over the
wretched tenantry whom they owned body and soul, and
even the far more civilized French noblesse exercised *le droit
de seigneur* and taxed and plundered their peasants without
mercy, two countries thought to free their slaves of the soil,
England by her Magna Carta and other laws, and Poland by
the Statute of Wislicki accorded by Casimir the Great. This
last contained the somewhat crude but none the less necessary
clause that a peasant was released from all obligations towards
a master who attempted the honour of his wife or daughter,
and further provided that his worldly possessions could not
be taken from him by his lord's armed troops.

But whereas the social system of England enabled her peasants to use their freedom so constructively that from them arose
the great yeoman class, the peasants of Poland were forced
by circumstances to occupy a place in the scale little above
that of the beasts they tended. All through the period of constitutional evolution when the West of Europe was slowly
beginning to recognize the rights of the individual, they were
kept chained, victims of a lax monarchy and a too powerful nobility. Instead of sharing in the development of the country, they were actually pushed backwards by it. The great
Polish grain trade which began in the latter half of the fifteenth
century, when the first cargoes of wheat were shipped down
the Vistula to Danzig to be sold in the foreign markets, while
it enriched the upper classes and turned an impoverished
knighthood into a prosperous wheat-producing landed gentry,
brought misery to the peasants. As more and more labourers
were needed to till the fields and cut the corn they became
valuable assets to their landlords, and laws were passed

binding them to conditions little better than slavery. Gradually they were deprived of first one privilege and then another.
A decree granted by the weak King John Albrecht in an
effort to curry favour with the landowners, establishing that
of a family of peasants only one child in each generation could
leave the estate on which he was born, harnessed them and
their descendants in perpetual bondage to their lords. Another
statute, excluding them from any court of law except a tribunal
presided over by their own masters, denied them even the pretence of justice.

As time passed the original code, which had always been
elastic where the landlord was concerned, was stretched still
further. The peasant who paid no rent for his little plot of
land and his miserable hut, but gave in return for it so many
days of labour a week, was forced to work longer and longer
hours, to toil from dawn to darkness in his master's fields
so that he had not time to cultivate his own holding on which
he and his family depended for food. Slowly he declined into
abject poverty. Whereas his forefathers had been free men,
comparatively well-to-do, able to send a son to the University
or provide a dowry for a daughter, he was able, even in the
best of seasons, to wrest only a bare livelihood from the soil.
Yet whether the yield from his ground was good or bad a certain proportion of it was claimed by the landlord as his due,
for nothing that the peasant had was his own, not even the
milk from his cow, if he was fortunate enough to keep one,
the eggs from his fowls, or the firewood he gathered. He was
only entitled to what was left over after his master had been
supplied.

Centuries passed. Centuries during which Europe was in
the melting-pot, when countries were shaped and reshaped.
Poland rose to the pinnacle of her greatness, declined slowly,
and lost her place among the free nations. But the peasants,
uneducated, brutalized, dulled into submission by toil and
hardship, remained in apathy, neither knowing nor caring
for the changing world outside their own small radius. They
lived out their span of years, resigned because their fathers
had never had anything better, unresisting because they were
unconscious of their own strength. Begat generations to drive

the plough and till the fields, and were absorbed back into the earth.

Then out of the drab background of their lives flashed the figure of the patriot Kosciuszko, the first leader to awaken in them love of their country. He gave them another perspective. He was a noble, one of the class they had been accustomed to fear and to obey. Yet he spoke to them as one of themselves. His words clothed them for the first time in dignity and self-respect for he appealed to them as the natural defenders of the soil, made them realize their own responsibility in the defence of their country. Thousands upon thousands of them flocked to his standard, fought heroically beside him and shared in his defeat.

But Kosciuszko, although he could not liberate them, left behind him the spirit of freedom in them and in their descendants. For a brief while they had been conscious of their own strength, and that consciousness was never wholly to leave them. Alexander II, one of the most astute of Russian Czars, realized it seventy years later and deliberately exploited it in an attempt to break the Insurrection of 1863.

One of the first acts of the Polish National Government which was set up during the Insurrection was to proclaim the liberty of the peasants, and give them free grants of their holdings of land, a measure which discontented certain of the great landowners who, alarmed at the prospect of an emancipated tenantry, held themselves aloof. This possible cause of dissension was immediately seized upon by the Czar, and Russian agents were sent far and wide through Poland with instructions to win over the peasantry with tempting offers, provided they would disassociate themselves from the revolt.

But the seeds of patriotism planted by Kosciuszko had not fallen upon stony ground. In spite of the wretchedness of their lot the peasants stood firm, loyal to the memory of the man who had led their fathers against the oppressor and to the love of their country which he had taught them. The blandishments of the agents met with negative results, and the peasant troops were among those who fought most gallantly in the ill-fated Insurrection.

When the terrible aftermath of 1863 had at length subsided and the Russian bayonets were satiated with blood, Alexander with a magnanimous gesture passed a measure giving the peasants their holdings of land in perpetuity, with the condition attached that they must pay taxes, a portion of which would be made over by the Government as compensation to the landowners. It was a move which met with the approval of no one except the agents who went about the countryside loudly praising the generosity of the Little Father. The peasants had suffered too bitterly in the Insurrection to have much enthusiasm for the future and saw in the prospect of taxation only fresh ground for oppression. The landowners on the other hand were angry at being deprived of the greater part of their estates and had no faith in the Russian Government's promises of compensation. As a means of *rapprochement* between the Czar and his Polish subjects, if indeed it was ever intended to be such, the scheme failed utterly.

It did, however, bring about radical changes in the social life of Poland. The smaller landowners found that their depleted estates no longer sufficed to keep them in even tolerable comfort, still less the luxuries which they had been accustomed to regard as their due. Little by little they were forced to sell their remaining lands, migrate to the cities and go into trade, or one of the professions. Their forefathers who had composed the proudest, most conservative nobility in Europe would have held themselves dishonoured by mere association with the commercial world, but the younger generation, after a vain attempt to exist on their patrimony, sunk their scruples and before long many of the oldest names in Polish history were identified with mills and factories. A middle class, hitherto non-existent in Poland, was created.

Curiously enough these pioneers whose families from time immemorial had never soiled their hands with anything remotely resembling work, revealed a surprising aptitude for trade and the professions. The abolition of the Russian frontier dues gave them a wide market for their wares. Their industries flourished despite the unjust and crippling taxes imposed by the Russian Government. Mines were developed, railroads built, Warsaw began to rank with the great commercial cities of the West of Europe, thriving cotton looms turned the ancient town of Lodz into the Manchester of Poland.

And with the migration of the landowners came the migration of many of their former serfs, for the peasants too were affected by the general reshuffle. The old social system, bad as it was, had at least assumed responsibility for them, even while it kept them in servitude. The great households of their masters had absorbed their ever-increasing families of sons and daughters. Forced to rely upon their own resources they found that they could scarcely gain even a bare living from the ground. So they, too, began to leave the land for the cities which had need of their youth and strength to feed the new looms and factories.

It was the old bondage in a new phase. Instead of tilling the fields and cutting the corn at the bidding of their master they hewed his coal or tended his machines. The slavery of the land became the slavery of a starvation wage and a thirteen-hour day. And they wore their chains in dull resignation as their parents had done because they had known nothing better.

CHAPTER VIII

AT THE beginning of this century there were scarcely any professions open to women even in the West of Europe and still fewer in Poland and Russia. Although a few courageous pioneers were blazing the trail into the spheres of University education, out of which was to emerge later the great figure of Marie Curie, they were regarded with something akin to horror by people like my Aunt Maria who held that mental activity of any sort was unfeminine and that every well-brought-up girl ought to find sufficient occupation in needle-work, painting lampshades, and reading light novels.

There was dire consternation then when on leaving the Gymnase I begged to be allowed to continue my studies with a view to earning my own living later. In the first place it would necessitate my going away for I had already reached the pinnacle of education in Suvalki, and secondly there arose the problem of where I was to go. There was no universities for women in Russian Poland and even if I wished to be admitted to one in Russia I should have to wait until I was twenty-one, another four years. The only alternative was the Commercial College in Warsaw, which was just then beginning to take a few girl students, and which gave much the same advantages as a University with the addition of a special business course.

When I broached the subject Aunt Maria was, as I had feared, shocked at the mere suggestion of any one in the family, least of all a woman, going into trade, but Grandmother unexpectedly proved my ally. I think that, although we never spoke of it, she realized that my ideal was the same as her own and was determined to let nothing stand in my way. Instead of opposing me she immediately set aside the necessary money and wrote to the Principal of the College. I entered it in the autumn term.

Although the old Polish University of Warsaw had been abolished after the Insurrection and a Russian University had been instituted in its stead, the penalties for "illegal education" were not so strictly enforced there as in Suvalki and other provincial towns. A number of private schools, entirely Polish in language and character, were enabled to continue without interference by the simple expedient of bribing the Russian functionaries. As most of the pupils came from wealthy Polish families, large sums were paid over regularly as the price of official silence.

The boarding-school to which I went, which was attached to the Commercial College, came under this category. Although it was sanctioned by the Russian Government, the principal, Madame Siemiradska, and all the mistresses and visiting professors were Poles. Lessons were, of course, given in Polish, but in every desk there were duplicate sets of text-books, one in Polish, the other in Russian. Whenever a Government inspector arrived at the school, which was several times in a term, the loyal old porter at the lodge would ring a bell which echoed in every classroom. Then the Russian books would be hurriedly taken out, the Polish ones put away, and the professor who was lecturing would immediately switch over into Russian. When the inspector entered he would find nothing to report even if he questioned the class, for all the front seats were occupied by girls who spoke fluent Russian and could answer him correctly. Much the same method of evading the regulations was adopted by every private school in Warsaw. In many of the fashionable *pensions de jeunes filles* lessons in the forbidden Polish history or literature were given during what appeared to be needlework or drawing classes. Immediately there was a warning books would be bundled out of sight and embroidery or sketching books got out.

My grandmother died just before the beginning of my first term at the Commercial College, but with her usual determination she would not even hear of my remaining at home on account of her illness and insisted on choosing my new dresses and embroidering my initials on the store of linen I was taking with me. She died as fearlessly as she had lived, ignoring her own suffering, reassuring poor distracted Aunt Maria and leaving careful instructions for the management of her estate.

I wanted to weep for her but I could not, perhaps because she had always been contemptuous of the weakness of tears and had neither shed them herself nor let any of us do so in her presence. So instead I remembered the promise I had given her on that night when she had put the patriot's ring on my finger. I think it must have been in her mind, too, for a few hours before she died she called Aunt Maria and my uncle to her and begged them not to oppose me in anything I might want to do, even though they might not agree with it.

To that last injunction of hers I owed the fact that I had much more liberty than any of the other students at Madame Siemiradska's school, for while they, in accordance with the strict chaperonage of those days, never went out alone, I was allowed, with Aunt Maria's consent, to go where I would in the city of Warsaw and to make friends outside the College. In this way I made my first contact with political work and also with what were known as "The Flying Universities," so named because professors and students were continually in flight and classes were never held at the same house twice. Their purpose was to teach the forbidden Polish history and literature and also sociology and political economy, subjects which were available to Poles only at the Russian Universities. They were attended by hundreds of young men and women drawn from all ranks of society. We would meet in the evenings or on Sunday afternoons, twenty or thirty of us at a time at the house of one of the students. Sometimes it would be in the salon or the garden of a beautiful country manor, sometimes in the stuffy little parlour behind a shop in the poor quarters of the city, or in an artist's attic where we had to squeeze ourselves in by sitting on the bed or on cushions on the floor. The teachers, too, varied from famous professors to obscure young writers, but all of them gave their services at the risk of imprisonment and exile. It was a widespread organization and a very practical one for it not only kept alive the sense of unity amongst us, but it provided a means of education for many who could not otherwise have afforded college fees. Above all it taught us to cherish the spirit of freedom as something precious which must not be suffered to die out.

Warsaw in those days was rent with political discussion,

particularly the milieu frequented by the students and intellectuals, for a number of rival parties were contesting the field,
each armed with its own program.

The group which held the greatest number of adherents,
especially among the students and young people, was the National Democrats. This was an offshoot of the National League,
founded by Colonel Milkowski, who had been one of the
leaders of the Insurrection of 1863. In its early days it had
been a purely patriot party, whose sole aim was the independence of Poland, irrespective of class considerations, although much of its propaganda was directed towards the
peasantry and the masses. But with the beginning of this
century the program of the party, which was by that time
under the influence of Roman Dmowski, underwent a change.
The insistence on national independence, which had been its
keynote, started to take second place to the plan for a closer
union with Russia and the party began to send its representatives to the Russian Duma. Basing its new policy on the as-
sumption that Poland had more to gain from Russia than any
other country, it conducted an energetic anti-German and
pro-Russian campaign, while at the same time it agitated
violently against the possibility of any Polish-Lithuanian or
Polish-Ruthenian collaboration. This was the party which was
diametrically opposed to the Polish Socialists, which was my
husband's party, and he and Roman Dmowski found themselves adversaries in nearly every crisis in Poland's destiny
from the time of the Russo-Japanese War.

A party which at that time gave little indication of the
importance it was to assume in Russia in the future was the
Social Democrats, which was a purely Socialist party, allied
to the Russian Socialists. In its ranks were Lenin and Trotsky
and most of the men who later became famous as Bolshevik
leaders, and a number of international Socialists among whom
was Rosa Luxemburg. Its propaganda in Poland was not
concerned with the issue of national independence, but with
gaining adherents among the working-classes to the creed of
Socialism, the destruction of the bourgeoisie and the improvement in the conditions of the proletariat. To this end it was
actually opposed to the restoration of Poland's freedom since

it would mean the loss of the Russian markets for her trade
and consequent unemployment in the great industrial centres
like Lodz. This attitude alienated the Polish patriots, while
its gospel of economic terrorism expressed in a series of unnecessary and cold-blooded assassinations lost the party many
of its more moderate supporters.

At the other extreme of the scale was the Conservative
Party, which was upheld by the entire Polish aristocracy and
was therefore most influential in Galicia where the landowners
were all-powerful. It was the one and only political party
in Poland which received unanimous encouragement from the
Russian, German and Austrian Governments, who were aware
that revolt would never menace them from the ranks of the
aristocracy. In return for that encouragement the party in
Russian Poland dutifully deplored the Insurrection of 1863
and echoed generally the opinions of St. Petersburg.

A party which was discussed at Madame Siemiradska's
school, because she herself supported it, was the Realist Party
whose leader was the writer Swetochowski. Its policy was one
of compromise, its sole ideal the material prosperity of the
nation. To attain this it was ready to sacrifice the fight for
independence and become absorbed into the Russian orbit on
the principle that Poland having been conquered ought to
adapt herself to existing circumstances, develop her economic
resources, and grow rich on her trade with Russia. . . .

"The existence of nations does not rest on the externals
of political independence" . . . wrote Swetochowski in sum-
ming up his program. . . . "If a people which has ceased to be
independent makes the fullest use of its spiritual forces and
discovers within itself reserves capable of benefiting civilization it can always declare proudly and hopefully, I exist still!
Fate has opened up to us a field of commercial and industrial
conquests which we have not yet fully explored, but in which
we shall win victories more lasting than those on which we
have hitherto set our hopes. . . ."

This doctrine of complacency and self-interest gained a
large following, principally among the middle class, but to me,
coming from a family of patriots, it appeared almost in the
light of a sacrilege. I had looked forward with youthful im-

patience to coming to Warsaw, believing, in my simplicity, that I should at once find myself at the very fountain-head of patriotism with a dozen political channels ready to make use of my energies. Instead I was tossed in perplexity from one party to another. At the end of six months, although I had waded conscientiously through masses of propaganda and attended meetings organized by the various rival groups, I was still uncertain as to which one to join.

In the meantime I studied hard, and read a great deal. It was at about this time that I discovered for myself the works of Karl Marx and Kennedy and Bebel, which brought me under the influence of Socialism. A course of Nietzsche and Renan resulted in a phase of agnosticism which was a cause of profound distress to Aunt Maria. She used to slip little religious books into the boxes of cakes and home-made preserves which Anusia sent me every week from Suvalki, but I put them away unread, tolerantly contemptuous in the light of my superior knowledge. Only at the end of long years and after many storms did my faith come back to me, and then it was firm and enduring.

The course which I took at the Commercial College included Commercial and Civil Law, Political Economy, and Chemistry. I had therefore several posts to choose from on leaving, but remembering the lesson of the Insurrection of 1863 . . . that any successful political movement must originate among the working class . . . I wanted to lose no time in making contact with them. The best way to do this seemed to be by becoming one of themselves, so I took a place as clerk in the office of a leather goods firm.

The factory which turned out all manner of leather goods from horses' harness to valises and ladies' reticules (as they were called in those days) was situated on the outskirts of Warsaw, so I and two other counting-house employees used to drive to work every morning in an old-fashioned barouche drawn by two horses. We used to set out soon after seven o'clock in order to be in our places by nine and when our day ended, at five in the afternoon, we would find it waiting at the factory doors to drive us home again. It was a thoughtful courtesy which we owed to the manager. He was an exceedingly considerate and liberal-minded man, very popular with his work-people, whose conditions were much above the average of that time. Viewed from present-day standards they were appalling. Both men and women worked from 7 A.M. till 7 P.M. for wages which ranged from the equivalent of $1.20 to $3.00 a week. But they were at least allowed an hour for dinner in the middle of the day, which was exceptional, for in the majority of factories there was only a fifteen-minute break, and the workers took their parcels of food which they ate standing by their machines.

In the early years of this century the lot of the Polish peasant who had exchanged the meagre livelihood of his little holding for the vague promise of the city was infinitely worse than that of his forebears. The soil had at least given them health and strength and a sufficiency of air and food; the mills and factories gave him none of these things. He lived in foul slums which grew every year more overcrowded with his increasing family, for he came of the most prolific stock in Europe, and died, generally before his time, of some disease born of the dust of the cotton looms or the grime of the furnaces which his country-bred ancestors had never known.

He had no unemployment relief and no health insurance. If he lost his job he had to find another immediately or starve. If he was taken ill he could only look to the charity of his individual employer. No matter how bad the conditions under which he worked might be, he was compelled to accept them because, not having learnt the value of unity, he had no trade union to fight for him and come to his aid if he went on strike. Such small unrecognized associations as existed were without funds, for there was no system of voluntary contributions among the workers, and in consequence the strikes which broke out from time to time were doomed to failure. Without any sort of organization behind them they petered out almost as soon as they had begun, and before news of them had penetrated even to the neighbouring towns the strikers had been forced by hunger to come to terms with their employers.

The insight into labour conditions which I gained from my experience at the factory made me realize that any political party which was to achieve practical results in the fight for

Poland's freedom would have to include in its program not only the issue of national independence, but also an extensive scheme for social reform. It was some time before I succeeded in finding one of this description. When I eventually did so it was unexpectedly.

While I was studying at the Commercial College I formed one of the happiest and most lasting friendships of my life with a girl named Janka. As we left at the same time, she to study music at the Conservatoire and I to go into business, we took a small apartment at a *pension de famille*. Both of us had a great many friends and it was crowded nearly every evening with young people. The majority of them were students, or ex-students just starting in one or other of the professions, poor perhaps where material possessions were concerned, but rich in hope and enthusiasm. We used to make coffee or tea and get out one of the hampers of country delicacies which Aunt Maria, who could never be convinced that I did not starve myself in Warsaw, sent me regularly. When the last morsels of home-cured ham and apple cheese had disappeared we would embark on long and earnest discussions lasting far into the night. Usually they were political in character centring on the propaganda of the rival parties, and in the course of one of them I first heard of the P.P.S.

The P.P.S., or Polish Socialist Party, had been founded in Paris in 1892 by a small group of Polish exiles, among whom were Yodko, Mendelssohn and Alexander Sulkiewicz. Its program embraced all the main points of Socialism . . . freedom and equal rights for all classes, and increased wage standard, shorter hours and better conditions for workers, and franchise for women. But in addition it was a patriot party, pledged to fight above all else for the independence of Poland.

This was the party which seemed to offer the practical plan of campaign I had sought in vain, and as Janka's brother belonged to it, I had no difficulty in gaining admission. Unlike most secret organizations it had no oath of allegiance binding its members till death, and any one who wished to leave it was free to do so without reproach, on the simple understanding that he, or she, would not betray the party. I was given work

to do almost immediately in the form of propaganda in the
suburb of Praga, which was then given over to the poorest of
Warsaw's poor, mill hands and factory workers who were
herded together in dark, airless slums. I used to go there every
Sunday afternoon and hold meetings for women and girls.
They were rough and uneducated, brutalized by the hardness
of their lives and the absence of any cultural influences, but in
them were the seeds of patriotism and a capacity for loyalty
for which I had cause to be grateful more than once. As time
went on my activities began to attract the attention of the
Russian Government spies, so that it became increasingly difficult to find a place for our meetings.

One Saturday evening I came home from my work at the
leather factory to find a rough-looking man in workman's
clothes waiting at the door of our apartment. I tried to appear as
unconcerned as possible when he stepped out of the shadows
and intercepted me, though I felt sure he was a Russian agent.
To my relief, however, he introduced himself as the father of
one of the girls who attended my meetings and explained that
he had come to warn me. He was a railway employee at Praga,
and on the previous Sunday he had noticed that when I left the
train two men waiting at the station had followed me at a
distance. Later in the day when I had taken the return train
to Warsaw they had been on the platform and one of them had
got into conversation with him, and questioned him about my
movements. He had replied that he had never seen me in Praga
before, and they had appeared satisfied, but he was convinced
that they were Russian police officers and intended to arrest
me. He had walked all the way into Warsaw to advise me not
to hold my meeting next day.

I was touched at his loyalty and took his advice. Later I
was very glad that I had done so, for I heard that the police
had in fact searched the house where I was to have held my
meeting, and had also kept watch at the station all day. From
that time onwards I knew I had been marked on the Russian
Black List as an agitator.

In those early years of the twentieth century the spirit
of political endeavour began to stir again in Poland. The tor-
por which had lain over the stricken and exhausted country

since the terrible retribution of the Insurrection had worn off, for as Joseph Pilsudski wrote: . . . "grass grows on tombs, new life rises from ashes and seeks sun and liberty. And Poland, too, which was one vast tomb, grew green again; a new life, a new movement arose, opening a new epoch."

Borne on the wings of that fresh impetus, the P.P.S. had become in the year 1904, when I joined it, the strongest political organization in Poland, with a membership which even then numbered several thousand, and which was increasing from month to month. All over the country stretched a network of local branches linked together by the Central Committee. Establishing communication between these was a lengthy and difficult process because, to avoid running the risk of letters, telegrams and telephone, it could only be done by conspiracy and word of mouth. Consequently those of us working in one centre, even in Warsaw, which was the largest and most important, saw little of the other members of the party. Not until after I had belonged to it for some years did I come into personal contact with the leaders, though I constantly heard of one of them, Joseph Pilsudski. When I joined the P.P.S. he had just returned from a mission to Japan which, although it had resulted in no material gain, had enormously increased the prestige of the party, since it was the first time since the loss of her independence that Poland had been accorded diplomatic status by one of the great foreign powers.

The outbreak of the Russo-Japanese War in February 1904 had been followed by wide repercussions in Poland. The prospects of thousands of Poles being mobilized and sent off to Manchuria to fight Russia's battles caused a fresh wave of resentment to sweep over the country, but the retribution of '63 was still green in the memory of the people. They submitted in silence to this new injustice.

Pilsudski, who could endure defeat but never submission, urged the P.P.S. to take action whether the time was ripe or not. He could not sit still in inertia while the flower of Poland's youth was offered up in sacrifice to Imperial aggrandizement. Better lead them to resist, even to die in resisting Russian tyranny as their fathers had done, than let them be slaughtered unwillingly in a war which was not their own! Burning with enthusiasm, he laid his plans before the Central Committee, strove to rally them to his point of view.

Their lack of response was a bitter disappointment. While some of the younger members of the party, fired by his example, stood behind him, the majority were cautious and apathetic. Some even maintained that a war between two bourgeois powers did not concern a proletariat organization.

But his was not the temperament to yield to discouragement and he had still another card to play.

The astute Japanese Government, realizing that the political situation in Poland could be turned to good account in dealing with Russia, had invited him to go to Tokio for a consultation. Accompanied by Tytus Filipowicz (who later became Polish Ambassador to the United States), he sailed in the month of May 1904.

"The precise object of the consultation was not stated," he wrote in describing his mission, "and I could have sent others, but I decided to go in person, because I realized that the conversation would hinge on the communication of information of a military nature to Japan, and I did not wish to entrust so delicate a matter to any one else. Japan would defray the cost of the journey.

"The crossing of two oceans and the continent of America from end to end lasted more than a month, and therefore I had time to reflect on the line of conduct which I intended to pursue in Japan. I decided in the first place that I would consent to organize an intelligence service only if Japan would give me technical aid in the form of arms and munitions. I was convinced that a war sustained in Russia could not continue without leaving its mark upon the Russian state, and that therefore we Poles, by resorting to force, could effect an improvement in the lot of Poland."

The Minister for Foreign Affairs received him cordially in Tokio. In the course of their interview, Pilsudski presented a memorandum which he had drawn up showing the ethnical composition of the Russian Empire. Only 75 per cent of its people were Russians; the rest had been annexed by conquest —Poles, Lithuanians, Estonians and Caucasians. He represented that of these Poland was the most capable of carrying matters to the length of open war with Russia, and that in that event she would bring in with her the other conquered nations. The question of Polish independence was therefore of the utmost significance to Japan. The Japanese Minister was favourably impressed with the plan, but the success of the mission was frustrated by Roman Dmowski who, as leader of the National Democrats, was already in Tokio with a rival memorandum, in which he stated that any insurrection in Poland could only be prejudicial to Japan's cause. Neither man was aware of the other's presence in the city until they met face to face in the street. They saluted one another casually, but from that moment it was a battle of diplomacy between them. Dmowski won.

"Nothing practical resulted from my interview in Tokio," wrote Pilsudski. . . . "All that I could obtain was the promise that Polish prisoners of war, many of whom had voluntarily surrendered themselves sooner than fight for Russia, should be united in one group and that one of the men of our party should be at the disposal of the Japanese General Staff to act as intermediary on behalf of these Polish prisoners. . . ."

That was the first clash of swords between Joseph Pilsudski and Roman Dmowski. Thereafter they were often to find themselves opponents. And more than once the fate of Poland was to hang in the balance while they struggled.

Meanwhile, in the summer of 1904 the first mobilization of Polish troops for the Manchurian campaign began. As in 1863 young men were torn from their families and packed off to Russian barracks to be hurriedly entrained as cannon-fodder. . . .

"But there was no question of our replying to it as our fathers had done in '63" . . . wrote Pilsudski. . . . "We were too weak and too ignorant for that. I knew that in spite of the reservists' hatred of the thought that they were to die for Russia against their own feelings, they would obey the order of the state. Like so many cattle led to the slaughter they would entrain and travel to the end of the world in order to die, to sicken, and to suffer, and sacrifice body and soul on behalf of their enemy. They would do all that without a protest, without uttering a word. I could almost have died of despair. . . ."

He was back in Poland now, consumed with a bitterness and resentment that would not let him rest. He rallied the Central Committee, urged them with renewed insistence to take action while there was still time, travelled openly and under his own name to sound all the branches of the P.P.S., although the St. Petersburg police had issued his photograph to every gendarmerie station with orders that he was to be arrested on the grounds of preparing a Polish rising.

In the end he had his way. The party agreed to let him organize a public manifestation against the Russian call-up of Poles for the war in the Far East. It was decided to hold it at the Plac Grzybowski in Warsaw on Sunday, November 13th, 1904.

The Warsaw branch of the P.P.S. naturally took the principal part in the preparations. Word was sent out to all branches of the party notifying them of the demonstration, and asking them to send representatives.

The manifestation was to take place outside the Church of the Holy Spirit in the Plac Grzybowski immediately after Mass. Hundreds of members of the P.P.S., students, working men and peasants from the country districts would assemble in the square during the morning, and at noon a procession which had formed in the Ulrica Bagno would march to the church doors singing the forbidden patriotic songs and carrying banners on which were printed the words . . . "We Will Not Be the Czar's Soldiers" . . . and "We Will Fight for Poland Alone." A small detachment of cool-headed men in the front ranks were to be armed with revolvers, but they were on no account to use them unless the Russian police first opened fire on the procession.

I and three other girls chosen to take part in the manifestation had been given instructions to attend the Mass but to remain in our seats afterwards instead of leaving with the rest of the congregation. I shall never forget the suspense of waiting there, watching the hands of my watch creeping slowly round to twelve, wondering what was happening outside and what we would be called upon to do. I tried to follow the Mass, but my thoughts kept going astray.

At length the Benediction was pronounced and people began to stream out of the church, but I remained kneeling in the pew as I had been told to do. Looking round cautiously, I could see the other girls still in their places, although we were separated from one another. The church was emptying rapidly now; the tall candles above the altar were being extinguished one by one. Suddenly I heard shouts from the square and a great many voices singing "Czervony Sztandar" and "La Varsovienne"—the songs that had echoed through the Revolution of 1830. The march had begun.

Almost immediately a volley of shots rang out, followed by the sound of horses clattering across the square as Russian lancers who had been hiding in courtyards rode out and charged the procession. People came running back into the church for shelter. A confused babel of voices arose round me. Then the great doors of the church clanged shut, and looking over my shoulder I saw police standing on guard before them.

Presently I heard hurried steps approaching my pew and a young man dropped on his knees beside me. I saw that he was a young doctor, one of the members of the P.P.S. He laid two revolvers on the seat, whispered "Hide them quickly," and was gone before I had time to reply.

I remained quite still with my head bowed in my hands, apparently in an attitude of devotion, but in reality wondering what to do. Looking out of the corner of my eyes I could see police subjecting every one to a thorough search before they allowed them to leave the church. No hope, then, of taking the revolvers out concealed on my person. I must either manage to leave them in the church or else be found in possession of them. Which would mean Siberia.

Luckily for me, in the pew just at my feet was an old-fashioned footstool, a heavy, cumbrous thing of mahogany with carved legs and a padded top, probably belonging to some old lady. The space beneath it would make an ideal hiding-place. Under cover of the folds of my skirt, which was a full one, I managed to take up the revolvers and slip them into it without being perceived. Then I got up and mingled with the people filing out of the church.

As I had expected, I was searched, but as nothing of an incriminating nature was found on me I was allowed to leave immediately.

The Plac Grzybowski was almost empty now except for the dead and wounded lying in the roadway. Mechanically I turned down the first street. A few feet away from me a mounted policeman was firing apparently at random. A bullet whizzed just over my head and a man dropped on the opposite sidewalk.

A mist swam before my eyes and for a few moments I was so dizzy that I could only stand still clutching on to some railings for support. Then my head cleared and I was able to go home. Later in the day I returned to the church and successfully retrieved the hidden revolvers.

The manifestation of Grzybowski, tragically as it ended, achieved its purpose. It had a far wider influence than any one realized at the time, for the Russian Government seeing in it the first public demonstration by a revolutionary party in Poland since the Insurrection of 1863, and uncertain of how far the unrest had spread, grew alarmed. Already involved in an unsatisfactory war in the Far East, they had no wish to take upon themselves the added strain of a revolution at their own gates. So by an immediate and drastic change of plans they reduced mobilization in Poland to a minimum.

PART THREE

★

THAT CERTAIN PILSUDSKI

CHAPTER IX

THE WINTER of 1904–1905 was a hard one in Russia. In towns and villages the poor died by hundreds from cold and starvation. The peasants huddled together in their huts at night and talked of what was to be done in a future that was as grey as the leaden December skies. And of their talk was born the conviction that one man could save them if only he knew of their plight. Their Little Father. They decided to send a deputation to him.

So on January 22nd, 1905, a procession of peasants and workmen led by the priest, Father Gapon, marched through the streets of St. Petersburg to the Winter Palace to lay their grievances before the Czar. It was an unarmed procession, peaceful and loyal in its intentions, but it never reached the Palace, for the way was barred by troops who fired volley after volley into its ranks until they dispersed in confusion, leaving their dead behind them.

The storm of indignation aroused by that needless and cruel massacre reached its climax in the Revolution which swept through Russia. Riots broke out in all the principal cities, thousands of workers, half-starved and underpaid, went on strike. The Government dealt with them after its usual ruthless fashion, shot the ringleaders and imprisoned the rest. But even so the revolt gathered strength. It spread into Russian Poland and there it changed character, took on a patriotic as well as an economic motive. Even the school-children joined in it. Over 100,000 of them went on strike as a protest against the prohibition of the Polish language. The Government ordered that an example should be made of them, so some were flogged with the utmost brutality while others were expelled from their schools, and thereby barred from every profession.

The children's brief effort was quenched in tears and suffering, but the revolt itself was not so easily suppressed. Instead, it gained a new impetus, extended to the furthermost

corners of Poland under Russian rule. Every industry was
affected. There were daily battles between strikers and police.
In Warsaw the Government proclaimed a state of siege,
mounted troops were ordered to charge any crowd of more
than five persons which assembled in the streets, but they
could not be in all quarters of the city at once. Agitators from
every political party stood on chairs and harangued the workmen in the dinner hour, there would be as many as five or six
separate groups in one street, each preaching a different program. Then there would be warning shouts and the Russian
lancers would sweep down upon them all impartially, striking
out to right and left, so that presently the street would be
empty enough except for inanimate bundles stretched out on
the stones.

The jails were full to overflowing with political prisoners,
the majority of whom were arrested merely on suspicion of
belonging to one or other of the different parties, and might
be induced after weeks of solitary confinement to reveal
the secrets of their organization. The police had their own
methods of extorting such "confessions." The application of
red-hot irons to the soles of the feet was considered to be one
of the most successful; boiling wax poured under the finger-
nails was another. If these failed there still remained the
knout.

One evening I went to the house of a student in Warsaw,
a member of the P.P.S., who had a little printing press. I
was to call for some cards which he had printed on it to notify
the local branches of our next manifestation. On my arrival
I found him very much agitated because only that morning
two of his friends had had a visit from the police who had
insisted on searching their rooms, though fortunately without result, for all their correspondence had been carefully
hidden. He was anxious for me to take away the cards though
he feared I might be stopped and searched on leaving the
house.

I hid the parcel in the front of my dress and hurried home-
wards, choosing unfrequented side roads in order to escape
observation. For once I was grateful for the fact that since
the Revolution there had been no lights in the city except

from the braziers set up at the corners of the streets where soldiers and police were posted.

I was nearing the pension where I lived when I heard sounds that made me stand still in horror. The street, which was almost deserted at that hour, was lighted only by the stars so that I could not see more than a few yards ahead, but horses were coming towards me at a walking pace. The ring of hoofs upon the cobbles was punctuated with the sharp crack of whips, followed by a low, sobbing, incoherent cry.

I shrank back into the doorway of a church, longing to escape, yet rooted to the spot by sheer terror of what I was going to see. A moment later two mounted Russian police came into view. Between their horses a man stumbled along blindly, plunging forward and falling heavily to the ground, only to be jerked to his feet again by the chains that bound him to each saddle. A man whose hands were pinioned behind him and whose shirt was torn to ribbons by the long nahajakas which the two policemen were wielding with rhythmic regularity. Every time the leather thongs cut through the air to flay the shrinking shoulders that despairing cry echoed in the stillness of the street.

As they drew level with me the horses slowed down a little. The man walking between them raised his head and I saw his eyes rest for a moment on the statue of Christ in the entrance of the church. His lips moved in supplication. Then the cavalcade passed on into the darkness. The cries died away in silence.

As month after month went by and the revolution showed no signs of abating, the Government grew alarmed and introduced still sterner measures. But one strike was no sooner suppressed than another broke out. In every part of the Russian Empire there were scenes of bloodshed and violence as men sought reprisals for the accumulated wrongs of centuries, and bombs and bullets took the place of speech that had been denied. In Russia the downtrodden proletariat had shaken off its docility and, like a slow and patient beast goaded beyond endurance, turned on its masters. In Poland, where the cause of the oppressed workers had become identified with the cause of the oppressed nation, the struggle gained

new impetus. Every political party increased its sphere. The
P.P.S. with an added membership of tens of thousands became
a force to be reckoned with, a definite influence in the life of the
nation, since it was the only party which was both Nationalist
and Socialist. Many of the most important strikes and manifestations of 1905 and 1906 were organized by it, notably the
General Strike of January 1905. All over the country its members took part in fights with the police and military in which
many lives were lost on both sides. In those days of storm the
militant organization of the party, the "Bojowka" (Association of Secret Conspiracy and Combat) came into being.

In its beginning it was merely an irregular armed group
created for the purpose of carrying on guerilla warfare against
Russian authorities. There was no thought of a disciplined
force or of any sort of military technique and training behind
it . . .

"To most Socialists it appeared ridiculous to speak of
artillery and rifles" . . . wrote Joseph Pilsudski in describing those early days. . . . "Any one thinking of an armed
rising was laughed at as a 'romantic' and a relic of the
insurrectionary traditions. The men were not even used
to assembling at a given time and place, so that to manœuvre
them was impossible. Another mark of the organization
was the lack of trained leaders, which made it a house
built on sand. Its first militants were chosen from the
district and factory organizations. They were entirely
at the disposal of the party. Their weapons were sticks,
their duty to collect at a certain point and carry out little manifestations. At a given signal a small group of them
would run out into the street, unfurl a red flag, and disperse before the police could come up. But these little
manifestations helped the party to gain control of the street
crowds. Events developed. The first shots were fired during the manifestation in the Plac Grzybowski, and after
that revolutionary methods were introduced into the P.P.S.
tactics. . . ."

The Central Committee of the party, which controlled this
militant branch, was at that time divided among itself over the

question of its policy. The great masses of the people, who were beginning to look to it for leadership, were in favour of a campaign of widespread demonstrations and incessant agitation against the Russian Government, a point of view which was shared by the majority of the Committee.

The opposition was led by Joseph Pilsudski, who was against any course of action likely to end in violence and clashes with the Russian authorities. He disapproved of terrorism in theory, and in practice, since he considered it of no use in achieving any definite results and calculated only to cause unnecessary suffering to individuals. The bombing of Government buildings and attempts on the lives of Russian officials, however great the provocation, were abhorrent to him, and he steadfastly maintained the view that the party ought to wait until such time as it should be strong enough, both in arms and in men, to take the field and challenge the Russian forces in open warfare. . . . "Let us fight by all means" . . . he urged . . . "but fight as soldiers in the open, not from the corner. . . ."

He was opposed therefore on principle to demonstrations and public manifestations since they invariably led to bloodshed and retaliations on both sides. The Bojowka, while it was more than capable of dealing with the armed Russian gendarmerie, was no match for regular troops and it was intolerable to him that lives should be wasted in futile skirmishes with the police.

In later years when he was the leader of the Polish Army instead of a small guerilla troop he had this same regard for the lives of his men. He would never risk even a single company without justification.

All through the year of 1905 therefore he held himself aloof from the party's campaign of terrorism and criticized it so steadfastly that he reached an open breach with the Central Committee which resulted in his withdrawing to Galicia. And because he was a man who throughout his life aroused the hot or the cold, but never the lukewarm in people, the party was rent with discussion. While some of the members of the Central Committee attacked him bitterly he had a tremendous following among the rank and file. The entire youth of the party stood solidly behind him.

The amnesty which was declared by Russia in the autumn of 1905 seemed to promise some amelioration in the conditions of Poland. It accorded a certain measure of liberty to the press and freedom of speech. The use of the Polish language was restored to schools (the poor children had at least achieved that by their strike).

But the declaration of the amnesty was marred by one of those pointless and apparently motiveless acts which have always characterized Russian policy.

In celebration of the amnesty a crowd, largely composed of students and young people, walked in procession through the streets of Warsaw, singing patriotic songs and waving flags. It was not an organized procession and had no political significance, just a spontaneous assembly of light-hearted people, rejoicing over the satisfactory end to months of strikes and disputes. But when they arrived at the Place de Théâtre they found it filled with police who fired upon them without warning, killing many of those in the front ranks.

There were casual apologies from the Government afterwards, and vague explanations laying the blame on first one official and then another, but the fact remained that whatever improvement had been effected in the relations between Poland and Russia was undone. With the passing of time, too, it became only too obvious that many of the promised concessions would never materialize.

Towards the close of 1905 the Bojowka had practically ceased to exist, for nearly all its members, with the exception of Pilsudski, who was still in Galicia, had been sentenced to varying terms of imprisonment. The Central Committee appealed to him to take over the Militant Organization of the party. He agreed to do so provided they would let him run it on his own lines.

It was the opportunity he had always wanted. He would create a trained and disciplined armed force capable of offering effective resistance to Russia's troops.

At his suggestion a uniform method of training was established to be used throughout the organization, and regular military schools were instituted in Galicia where selected recruits from all parts of Poland were taught tactics and prepared for guerilla warfare. Not until they had passed an examination corresponding to those of the recognized military colleges could they be admitted to the ranks of the Bojowka. Those who graduated successfully were appointed officers and sent through Russian Poland to form provincial groups composed of men of the working classes whom they drilled and trained in the use of arms. At first no group, even in the big industrial cities, contained more than five members, but so great was the demand that before long each group began to organize in its turn sub-groups until the association numbered several hundred men.

It was an ambitious undertaking, this transformation of a revolutionary band into an efficient and disciplined military force, for the entire training and organization could only be carried on in the utmost secrecy. The recruits had to assemble under the most difficult conditions; drilling took place in warehouses after closing hours, revolver practice was held in deserted woods and country lanes. But the venture succeeded almost beyond belief. . . . "In spite of the inexperience from which even the leaders suffered" . . . wrote Joseph Pilsudski in describing those early struggles . . . "in one respect a miracle was achieved, for the men acquired an extraordinary discipline, capacity to obey orders, self-control and resolution." . . .

Out of the ranks of that first Bojowka emerged men who were to rise to fame in the future Polish State . . . Walery Slaweck, and Colonel Prystor, both of whom held office as Prime Minister, and General Sosnkowski, Chief of Staff of the First Brigade of the Legions and subsequently Polish Minister of War.

As the numbers of the Militant Organization increased from scattered units to hundreds of men, dispersed over the greater part of Russian Poland, the provision of arms and ammunition became a vital necessity. The P.P.S. was well supplied with funds by its members and sympathizers, who included a number of landowners and well-to-do young men. The difficulty therefore was not unsurmountable. Quantities of Mausers and revolvers were purchased in Belgium and smuggled into the country, knives were imported from Finland and bombs and cartridges were filled at secret laboratories which were opened in Warsaw and other cities. The work of transporting these arms from the frontier and to the different depots and distributing them to the provincial centres was carried out by men and women specially chosen from among the members of the party. At first it was only a question of hiding a few Brownings, but as it grew in proportion to the growth of the military force which it had to equip it involved before long the organization of a whole chain of secret arsenals and magazines.

I was given charge of the central arms depot in Warsaw which controlled all the provincial distribution centres, and thousands of rifles and revolvers and tons of ammunition passed through my hands in the course of a year. I was responsible not only for storing and issuing them to the different branches of the Bojowka, but also for arranging for their transport and collecting them at the final clearing house. I had of course a number of helpers, both men and women, who assisted in the actual conveying of the arms, but I alone knew the full route of each consignment and the identities of the different people who acted as links in the chain.

In May 1906 Joseph Pilsudski, who was visiting every branch of the Bojowka and selecting recruits for the training school in Cracow, came to inspect my depot. I remember that when I was told to expect him I felt some curiosity to see this man whose name was fast becoming a legend in Poland.

In looking back on that first meeting I realize that for a long time my impressions were always of the leader, never of the man himself. That I should love him one day never even occurred to me. We were completely impersonal, two people working side by side for the same cause.

Yet my picture of him on that spring afternoon as we stood surrounded by stacks of rifles and boxes of cartridges is as vivid still as it was thirty-four years ago. I remember that my first thought of him was that here was a man whom Siberia had failed to break. It had not set its seal upon him either mentally or physically, as it had upon all the other returned exiles I had met. There was neither bitterness nor resignation in his face. Then I became conscious of the tremendous force of his personality, of that indefinable magnetism which enabled him, all through his life, to sway the minds of men, even against their will.

I had somehow expected him to be a big man, powerfully built. I was surprised to find he was of medium height only with broad shoulders, a slender waist and a step as light as a girl's. He had a feline grace of movement which he retained even in old age. He glided over the ground with an easy buoyancy so tireless that he could outmarch men far more robust than himself. For the rest I saw he had a small head with ears that were slightly pointed and very sensitive, grey-blue eyes, deep-set and penetrating, and a face so mobile that it reflected every passing thought.

But in that first impression of him I noticed more than any other characteristic the curious contrast between his right and left hands. The left was fine and narrow, with delicate, tapering fingers, like a woman's, useless and nervous. The hand of an artist and a dreamer. The right was so much larger that it might have belonged to another man, forceful and brutal, with broad, square-tipped fingers so strong that he was able to bend a horseshoe easily in them. The hand of a soldier and a man of action.

In later years I used to think that nothing could have better expressed Joseph Pilsudski than those contradictory hands, for I believe few men have combined so many opposing qualities. He was a soldier and a realist, far-sighted, essentially practical, ruthless when the occasion demanded. He was a dreamer and an idealist, a lover of poetry and of beauty in every form, sensitive, impressionable to the point of sentimentality where his affections were concerned, too generous in his judgment of those whom he trusted.

That first meeting left me with only a fleeting impression of that restless, dynamic personality, for our few minutes' conversation was confined to counting Mausers and Brownings, but before two months had passed I was to see much more of him.

In July 1906 the Bojowka summoned representatives from every branch of the party to a Congress in Cracow. Joseph Pilsudski attended it both in the capacity of leader of the Bojowka and as one of the delegates from Galicia, and as I had been chosen to act as secretary to the Congress we were constantly working together.

Under the friendlier, more tolerant rule of Austria political enterprise of every description flourished in Cracow and a number of different parties managed to carry on their activities there with very little hindrance from authorities. For this reason it had been chosen as the headquarters of the Bojowka, and also as the most convenient refuge for any members of the party who were in flight from the Russian authorities.

It was my first visit to Cracow, once the Polish capital, the loveliest and most venerable of our cities. So much that has been lost to us lives still in Cracow, enshrined in memories of the past. It seems to hold the very spirit of Poland, unchangeable, unconquerable. It has known war, fire and tempest, but they have not disturbed its serenity. It is too old, too rich in wisdom for that. The swastika may float today over its ancient castle, steel-helmeted Nazis may patrol its winding streets lined with stately houses washed in soft greens and greys, bleached by the rains and sunshine of centuries, but they will leave no lasting trace on its calm face. It has seen other conquerors come and go and outlived them all.

I can still recall the happiness of discovering for myself the gracious, mellow charm of the city. I wandered about the market-place which had housed the great trade guilds of the Middle Ages, and whose pillared arcades had sheltered from sun and wind the first merchant princes come from the rich towns beyond the Danube to barter their wares for good Polish cloth. I walked up the hill to the Wawel Castle, that gem of Italian architecture set on the misty banks of the Vistula to console a queen of Poland who had been born a Sforza and longed for the warm lands of her youth, and stood on the balcony remembering the story of that Christmas Eve in the year 1683 when a watchman had strained his eyes over the snow and run back with the joyful tidings that he had seen a great company of men approaching across the plains: King Sobieski's army coming home in triumph from the rout of the Turks.

I spent an hour in the University which had been built by

King Casimir in the fourteenth century when the Academy of Prague was the only stronghold of learning in Central Europe. Tradition says the King founded it at the earnest entreaty of his daughter, the beautiful Jadwige who even sold her jewels to contribute to its cost. If that is true the professors and students were sadly ungrateful more than a century afterwards, for when they discovered the presence among them of a young girl who, in her determination to share the privileges of learning denied to her sex, had disguised herself as a man and attended the lectures with the other students, they were at first disposed to burn her at the stake. However, when it was proved that she had conducted herself "modestly and discreetly and had caused no harm or annoyance to any of her fellows"—she was allowed to live, but for her presumption was immured in a convent for the rest of her days. I thought of her sad fate (from which Aunt Maria would surely have drawn a moral) when I walked through the shady cloisters of the University, famous for its associations with the two great astronomers of the Middle Ages, Wojereck Brudzswa and his pupil Copernicus. The pavements of the courtyard have been worn thin by the feet of generations of scholars, and I pictured Copernicus pacing up and down them, pondering over the pages of Aristotle, which he had been studying, getting, perhaps, as he watched the slowly deepening twilight, the first inspiration for his theory of the daily rotation of the earth round the sun.

I got up early in the morning because that was the only means of finding time to visit the lovely old Gothic cathedral, the last resting-place of Poland's kings and heroes. I was rewarded for sacrificing my sleep by hearing the silvery notes of a trumpet ringing out clearly in the silence of the slumbering city—the "Heynal," which is still sounded from the Marjacki Tower, after seven hundred years, in memory of the brave trumpeter who warned the city of the advancing Tartar hordes.

We were unable to remain in Cracow longer than a day or two, because it was obvious from the beginning that our congress was an object of suspicion to the authorities. Word had evidently been passed along the chain of secret service agents operating in Russian and Austrian Poland. Within the first few hours we became aware that we were being spied on. So we decided to move to Zakopane. There, in the heart of the mountains, we would be safe.

I travelled up from Cracow in the same carriage as Joseph Pilsudski. It was the first time I had spoken with him since our meeting in Warsaw, and before the end of the journey I revised some of my impressions of him. To begin with, I saw that he was younger than I had supposed, certainly not more than thirty-nine or forty, though his beard and moustache and the deep lines etched round his eyes made him appear older. When he laughed, which he did often, it was the laugh of a young man. He was a much gayer and more amusing companion than I had expected. There was nothing of the fanatic or zealot about him. His conversation was not, like that of most of the other leaders, centred on the party and on politics in general to the exclusion of all else. He talked lightly and easily, showing a keen sense of humour and knowledge of the world.

As we approached Zakopane I was enchanted with the glimpse of high peaks sprinkled with little lakes and fringed with lush green valleys. But he told me that the scenery of Siberia was much finer. "I never even imagined such beauty until I went there," he said, and gave me a vivid picture of white-capped mountains towering over immense tracts of plain crossed by mighty rivers like oceans, where the ice broke in spring with the roar of cannon. And of the loneliness of dark silent forests, inhabited only by wolf and bear, and where no shaft of sunshine ever penetrated the dense growth of the trees. As he talked his face lit up with enthusiasm, and I remember thinking that although I had heard many men speak of the miseries of Siberia, this was the only one who had ever told me of its beauty.

Later that evening I heard him give an address to the delegates, and then I looked at him and marvelled because he was a different man from the one who had travelled in the train with me. In his speech he quoted several verses from one of the patriotic poems of Slowacki, and I thought that surely they could never have been spoken more beautifully or with such depth of feeling. I knew then as I listened that whatever might be the virtues or faults of this Joseph Pilsudski of whom

I had heard so many conflicting opinions, his whole heart was given to Poland.

The Congress had been summoned with the main purpose of discussing the line of policy to be followed by the Bojowka in view of the influence of the revolution on the Polish national situation. A difference of opinion had already made itself felt in the ranks of the party, which was gradually dividing into Right and Left wings.

The Left was in favour of working in close harmony with the Russian Socialists and therefore it was willing to substitute for the claim of Polish independence one for autonomy, and to carry on the struggle against the Russian Government on economic grounds alone.

Pilsudski, as the leader of the Right wing and a passionate champion of complete independence for Poland, was in violent opposition, not only over the question of policy but because they wished to use the Bojowka to further it. Their argument was that since the masses of the revolutionists desired a campaign of agitation against the Russian authorities it was the duty of the party, as a Socialist organization, to support them with its armed force. Pilsudski retorted that the Militant Group had been formed to serve as a framework for the ultimate aim of an armed revolution, and that since the party, at that stage, could not possibly create a fighting organization large enough to assimilate and discipline the masses, a program of indiscriminate terrorism with the Bojowka lending itself to local demonstrations and carrying out their requirements could achieve no good purpose. It could only lead to reprisals from the Government which we should not be strong enough to counter.

His views received the support of the entire Bojowka and all the more moderate members of the party, but the Left wing won the day. A few weeks later their victory bore bitter fruit in the tragedy which caused August 6th of that year to be ever afterwards known as "Bloody Wednesday." Against the advice of Pilsudski, a section of the Bojowka, acting on the orders of the Leftists in the Central Committee, organized a series of risings in several towns in Russian Poland during which eighty police officers lost their lives. The Russian authorities immediately retaliated with the terrible pogrom of Siedlce on September 8th, which, despite the flimsy excuse that it was an act of vengeance perpetrated by troops acting on their own initiative, was undoubtedly inspired, if not actually ordered, by the military command.

Pilsudski's misgivings had received ample justification. . . . "It was a blow to which we could make no response" . . . he wrote of it. . . . "A moral defeat followed by a material defeat. It caused dismay in the whole party organization because it was realized that with the help of the military the Government could organize such a massacre at any part of the country. The Bojowka had not sufficient means to counteract it, and the Government, aware of its weakness, set about liquidating the revolutionary movement. . . ."

"Bloody Wednesday" and its sequel brought to a head the disputes within the party. The Left wing continued to urge alliance with Russia until matters reached a deadlock. In November 1906 a meeting was held at Lwow to take a decisive vote on the future policy of the party. Pilsudski, in an impassioned speech, defended the ideal of national independence which had been the principal motive of the P.P.S. since its formation, but the majority were against him.

He rose to his feet very pale. . . .

"Over any other question I am ready to meet you . . ." he said. . . . "But in this one matter there can be no compromise. If you are resolved to abandon the fight for our freedom I will not remain in the party." . . .

He walked out of the meeting, followed by a number of others who shared his views.

The split in the party was definite and final. The Left wing continued as the P.P.S. with its changed course of policy. The Right, which included the entire organization of the Bojowka, remained faithful to the original program of independence and vowed not to lay down their arms until it had been achieved. And of this party, which became known as the "Revolutionary Fraction," Joseph Pilsudski was unanimously elected leader.

I, too, remained with the Bojowka.

CHAPTER X

THE IMPORT of arms for the Bojowka, which had begun as the thin trickle of a few Brownings brought into the country at irregular intervals and with great difficulty, developed to such an extent that in the spring of 1906 I was receiving consignments nearly every day, and distributing thousands of arms not only to Warsaw but to the provincial centres of the Militant Organization—Radom, Lublin, Kielce, and many others. It was no small task to arrange all the details of transport and distribution, and finally I decided to give up my work in the office of the leather goods factory in order to devote more time to it.

As it was still necessary for me to earn my own living, I took a few pupils for private lessons in languages, science and mathematics. They were all daughters of rich families in Warsaw, and sometimes I used to laugh at the curious contrast of the two roles I played, and think how surprised they would have been to hear that the conventional young governess who corrected their French translations and set them problems in algebra was a revolutionary, who addressed secret meetings in the poorest quarters of the city, smuggled guns and ammunition and fled at the approach of the police.

The transport of arms was organized as a network to cover the greater part of Russian Poland, and hundreds of people acted as intermediaries and messengers, people drawn from all walks in life, from landowners to peasants, from working men to intellectuals, students, doctors, and professional men and women.

The Mausers and Brownings which formed the bulk of the consignments were bought in Belgium by men belonging to the party, and transported across Germany and into Austrian Poland as far as Cracow or Sosnowiec by various representatives and agents. There they were collected and brought across the Austro-Russian frontier, generally by workmen or railway employees, some of whom were members of the party, while others were professional smugglers. This last was a simple matter of arrangement, for many of the inhabitants of the frontier districts took part in some form of smuggling. Once they were "over the line," as it was called, the arms would be stored in some house in the locality owned by a member of the party. A message would then be sent to me either by word of mouth or by a secret code, since it would have been too dangerous to trust such information to writing, and I would send one of my helpers for them. He (or more often she) would take them to still another hiding-place, this time much nearer to Warsaw, and there I would collect them and take them to one of my depots to be stored until they were needed for distribution. I had several of these secret arsenals in different parts of Warsaw and the suburbs; in some of them I would leave only twenty Brownings and a few boxes of cartridges; in others two hundred or more rifles. I kept all my records and inventories and the addresses of consignees in books worded in code, so that in the event of the police discovering one depot they would not be able to link up the chain. For the same reason no one but myself and one other member of the party was ever allowed to know the final destination of each consignment or the identity of those responsible for its transport. In that way there was less chance of betrayal, either unconsciously through some stupid slip or in a "confession" after Russian "third degree" methods had been successfully applied. The penalties were too heavy . . . from four to ten years' solitary confinement in the Katorga followed by exile to Siberia for life . . . to permit our taking unnecessary risks.

The chief difficulties were encountered in the actual transport of the arms, for whether they were brought by road or by rail it involved running the gauntlet of a series of customs barriers and an army of officials.

The Imperial Russian system of frontier control was, I believe, the most complicated and at the same time the most inefficient in the world. It was divided into three lines, the first of which was situated at the actual frontier which bristled with the rifles and bayonets of soldiers, gendarmes and armed troops of every description. No sooner had the traveller successfully negotiated the customs station there than he found himself confronting the officials of the second line, which was only a kilometre or two behind it.

This second line, or "line of cordons," as it was known, crossed every road leading from the frontier, and its principal function was to send out horse patrols authorized to search at their own discretion the baggage of any one passing along the road. As the first and second lines operated quite independently of one another one might be searched by both or by neither. It was largely a question of luck.

The third frontier was an institution peculiar to Czardom. It covered a zone of over a hundred kilometres inside Russian Poland and consisted of an elaborate organization of customs who operated at all the principal railway stations, on all trains coming from the frontier, and on many others running between the big provincial cities. They would walk through the compartments when the train was in motion, selecting at random passengers whom they would order to open their bags.

It required some ingenuity then to transport consignments of two or three hundred Mausers and seventy or eighty pounds of dynamite past these different controls, and it could be done only by taking them in small quantities at a time, divided among several people. As a rule we considered it too dangerous to trust our contraband to bags or valises which were likely to be searched either on the train or at one of the stations, and therefore we carried it on our persons. Mausers were strapped down our thighs so that we could conceal under our skirts two or even three at a time; revolvers and cartridges were sewn into wadded bands and worn round our waists; blocks of dynamite were encased in wrappings and padded into our corsets. Luckily the mode of those days favoured us. The long full skirts and fashionable "pelerins" could hide a surprising amount, and we grew so expert in manipulating them that we were able to travel for hours in a train with a load of arms and ammunition weighing up to forty pounds distributed over our persons without any of our fellow-passengers even suspecting us. I have often carried a thousand or twelve hundred Browning cartridges at a time.

Dynamite was the most dangerous and the most uncomfortable contraband to carry. In the first place, it necessitated being continually on the alert lest one of your fellow-passengers should throw down a cigarette-end, when you would have to make good your escape into the corridor. Neither could you, if you were possessed of imagination, dismiss altogether from your mind the possibility of disaster caused by the friction of a hook or safety pin, even a corset busk. With every mile of your journey the tightly packed bricks that encased you like a vice of steel seemed to weigh heavier; the muscles you were afraid to stretch grew more cramped until you felt that you could scarcely breathe. But nothing of your discomfort could show itself on your face, for only with a light and confident step and a mien of careless indifference could you hope to get past the customs men at the end of the journey.

This transport of arms, even though the Devil held the dice, was not without its comedies.

I shall never forget one occasion when I went with one of the members of the party to transfer a consignment of revolvers and ammunition from a depot in the suburbs to one in Warsaw. My companion was a very zealous lady of middle age and weighing about 250 pounds. Because of her proportions and the voluminous clothing she wore, it was easy for her to conceal large quantities of contraband successfully, and therefore she asked to be entrusted with the entire consignment of dynamite which was in blocks weighing altogether over forty pounds, while I took the revolvers. We draped our coats carefully over our packages, and set off together.

We had not covered half the distance when as we crossed a road my companion caught her heel on the curbstone and fell in a sitting position. Fortunately, she was not hurt, but the weight of the dynamite, added to her own very considerable one, made it impossible for her to get up. I grasped her by the arms and heaved and tugged until I nearly lost my own footing, but try as I would I could not move her even an inch.

We were both struggling desperately when to our dismay a Russian officer came up and gallantly offered his assistance. He, too, placed his hands beneath her arms and attempted to lever her to her feet, but as he felt her weight an expression of amazement spread over his face, and after three or four valiant efforts he was obliged to let her sink back on to the ground again. At that moment I looked round and saw a policeman approaching from the opposite side of the road. The sight spurred me to a fresh endeavour. . . .

"Let us both try together" . . . I said to the officer, and without waiting for an answer, grasped the prostrate lady firmly by one arm. He took the other and this time between us we succeeded in getting her upright. We parted with mutual compliments, and I do not suppose that to this day he has ever guessed that he was instrumental in the transport of arms for Polish revolutionaries!

On another occasion I and another girl in the party named Hanka had to take a large consignment of cartridges from the principal arms depot in Warsaw to one of the Bojowka's provincial branches. As usual, we decided to carry them on our persons. I sewed about eight hundred into bands which I wrapped round my waist and advised Hanka to do the same, but she insisted on carrying them all in a special pair of knickers which she had made after the fashion of Zouave trousers with wide folds over the knees. I pointed out that she ran the risk of having the ribbons break under the weight, but she assured me that she had often carried them in this way before, and had found it better than any other.

On our way to the station we went through the busy street of the Marsalkowska. Ever since the outbreak of the revolution it had been strongly patrolled by police and military. Policemen stood outside the station, surveying the passengers entering and leaving it, from time to time picking out some man or woman to be searched. Soldiers were posted at frequent intervals on the opposite pavement along which we were walking.

We were nearly at the station when Hanka stopped suddenly and gave a gasp of dismay. . . .

"The ribbon of my knickers has broken!"

Already a cartridge was lying at her feet. Even while we stared at it in consternation another fell from beneath her skirt and rolled to the very heels of the soldier who was standing only a few feet away, mercifully with his back turned to us.

Then another fell and still another, until presently she was showering cartridges in all directions. They bounced off her shoes and rolled into the gutter, to the amazement of the passers-by.

The soldier, with true Russian military imperturbability, had not yet turned, and probably nothing short of a bomb would make him do so. He had been posted outwards and facing outwards he would remain. But the policemen guarding the station on the other side of the street were already showing interest in us. I saw two of them pointing in our direction and summoning a couple of soldiers. Presently there would be others. The very sight of a cartridge, to say nothing of dozens of cartridges, was enough to bring down a whole regiment on us.

There was not a second to lose. I seized Hanka's arm, for she was still standing in dazed contemplation of the disaster, holding on to her skirt. "We can't stay here," I said. "We shall have to run for it. You go one way and I'll go another."

I hurried off towards the right, crossed the road a little farther down, and went into a draper's shop, where I ordered the first thing that came into my head. While the assistant was getting it for me I stood by the window, screened by the array of boxes and bales of material, and took survey of the position. On the opposite side of the street I could see a crowd collecting, and soldiers, of whom by this time there were several, picking up cartridges from the gutter. But there was no sign of Hanka and I could not tell whether she had made good her escape or been arrested and taken away.

I waited in the shop as long as I could, asking to be shown first one thing and then another, until the assistant must have thought me the most inconsiderate customer he had ever had to deal with, and then, as the street was quiet again, I decided to go to a lady doctor who had a nursing home not far away, and who was in secret a member of the party. It was obviously out of the question to attempt to continue the journey and deliver over my share of the cartridges, since every one entering the railway station would now be searched. On the other hand, I could not return home without news of poor Hanka, whom I pictured as already being interrogated by the police, and as it would be unsafe for me to make inquiries I must get some one else to do so.

The lady doctor, on hearing what had happened, immediately telephoned to a friend who went round to the flat which Hanka shared with her sister. After what seemed an interminable time, she came back with the welcome news that Hanka had just arrived home in safety.

Later I heard from Hanka the story of her escape.

When I had hurried off to the right she had gone in the opposite direction, still shedding cartridges in her path. She had only taken a few steps when she saw a policeman coming towards her, so instead of continuing her way she turned down the first side street and walked boldly into the house which fronted the corner. It was a big block of apartments, and to her relief she saw that the porter was not in his lodge. Without pausing, she ran up to the second floor and sat down on the stairs to try and evolve some plan. Presently she heard voices in the hall below her. One evidently belonged to the porter, the other to a man, probably the tenant of one of the apartments.

"Will you believe it, I had only just gone down to the basement for a moment and when I came back I found a couple of cartridges on the floor here . . ." said the porter. . . . "What do you think I ought to do about it?"

"Oh, I should not bother about it," answered the other voice. . . . "Some one must have dropped them, but it is not your affair. . . ."

The porter was not satisfied.

"If trouble comes of it the police will blame me," he said. . . . "I think I shall go and inform them. . . ."

"Why not have a look first?" said the other voice. . . . "The person who dropped them must have gone upstairs. It won't take you five minutes to search every floor. . . ."

Hanka held her breath and prepared for the worst. But the porter was evidently a cautious man.

"No, no, I shall be on the safe side and fetch the police," he replied. . . . "I shall go now so that they cannot accuse me of losing time. . . ."

She heard retreating steps and the slamming of a door and

waited for no more. She slipped downstairs and out into the
street. Once there she was able to mingle with the passers-by
and eventually reached her home. But not for several days did
she dare to leave the house or to communicate with any one in
the party.

Loneliness was one of the minor penalties attached to the
transport of arms, for those of us engaged in it could never visit
one another in an ordinary way lest the Russian secret service,
whose long, inquisitive fingers poked into every nook and
cranny of the country, should establish a link between us. We
were afraid, too, to make friends outside the party, for it would
mean exposing them to suspicion and perhaps danger on our
account. We used to welcome the summer because then we
could take rowing-boats and go out on the Vistula. There in
some cool shady backwater we could meet and talk for as long
as we would with no danger of being overheard. Sometimes on
Sundays we would go down the river to picnic in the orchards
of Saska Kempa and laze under the trees all the afternoon. Then
we would drink tea or beer on the terrace of some little café
crowded with the simple working-class people of Warsaw in
holiday mood and watch the young men and girls dancing the
polka to the strains of an overtaxed violin. Then when the
evening shadows were beginning to fall we would row back
slowly along the Vistula, lovely and mysterious as an enchanted
river with the last rays of the setting sun throwing great columns on the water, turning the yellow of the sandy shores to
bright gold.

Occasionally we dared to meet one another at the Art Exhibition. For some reason or other Government espionage was
not active there, although, as a matter of fact, many of the
exhibitors were members of our party, and of other revolutionary parties.

Among those who sympathized with us in secret was the
painter Stabrowski, whose work was already becoming famous
both in Poland and in other countries. I shall always remember a picture which he painted at about that time, a landscape
of fields fringed by forests, the eternally fertile fields of Poland,
but above them hung a cloud whose shadow fell upon the
earth in the form of a cross. I loved this picture more than any

other in the exhibition, and I used to dream of having the money to buy it one day. But although my husband gave me several of Stabrowski's works I was never able to have that particular one, because it was destroyed during the Russian Revolution of 1917.

The shadow of the Katorga was always in the background of our lives, although by tacit understanding we never spoke of it. It was a risk which we accepted gladly and willingly. Yet we were neither sentimentalists nor fanatics, only ordinary men and women with one consuming purpose. To free our country. And for that no sacrifice seemed too great.

One of the women who was most successful in concealing arms was a young and pretty dressmaker who had a fashionable clientele in Lodz and afterwards in Warsaw. Naturally enough it never occurred to the police who passed her smart little shop dozens of times in a day that the French models in her show-cases were screening stacks of Mausers, or that there was anything worth a search in the cardboard boxes which she used to deliver to her clients. But one day a workgirl whom she had dismissed spied upon her, with the result that she was arrested and condemned to four years of the Katorga, followed by exile to Siberia for life. To any one of her temperament the sentence must have been harder to face than death; yet she received it without flinching and went down to the cells with a light and joyous step, singing patriotic songs as she went.

Another woman who succeeded in smuggling large quantities of arms to the provinces was a spinster of middle age who lived with her widowed mother in a small apartment in Warsaw. Both were fervent patriots, and the old lady had in her youth played an active part in the Insurrection of 1863. The daughter began by carrying bibula (that is to say, illegal printed matter), but after a while she begged to be trusted with arms and ammunition. She decided not to tell her mother of what she was doing, partly because she did not want to alarm her, and partly because she had always appeared to disapprove of her activities in transporting bibula. But one day she forgot to lock the cupboard in which she had hidden a number of revolvers, and on arriving home found her mother sitting with them spread out on the table in front of her. Instead of being angry the old lady was delighted. . . . "Now at last you are doing something really useful," she told her daughter. . . . "I never had patience with your foolish Socialist papers. This is much better. This is the argument we used in '63." . . . And she fingered a revolver lovingly.

As I have already explained, the transport of arms was carried out by men and women of all types. One of my helpers, for example, was a music teacher, another was the wife of a professor at the University, a third was a prosperous business man, a fourth a young artist. All of them were prepared to leave their homes and ordinary occupations at a moment's notice and travel to any part of the country to collect a consignment. They did it without any thought of reward. All the adventure had to offer them was danger and discomfort, with exile as the penalty for failure.

Those who stored arms ran a risk as great, if not greater, yet any number of people were willing to provide accommodation for this purpose. One of them was the lady doctor whom I have already mentioned. I would often ring the night bell of her surgery and she would steal downstairs in her dressing-gown to take from me a box of Brownings. Another of my depots was concealed in a carpenter's warehouse in one of the poorer suburbs. A veterinary surgeon used to hide Mausers in his empty dog kennels, the owner of a music shop let me leave parcels of ammunition among his pianos, a railway engineer lent his shed for my principal depot in Warsaw.

The bombs were made in a small laboratory owned by two brothers, one a chemist and the other a medical student. Their father had been exiled to Siberia many years before as a persistent agitator against the Russian Government, and their mother who lived with them and had brought them up in the traditions of patriotism was overjoyed to see another generation taking up the battle. She helped her sons in their work, and I shall always recall my first meeting with her in the laboratory and how I was struck by the contrast between this frail, gentle little woman and the bomb which she held in her hand.

Although the party emphasized in its program complete

equality in franchise and in working conditions for both sexes it was, unlike the Russian Socialist parties, opposed to letting its women members take any part in combative measures, and all armed demonstrations were carried out by the men alone. I can only remember one exception.

Among the men of the Bojowka was a young student in Warsaw who was engaged to a beautiful girl named Jadwiga Krachelska, a pupil at the École des Beaux Arts. She joined the P.P.S. not only because it was her fiancé's party, but because she was a sincere convert to Socialism, and very few people in the party were aware that she was the only daughter of a rich landowning family, and had a big estate of her own.

Within a few days of the date fixed for their marriage her fiancé was imprisoned. He was brought before the prison examiners many times for interrogation, but always with the same result. He refused to betray the names of any of his associates in the party. The usual Russian modes of inducing unsatisfactory prisoners to talk were resorted to, but even under torture he remained silent. Eventually, either for lack of direct evidence against him, or because the police grew tired of questioning him, he was released. Wrecked in health, haunted by the shadow of the Katorga, he went home and shot himself.

Jadwiga took the news of his death outwardly calm and resigned. But from that day her whole life was dedicated to avenging him. She never ceased to importune the Central Committee to let her take part in the reprisals against the Russian authorities. For a long time they refused, but in the end she persuaded them to let her make an attempt on the life of Scallon, the Russian Governor who had ordered the torture of her fiancé.

She took an apartment in Warsaw with her servant, Maria Owczarkowna, the only person in whom she confided, and who was also a member of the P.P.S. There she laid her plans carefully, and when the Governor drove past in his carriage one day she threw a bomb at him. It missed him, but his aide-decamp and a policeman were wounded.

Scallon was one of the most hated men in Poland and the crowd which collected deliberately misled the police so that the two women were able to escape. The servant was arrested later, but refused to betray her mistress, who had, by that time, crossed the frontier into Austrian Poland and taken refuge in Cracow.

The Russian Government accordingly sent an official mandate to the Austrian Government, demanding that Jadwiga Krachelska should be sent back to Warsaw for trial. But the Austrians, more chivalrously inclined, had no wish to deliver up to punishment a young and beautiful girl who had not offended against their own laws, and answered that they would try her themselves. Thereupon ensued a solemn exchange of letters and formalities lasting several weeks. But before anything definite had been arrived at, the prisoner, who had been allowed bail, gave a new turn to the proceedings by going through a civil marriage with a young Galician artist. They parted immediately after the ceremony, but the bride had now became an Austrian subject, and therefore there was no longer any question of her being extradited for trial by the Russians. When she was eventually brought before the Austrian courts she was acquitted. Some years later she married Tytus Filipowicz, who became Polish Ambassador to the United States.

While I was taking part in this transport of arms I had an unpleasant experience which might have put an end to my story.

I had hidden a large number of Mausers in the attic studio of a young artist in the party, and one afternoon I and another girl went there to collect some of them, which we were going to deliver to one of the provincial branches of the Bojowka. We took with us a load of revolvers, which we carried through the streets in a laundry basket, over which we placed a few clean pillow-cases and a layer of the coloured tissue paper most laundries use. We were very proud of the ingenuity of this device, for it enabled us to pass right under the eyes of the police, and we reached our destination without misadventure. The artist's studio was on the top floor of apartments. She was out when we arrived, but I had a key and we let ourselves in. We deposited our revolvers in a cupboard, and then turned our attention to the Mausers which were packed in two chests. I picked out the number I wanted, and then noticed that the

cock of one of them would not close. I knew how to handle
both rifles and revolvers, because at Pilsudski's suggestion all
the women engaged in the transport of arms had been given a
short course of instruction in cleaning and caring for them, and
in marksmanship if they wished. So I set to work to examine
this refractory Mauser. The possibility of its being loaded never
even occurred to me, for all the arms which we smuggled from
place to place were examined first as a matter of course, and I
myself had deposited this particular consignment only a couple
of days earlier. But I had no sooner taken it into my hands to
examine it than a shot rang out.

For a moment I was so appalled by the noise, which I thought
must betray our secret to every one in the house, that I felt no
pain, and it was not until the girl who was with me cried out in
horror that I looked down, and saw that my left shoe was full
of blood. The bullet had passed right through my foot, between the boards of the floor, and through the ceiling of the
room below.

We waited in an agony of suspense, expecting to hear the
sound of people running upstairs, followed by knocking on the
door. But nothing happened, and we began to breathe more
freely. We did not dare to call for help and send for a doctor,
but we found a towel and tied it tightly round my ankle, and
that checked the flow of blood a little. We decided that the
only thing to do was to leave the apartment as quickly as possible, and to go to my own doctor, who was a member of the
P.P.S., and could be trusted not to give us away. But then we
remembered the bullet. Perhaps it had killed or wounded some
one in the room below! We could not go until we were reassured on this point.

The artist's studio was naturally not equipped for experiments in masonry, but we found a chisel and a palette knife,
and with the aid of these we managed to scoop out enough
plaster between the floorboards to enable us to see into the
room below. To our unspeakable relief it was empty. There
still remained the question of how I was to get out of the house
and along the street to a cab without arousing suspicion. Fortunately, the skirts of those days touched the ground, and
after we had washed the blood from my shoe and put on one

of the artist's thick stockings over my own stocking, there was very little to be seen. So I began to hobble slowly and painfully down the five flights of stairs to the ground floor, praying fervently that we should meet no one on the way. Again luck befriended us. We were able to get out of the house unobserved.

We were obliged to walk more than half a mile before we reached a cab rank, and to this day I do not know how I did it, for every step was excruciatingly painful. By the time we arrived at the doctor's surgery I was almost in a state of collapse.

Fortunately for me the bullet had passed straight through my foot, making a clean flesh wound but not breaking any bones. After it had been dressed I was able to drive home, but I had to remain in bed for nearly a fortnight.

Later I discovered the cause of the accident and cursed artistic irresponsibility. The painter had lent the gun to one of her friends on the previous day and had forgotten to ascertain whether it was unloaded when she put it away.

All through the restless, revolutionary years from 1906 to 1910 Joseph Pilsudski continued to train and organize his little armed force that seemed so frail an opposition to the might of Russia, and I and those who worked with me travelled all over the country to equip it. We could judge its growth from its increasing needs; the military schools and provincial branches absorbed our consignments of arms as quickly as we could supply them. In that we had our reward.

CHAPTER XI

THOSE YEARS of transporting arms brought me many adventures. At one time when the Bojowka was threatened with extinction and all its leaders were in prison or had fled over the frontier, I had to carry on the organization almost alone, for it was a vital necessity to keep up the import of arms and replenish those that had been lost in order that the troops could be re-formed as quickly as possible. While I was familiar with the whole routine of smuggling arms I had never had anything to do with the buying of them; however, I knew the names of the factories in Belgium which were our main source of supply and got in touch with them. They agreed to go on furnishing the usual consignments provided I could make satisfactory arrangements for their transport.

This was a difficulty which at first seemed unsurmountable, for while I and my helpers could easily deal with the arms once they had arrived within our radius, I had no idea of how to get them over the frontier, and the men who had formerly been responsible for this stage of the transport were all under arrest.

Finally, I decided that it would be safer to form an entirely new chain of clearing-houses and intermediaries than to try to piece together the old one, for I did not know how many of those connected with it had been marked down by the police. I would strike out on fresh ground and bring the consignments through German Poland.

I went to open up negotiations and chose the town of Bytom as being the best suited to my purpose. It was my first visit to one of the districts under German rule, and in later years I realized how accurately Joseph Pilsudski had described it when he wrote:

"The German occupation weighted us down with a paw which if not the most cruel and the most terrible was certainly the strongest of all three of Poland's conquerors, as it

137

was the most powerful, the most relentless, and the most changeless."

There was nothing of the incompetence of the Russian system in this German-ruled Poland, and nothing of the easy-going spirit of tolerance which characterized the Austrian provinces. The regime was ruthless, efficient and brutalizing. The industrial towns were prosperous and inexpressibly dreary, the populace thrifty, hard-working and joyless. A people whose blood had not been shed, but slowly drained from them, whose patriotism had not been crushed to rise again as in Russian Poland, but burnt out so that nothing but ashes remained. Years later these seemingly dead ashes were to be rekindled and to burst into a new flame.

I went to the first gunsmith's shop I came upon. It was stocked with a curious medley of ironware. Rifles and revolvers shared the window with kettles and pans and gardening tools. The proprietor was alone when I entered, and I went straight to the point. I had bought a quantity of arms and ammunition in Belgium. Would he undertake delivery of them and arrange for their transport to Cracow? I would pay him well for his trouble.

At first he stared at me open-mouthed, then when he grasped the full import of what I was asking a look of sheer terror overspread his face, and almost running from behind his counter, he threw open the door. "I would not dare to do such a thing!" . . . he exclaimed in a trembling voice. . . . "Even your coming here is dangerous. You may have compromised me." He looked round fearfully though there was no one in the shop. . . . "Go. Go quickly" . . . and he almost pushed me outside.

I went to three other shops in Bytom with no more encouraging results, and then decided to try the busy industrial town of Katowice. There I was more fortunate. The first arms dealer I went to received my proposition with a smile. . . .

"Are you a revolutionary?" . . . he asked. I told him that I was.

"I had a good friend who was a revolutionary," he said slowly. . . . "That was long ago, before you were born, young lady. We were at school together, and then he went to live at Warsaw and got himself mixed up with politics instead of sticking to business like me. So he went to prison and died there. He was a foolish fellow, but still I liked him. . . . I will handle your arms and ammunition for you. I will undertake delivery from Belgium and you may collect them from me once a week." . . .

He was as good as his word, with the result that at the end of a few months we had replenished the equipment of the Bojowka.

.   .   .   .   .

One day in January 1907 I sent one of my helpers, a young man who was studying at the Commercial College, to collect a consignment of arms which had just been brought over the frontier. The arrangement was that he was to deposit them at one of our depots in the suburbs and then to notify me at the central office. In order to guard against spies this central office was changed every few days and its address was never given to any one unless he or she called in person at the little stationer's shop which was owned by a member of the party, and used as a sub-office for the re-direction of correspondence. When at the end of the morning there was no sign of the young man, my first thought was that he had probably missed the train and had not been able to communicate with me. But as hour after hour passed without news, I began to grow anxious, and finally I decided to call at the house of his parents, whom I had often visited. They were ardent patriots and knew of his work in the party so that I had no fear of betraying him.

It was late afternoon when I walked up the garden path of their pleasant little villa on the outskirts of Warsaw and rang the bell. The door was opened immediately, not by the usual peasant girl, but by two men. Before I could draw back they seized me by the arms, pulled me roughly inside and shut the door behind me. I knew even before I caught sight of the uniformed gendarme behind them that I was in the hands of the Russian police.

One of them still kept a detaining grasp on my sleeve as

they took me into the salon, which looked as though a hurricane had swept through it. All the furniture had been turned upside down. Cushions and chair coverings had been ripped open, pictures and curtains had been torn from the walls and thrown on the ground, the contents of drawers were strewn all over the floor.

In the midst of the chaos on two chairs facing one another sat the boy's parents. The mother's face was white and drawn, but not a flicker of recognition crossed it as her eyes met mine.

One of the police agents signed to me to stand beside her and began his interrogation.

"Who is this young woman?" . . . he asked.

"I do not know. I have never seen her before" . . . she replied.

"Then why does she come to your house?"

"You must ask her if you wish to find out. I cannot tell you."

"She is a friend of your son's?"

"My son has a number of friends, but if this lady is one of them I am not aware of it. I have told you that I do not know her."

The agent turned to me . . .

"Who are these people?"

I told him that they were strangers to me.

"Then why do you come to their house?"

I replied that I was a governess and that I had come in answer to an advertisement for some one to give lessons in French. It was, of course, a lame explanation, but it was the best I could invent on the spur of the moment, and although he returned to the point again and again I persisted in my story.

After an hour or more of the same questions and the same replies I was put into a carriage with a policeman on either side of me and driven to the Danilowiczowska Prison. There I was first searched and then shown into a small room containing only a table and a couple of chairs. A Russian commissioner was seated in one of them, and after signing to me to take the one on the opposite side of the table, he opened the conversation in a suave and disarming manner.

I waited. During the drive to the prison I had had time to marshal my forces and decided that the wisest course was to say as little as possible until I knew what evidence they had against me.

"You are Alexandra Szczerbinska, and you are known as Ola in the party, are you not?" he began.

"I do not know to what party you refer. I have been called Ola since I was a child" . . . I answered.

"How long have you worked for the party?" . . . was the next question.

I answered that I worked for no party but that I had earned my own living first in an office and then as a governess since I left school.

"You are being childish in pretending that you do not understand me" . . . he said, dropping his suave manner. . . . "You must answer these questions sensibly or we shall have to find means of compelling you to do so. . . ."

As I remained silent he frowned and took up a sheaf of papers which lay on the table in front of him. For a few moments the only sound in the room came from the ticking of a clock over the door. Then suddenly he looked up and began to question me again.

Where were the party's headquarters? Who were its leaders? Was Joseph Pilsudski one? How long had I known Pilsudski? When had I last seen him? In answer to everything I professed ignorance until at length he appeared to tire of the inquisition and summoned a policeman. . . .

"Take this woman to the cells. I will examine her again tomorrow. . . ."

The man conducted me through iron gates which clanged to after us and delivered me into the custody of a jailer who wore a bunch of keys round his waist and carried a lantern.

By this time it was midnight and all lights in the prison had been extinguished except an occasional oil lamp set in brackets on the whitewashed walls of the corridor, through which we passed. It was as cold and damp as a vault, and on looking up I saw that there were no panes in the windows, only bars, and the biting wind of the January night swept through them. We stopped in front of a heavy oak door with a grille near the top through which the jailer shone his lantern. Then he fumbled for the key from the bunch at his belt, opened the door and pushed me inside. I heard the key turn in the lock behind me and the sound of his footsteps retreating down the corridor.

The room in which I found myself was so ill-lit that for a moment I could see nothing. Then by the glimmer of one flickering oil lamp at the far end I made out row upon row of straw mattresses laid out on the floor so closely together that it was almost impossible to walk between them without stepping on them. And on each mattress was a sleeping woman. Lining the walls were pegs with the vague shapes of clothes suspended from them. The atmosphere of the room was appalling, for its sole ventilation came from three tiny grilles of about six inches square, and over a hundred women were penned up together in it night and day. No one was allowed to leave it for any purpose after sunset, and one large earthenware vessel served as a common receptacle. As it generally overflowed on to the mattress of those nearest to it before the morning the filth of the room was indescribable.

I stood for a while by the door until my eyes grew accustomed to the gloom and then tried to grope my way over the floor in the direction of the grille. But I stumbled over one of the mattresses and the occupant sat up and cursed me shrilly. Other women whom she had awakened abused both her and me impartially, and minutes passed before quiet descended on them all again. Determined to risk no further *contretemps*, I sank down on the floor by the wall and leant back against it. But I could not close my eyes, try as I would. The closeness of the room; the nauseating odours compounded of perspiration, stale scent and unwashed humanity; the sounds that came out of the shadows where women talked and tossed uneasily as they slept or lay awake sobbing into their mattresses, made sleep impossible. The hours passed while I sat crouched uncomfortably against the wall, longing for morning.

Suddenly I felt some one pulling my dress. I looked round. A girl on a mattress a few feet away from me was sitting up and trying to attract my attention.

"You'll get stiff sitting up there," she whispered. . . .

"And the cells are damp enough to give you a fever. Come and lie down beside me. There's room enough for us both. . . ."

She made a place for me on her mattress and I lay down beside her thankfully enough.

"I know what it feels like, your first night here" . . . she said as she drew the worn blanket which served as a covering over us . . . "But you'll get used to it. You're a 'political,' I suppose?" I assented. . . .

"That's not so good, because they can send you to Katorga. It's better to be like me. . . ."

I discovered that her name was Marietta and that she was a prostitute . . . "But I'm patriotic too . . ." she said proudly . . . "I wouldn't have anything to do with a Russian no matter how much he paid me. . . ."

She turned over and fell asleep. I tried to follow her example, and told myself sternly that it was only imagination when I seemed to feel something crawling all over me. At length under the warmth of the blanket I, too, dozed off, and did not wake until the grey light of the January dawn was coming through the grilles. All around me women were yawning and shaking themselves like dogs. Those who had undressed were getting into their clothes. My friend of the night before was struggling into a torn and crumpled blouse. I saw that she had a pretty little face framed by a cloud of tangled auburn hair.

"I thought you were never going to wake" . . . she said . . . "Hurry up. They will bring breakfast in a minute, and I can tell you that you will have to fight for it if you want any. . . ."

As she spoke there were footsteps in the corridor. The grille in the door opened and two jailers pushed in the morning meal. The women rushed in a body to get it, thrusting and jostling each other out of the way, and quarrelling shrilly among themselves. I should have got nothing but for Marietta, who hurled herself into the mêlée and came back with my share as well as her own. But when I looked at the breakfast, which she set down on the floor beside us, for there were no chairs or tables or any other furniture but the rows of mattresses, I said that I was not hungry. Even though I had fasted for many hours I could not eat the chunk of dry bread, or drink from the bowl of hot water covered with a thick scum of grease.

The morning hours passed slowly. The grey of dawn gave place to a pale sunlight that filtered through the grilles to fall cruelly on unwashed faces and unkempt hair. At about eight o'clock the door was opened and we were allowed to go into the corridor and to the lavatory, which was just a couple of boards over a hole in the earth. It was in such a state of filth that I could scarcely summon up courage to make use of it. There was only one wash-basin for all of us, and that emitted a thin trickle of ice-cold water. Soap or towels were un-dreamed-of luxuries unless they were supplied by friends out-side, and most of the women either dried their hands on their underclothes or did not wash at all.

I was going back to the cell after a discouraging attempt at a toilette when a woman with a pale intellectual face came up to me and asked me whether I was a political prisoner. When I replied in the affirmative she took me over to what she called "the political corner" and introduced me to several women there, most of whom belonged to the Social Democrat Party. Some of them had been in the prison several weeks awaiting trial, and they primed me with advice over the dif-ferent modes of interrogation. They also warned me of the danger of conversing with the other inmates, for the Russians often employed the method of getting one prisoner to spy on another.

One of them lent me soap and a towel and another produced a comb. I drew it through my hair and to my horror it came out full of vermin even though I had only been in the prison a few hours.

With the exception of this political group most of the prisoners were drawn from the dregs of society, thieves, pros-titutes and criminals of all types. They used to huddle to-gether over the one small stove which was all the heating we had, gossiping from morning till night, when they were not wrangling or abusing one another. As we were never allowed out for exercise and had no books or anything with which to occupy our time they grew nervous and hysterical and gave way to violent outbursts of mass emotion. When one of them began to cry they would all cry with her and continue sobbing in chorus, sometimes for hours. Yet later in the day one of them would start laughing at nothing and they would all copy her and make so much noise that the jailer would come to the grille and shout to them to be quiet. Sometimes they used to sing. Among the political prisoners was a Jewess of the Bund Socialist Party, a dark girl with a pale, brooding face, the sad eyes of her race, and one of the most beautiful voices I have ever heard. In the evenings when most of the jailers were at supper she would sing song after song, with the other women joining in the chorus. Her favourite was the lament of the Jews for their comrades killed in the pogroms . . . "Scattered upon the ground are the bodies of our people who have been slain. . . ." She used to sing the melancholy, haunting air with such tragedy in her voice that most of the women who sang with her were reduced to tears even though they were not of her race.

The worst quarrels took place over the food, because there was never enough to go round. I rarely took my share, for hungry as I was I could not force myself to eat it. The breakfast of dry bread and greasy hot water was never varied, and we had only two other meals in the day, a plate of kascha (a sort of oatmeal) which was served at noon, and in the evening.

The nights were the worst ordeal, to political prisoners at least, for we never knew when we were going to be questioned. Four or five times a week the door would be thrown open at about two in the morning and the jailers would come flashing their lanterns on us, hauling off first one woman and then another for interrogation. I used to dread their coming so much that I lay awake hour after hour listening for footsteps, afraid to sleep lest I should be at a disadvantage, for the whole object of these night-time examinations was to get the prisoners when they were sleepy and off their guard and then to fire a string of questions at them. Although I was interrogated in this way several times, I always succeeded in standing my ground and neither giving myself away or any one in the party.

I and all the other women in the common cell had an almost daily foretaste of Russia's Third Degree methods, for next to us was the room in which what were known as "compulsory measures" were applied to the male prisoners awaiting trial. The cries which used to come from it were so terrible that most of the women were hysterical for hours after hearing them.

I had been in the Danilowiczowska for nearly three weeks when two jailers came to the door early one morning and told me brusquely to put on my coat and come with them. I obeyed with the sinking sensation which all of us who were political prisoners felt whenever we received a summons. Because each time it might be a prelude to torture or the Katorga.

In this case, however, it was only a transfer to another prison, the Pawiak, where I was to remain until my trial.

Conditions in the Pawiak, one block of which was a women's prison kept separate from the men's, were very much better. Instead of one big common cell there were a number of small ones, which were comparatively comfortable with wooden chairs, a table and folding beds. We were also given half an hour a day for exercise in the courtyard and allowed to have our own books. I was put into a cell with five other women, all of them political prisoners like myself. We used to speculate on the probable length of the sentences we would receive. We were all certain that I should get at least five years of the Katorga followed by Siberia, for the transport of arms came into the category of the most serious political crimes. But the unexpected happened.

Among the women who shared the cell with me at the Pawiak Prison was a young student of the Conservatoire who had been arrested as a Socialist agitator. She was keenly interested in spiritualism, which at that time was just beginning to be seriously accepted, and endeavoured to convert the rest of us to it. To pass the long evenings we formed a little circle among ourselves and started to experiment in automatic writing and table turning.

One evening a message came through addressed to me . . . "Ola, you will be released a month to-day. . . ." It was signed Jan Zelinsky. I asked who Jan Zelinsky was, and received the answer that he had been imprisoned in the cell which we now occupied, and had died there.

At the time I did not pay much attention to this message, for on the face of things it seemed absurd.

Even though I might have the good fortune to escape being sentenced to Katorga, which was highly improbable, no Russian judge could possibly give me less than four years' imprisonment for smuggling arms. Apart from that the Pawiak had always been a woman's prison so that it appeared most unlikely that any such person as Jan Zelinsky had ever been imprisoned there.

The other girls, with the exception of the little music student, treated the message as a joke, but as the days passed the conviction came to me that it was true, and almost without realizing it I began to hope. But the weeks crawled by without any prospect of release for me; I had not even been taken before the magistrates for my preliminary examination. On the evening before the date which "Jan Zelinsky" had named I went to bed with a sense of disappointment, and responded rather halfheartedly to the teasing of the others who kept reminding me that it was my last day in prison.

I was awakened very early by loud knocking at the door and some one calling my name. A jailer was flashing his lantern through the grille. He told me to dress and come with him to the office of the Administrator of Police. I threw on my clothes, not daring to hope, telling myself that it only meant another interrogation.

The Administrator of Police was occupied with some papers when I entered his office. He looked up from his writing only for a moment to say . . .

"Alexandra Szczerbinska, you are to be released this morning. You may leave immediately. . . ."

I walked out half dazed, still thinking that I must be dreaming. But as I was crossing the quadrangle to the gates I remembered something. I turned to the jailer who was accompanying me . . .

"Have men ever been imprisoned here?" I asked . . .

"Why, yes" . . . he said . . . "It was long before my time. But I have heard some of the others speak of it. They had a lot of young men, political prisoners, in here after the Insurrection of 1830. There was an epidemic of cholera and most of them died. . . ."

It was not until some years later that I heard the reason for my sudden release.

I had been arrested as a result of information given by a spy in our own party, a young man who was the son of a patriot family. As his parents had both belonged to the P.P.S. for several years, he had been received into it almost without question. In reality he was a spy working in the pay of the Russian authorities. Thanks to my system of organizing the transport of arms in a series of watertight compartments so that no depot could be linked up with another, he had not been able to secure much evidence, but even so it would have been enough to convict me. Over my trial, however, there arose a dilemma.

By the Russian law I had to be confronted with two witnesses for the prosecution. The police had hoped during the time I was in prison to pile up indisputable proofs of my revolutionary activities either by discovering my arms depots or by getting some one else in the party to betray me. But they had not succeeded. The young man and his parents, at whose house I had been arrested, had stood firm under repeated interrogations, and the depots were too well hidden. There remained, then, only the evidence of the spy who had accused me. But he could not give it without exposing his own role in the party, which would mean that the secret police could no longer make use of him. They decided that the information with which he was able to furnish them from time to time was more valuable than my conviction, and therefore released me without trial.

On leaving the prison I did not return to my own apartment but went instead to the house of friends, for I knew that I should be subjected to strict surveillance. The Russian police had a trick of releasing political prisoners in the hope that they would be thrown momentarily off their guard and betray either themselves or their associates. So I remained indoors for a week or so, then dyed my hair blonde and departed for Kiev, carrying with me a whole consignment of revolvers and ammunition for the branch of the Bojowka there.

Another girl, who was also a member of the party, travelled with me part of the way, and I remember that we were both in very high spirits and talked and laughed so much that an old Russian lady who shared the compartment with us said suddenly to me . . .

"I am quite sure that you have never been in love. I can tell it from your laugh. No woman who has loved ever laughs like that."

"No. I never have been" . . . I answered, amused . . . "I am too much interested in my work to fall in love. I have not the time. . . ."

She had a mild and kind face which reminded me of Aunt Maria. Evidently they had the same views, because she answered me . . . "I do not know what your work is, but I think that any one as young as you must be wasted in it if it leads you away from the thought of marriage, which is the only career for a woman. . . ."

I laughed again, imagining how shocked she would have been to know that my work at that moment was carrying arms which were to be used in an attack on a Russian bank which the party was planning.

Joseph Pilsudski was at Kiev, and it was there that our acquaintance passed on to the plane of friendship. We used to go long walks together.

The friend with whom I was staying in Kiev, a woman of middle age, had little patience with my going for walks with Pilsudski, in the first place because they usually made me late for supper, and secondly because she disliked him. . . .

"I can't imagine what any one sees in him" . . . she used to say crossly . . . "There are other men in the party with far more brain, and he is so conceited."

Later I found out that she was wrong in that at least. Actually he was the least egotistical of men, pliant in his outlook, always ready to listen to the opinions of others, even of those much younger than himself. And he was intensely shy. To the end of his life public speaking was an ordeal to him. He must have made altogether some thousands of speeches to every type of audience and on diverse subjects, but he never made one without undergoing acute misery beforehand. He set himself to conquer what he considered this weakness in his character, but it was only by a conscious effort of will that he succeeded.

That was one of the things he confessed to me during those walks in Kiev. At first our conversation was confined to general subjects, for he was not a man who gave confidences easily. But afterwards he lost his constraint and told me of his plans for the future and his dreams for a new Poland that would rise from the ashes of the past. In looking back I realize how many of those dreams were afterwards fulfilled, and also that I never doubted even then that they would be. It never struck me as incongruous that this man, who was only the unknown leader of a little revolutionary group, should talk of laws he meant to pass, of the University he would found at Wilno, and of the Polytechnic he would build at Lodz. . . .

"Our slavery will come to an end before long" . . . he used to say . . . "because we shall profit by the general upheaval there will be in Europe. A big war is bound to break out any time within the next ten years. Germany and Austria will certainly be involved in it, and probably Russia. And that will be Poland's opportunity to free herself. Until then we can only carry on constant guerilla warfare against Russia, and wait. But above all else we must prepare ourselves so that when the moment for a greater and wider conflict comes we shall be ready for it. . . ."

He talked of the Polish state that would be created and of the form of Government that would be best suited to it. He thought that of the United States . . . "The democracy you get in England is older and of finer traditions, but it is not plastic enough for a people as unused to self-government as we shall be. We need a democracy based on Socialism. The average Englishman does not understand Socialism. A Socialist is to him a man who wears no collar and needs a haircut, mouthing principles with which he has no patience. He does not realize that the Socialism for which we fight is only another form of democracy, that we are only reaching out for the freedom which England has had for centuries and France since the Revolution. . . ."

There was one subject which always ended in an argument between us. The question of women's franchise. He had already decided that in the new Poland women would have equal rights with men in the government of the country. But he always maintained that they would not use their vote wisely because the feminine mentality was by nature intensely conservative and too readily swayed by personal considerations. I being an ardent feminist used to fly to arms at this, and the walk generally ended in a heated dispute. On those days I used to tell myself that my friend was right and that Pilsudski was conceited. But one day the wind was taken out of my sails, for I was out shopping when he called at the house and she entertained him at tea. When I returned later I found that she had completely revised her original opinion of him and was enthusiastic in his praise. . . .

"What a charming man he is when one gets to know him better" . . . she explained. . . . "Such a brilliant brain. Really it is absurd how people misjudge him." From that time onwards he could do no wrong in her estimation.

I was amused at the fact that he had evidently sensed her antagonism and instinctively overcome it. To him the human soul was a harp with many chords and he knew unerringly which one to touch in making a friend or winning over a political opponent. It was because of this that he was able all through his life to reconcile men with widely opposing views and to set them working harmoniously together.

CHAPTER XII

JOSEPH KIEMENS GINET-PILSUDSKI came into the world on December 5th, 1867, at Zulow, his father's estate in Lithuania. His infant eyes opened on a vast panorama of snow-clad plains backed by gently sloping hills and threaded with forests of pine and birch, the heritage of a people rich in folk-lore and steeped in tradition, clinging tenaciously to the ways and the speech of their forefathers, still practising among themselves customs founded on the primeval worship of the gods of the woods and the rivers.

The Pilsudski property consisted of a rambling one-storied manor house built of larchwood and set on the banks of a stream. Flanking it were rows of tall chestnuts and fragrant limes; in front was a lawn where the children played and had their swings in summer. Behind it were the outbuildings, the barns and carpentering sheds, the vats and presses, for among the industries of the estate was a brewery. But the value of the land was decreasing, the crops were dwindling with each harvest through lack of proper handling, for the owner, Joseph Pilsudski, had no idea of how to manage the estate.

He was a handsome man, descended from a long line of Lithuanian nobles, with a strain of Scottish blood from an ancestor who had belonged to the ancient house of Butler and had come out to Poland as a fugitive after the Jacobite rebellion of 1745. But this intermingling of blood had left behind it a legacy of superb physical vitality, and a tradition of gaiety and undying fidelity to an ideal rather than the Scot's accepted qualities of energy and tenacity. The younger Joseph had to acquire these from his mother. His father was a man of considerable mental gifts, cultured, extremely well-read, a brilliant pianist and a talented composer, but he had the irresponsibility that so often accompanies the artistic temperament, and a mercurial disposition, usually sunny but given to violent gusts of rage that shook the whole household while they lasted. He was the kindest and most indulgent of fathers, welcoming with undiminished enthusiasm the arrival of each of the new babies who made their appearance at the manor with the regularity of the spring flowers or the winter gales. He used to invent games for them and tell them wonderful fairy tales, and generally succeeded in making their world a colourful and adventurous place.

His wife, Maria, who was his second cousin, was delicate, intellectual and witty, lame in one foot as the result of a lingering and painful form of tuberculosis from which she suffered all her life, and with a small face covered with freckles, considered in those days an unredeemable blemish. A woman of an ethereal type of beauty but with great force of personality and a gay dauntless courage which dominated her frail body.

Joseph, who was given his father's name, was her fourth child and between them was a tie so strong that although he was only fourteen when she died her influence lasted throughout his life. Whenever he was faced with a difficult decision he uesd to try to imagine what she would have wished him to do and then do it . . . "As long as I can feel that I have done right in her eyes I do not care if the whole world is against me" . . . he said in telling me of her in those days at Kiev.

She was, he described her, "an irreconcilable patriot," and it was from her lips that he first heard the story of Poland. Her family had fought and suffered in the Insurrection of 1863 and memories of its terrible aftermath were still green at Zulow and in all the Lithuanian countryside where the savage cruelties of Muraviev, the Russian General, had earned him the name of "The Hangman."

"The impression of his rule was still so fresh" . . . wrote Joseph Pilsudski, "that people trembled at the sight of an official uniform, and their faces lengthened at the sound of a bell announcing the arrival of one of the representatives of the Muscovite Government" . . .

In the manor at Zulow, as in every Polish and Lithuanian home, patriotism could only flower in secret. In the evening when the servants were safely in the kitchen Maria Pilsudski would unlock a drawer in her cabinet and take out the forbidden books of Polish history and literature to read them to her children. She loved best of all the works of the patriot poets Krasinski and Slowacki and she taught her son Joseph to love them too. When he grew older he used to read them to her as she lay on her couch in the garden.

In accordance with the usual custom of the Polish nobility of maintaining large households of poorer relatives and dependents the family at Zulow included besides the twelve children, two aunts, one of whom was known as "The General" because of her exploits in the Insurrection of 1863, several cousins and two governesses, one French and the other German. Discipline was not rigidly enforced and the younger generation at least led a happy carefree existence, roaming about the estate, helping the peasants in the hayfield, and stripping the cherry trees in the orchard. Joseph was the ringleader in everything. Of them all he had most strongly the heritage of the countryman. Every glade of the forest was home to him. There was not a path which he could not follow in the darkness, not a bird's call which he could not identify. He alone of all the family loved hunting, and he used to go out fearlessly after wolf and boar. It was only in later years that the taking of life became so repugnant to him that he would neither shoot nor permit any one else to shoot on his estate.

By the time Joseph reached the age of twelve the Pilsudskis' affairs had gone from bad to worse. His father sent for books on the technique of farming and agriculture, introduced new scientific methods and bought modern machinery. His reaping and threshing machines were a source of wonder to the peasants, but they only succeeded in dissipating still further his capital. The climax came with a fire which broke out one night and raged for hours, burning to the ground the wooden manor house, the outbuildings and the newly-gathered harvest. Rebuilding was impossible, so collecting what little was left of the library and furniture the family moved to Wilno and rented a house in the city.

Joseph was sent to school at the Wilno Gymnase (the

Russian Secondary School) which was housed in what had once been the ancient University of Wilno, sacred to Poles because of its associations with Mickiewicz and Slowacki. His sister described him to me as a quiet, rather stocky little boy, inclined to be lazy except in studying the subjects that interested him . . . history, literature and mathematics. Of his unhappiness and the bitterness that consumed him he gave no sign, in those days. It was only years later that he wrote . . .

"For me my time at the Gymnasium was a sort of penal servitude. The masters there were Czarist schoolmasters, teachers and trainers of youth who brought all their political passions to school with them, and whose system was to crush as much as possible the independence and personal dignity of their pupils. The atmosphere crushed me, the injustice and the politics of the masters enraged me. A whole ox's skin would not contain a description of the unceasing humiliations and provocations from our teachers and the degradation of all that I had been accustomed to respect and love.

"My hatred for the Czarist administration and the Muscovite oppression grew with every year. Helpless fury and shame that I could do nothing to hinder my enemies often stifled me; my cheeks burned, that I must suffer in silence while my pride was trampled upon, listening to lies and scornful words about Poland, Poles and their history. The feeling of oppression, the feeling of being a slave who can be crushed like a worm at any moment, weighed on my heart like a millstone. I always count those years spent in the Gymnasium among the most unpleasant of my life."

He turned to his mother for help. She did not fail him, but there was nothing of the sentimental in her love. She gave him such comfort as a mother of Sparta might have given . . . "Endure, remember and wait. . . .

"One day this tyranny will end. One day Poland will be free. . . ."

"When will that day come?" he used to ask her . . .

"When we shall show ourselves worthy of it by fighting for it. . . ."

Together they would make plans for the dawn of a new and glorious day, the frail invalid lying on her couch and the little schoolboy . . .

"In these moments she seemed inspired, as though her eyes could indeed see into the future . . ." he said.

She taught him patience and self-restraint and to find consolation in the books she loved. He read incessantly. He used to come home from school and go up to his attic bedroom. There he would sit up far into the night studying by the light of a candle the forbidden history and literature. The story of the French Revolution gripped him. . . .

"I read whatever I could get hold of about it . . ." he wrote long afterwards. "Naturally I did not then understand the social basis of the movement, but I was enchanted by the enthusiasm and revolutionary fury and by the part taken by the great masses of the people. When I asked myself why we Poles could not achieve such revolutionary energy I could find only one answer . . . that we had been, and still were, inferior to the French. This was a great blow to my national pride. . . ."

The figure of Napoleon dominating that colossal background of turmoil and struggle became his inspiration. He read the history of his campaigns until he knew every phase by heart. They woke in him the passionate longing for an army career which was denied to him since as a Polish patriot he would not serve in a Russian regiment. But because he was a soldier by instinct loving "the whole art and tradition of warfare," as he described it, he set himself to study every book he could procure on military tactics.

At that stage of his life most of his friends were drawn from the books he read. The death of his mother, which was a crushing grief to him, made him withdraw into himself. The Gymnase, now that she was no longer waiting for him at home with words of comfort and encouragement, seemed still more intolerable. But his reading had opened a new world to him. At night the bare little attic was peopled with the splendid figures of history. It was often nearly daybreak before he reluctantly extinguished his solitary candle. Most of his father's books had been destroyed in the fire at Zulow but he saved up his pocket money to buy more, and borrowed others from the school library and from friends. He read the plays of Shakespeare so often that he could repeat whole Acts from memory. He read Alexandre Dumas and Victor Hugo and Alfred de Musset who introduced him to the beauty of French verse. He had even in those school days a great appreciation of poetry, and later he learnt to know and love the poets of every nation, but Slowacki was always the dearest to him.

During his last years at the Gymnase he began to take up the cause of Socialism. It was a step without precedent for a member of a noble family, for it entailed breaking down centuries-old barriers of tradition and inherited prejudice.

The Polish nobility into which he was born was a conservative class, the remnants of a ruling order that had been without equal in power and privileges. In time past they had exercised a power over the country which was far mightier than that of a king, for the king was elected by them, chosen from candidates to be the puppet of the state while they were the state itself. They used to come to these royal elections, followed by their armies of retainers, sometimes numbering as many as twenty thousand men, resolved to support the aspirant, who was most likely to prove amenable in safeguarding their prerogatives and lightening their taxes. Thus laws were made and unmade to suit their convenience. The peasants were kept in serfdom to enrich them with their labour, the merchants and artisans were ground down to pay the revenues to which they refused to contribute. In their splendid castles they lived in regal state, surrounded by their hundreds of servants and peasants, followed by their retinues of young men of noble birth whose swords were pledged to their service.

They travelled extensively and their journeys had all the pomp and dignity of a royal progress with long cavalcades of coaches and outriders escorted by men-at-arms. From their tours in foreign lands they returned with treasures to enrich their castles. The weavers of Arras made tapestries for them, the armourers of Toledo and Bilbao hammered out their finest blades for them, the goldsmiths of Paris searched for rare gems to adorn their costumes. Sometimes one of them brought back a foreign wife with her train of female relatives, maids and attendants to swell the already enormous household. They were, in fact, magnificent and picturesque figures.

They ruled their great estates in patriarchal fashion, dispensing hospitality, money and aid to all who came to them. They endowed schools and hospitals, were great patrons of art, learning and the church, and kept open house to hosts of poor relations and impoverished lesser nobles. Any one who could claim kindred with them, no matter how remote, was entitled to share their privileges, for long-established custom had built a fence round their entire class, made of it a close and jealously guarded preserve. Those born within the fence could never be put outside it even though they might lack lands and money. So the household of every great magnate was full of dependents . . . sons of cousins seven or eight times removed who must be educated with his own son, penniless girls, vague relatives who must be given dowries and provided with suitable husbands; elderly spinsters unwanted by the rest of the world but who, because they bore his own name, must not be left in undignified poverty.

Only a degree less in importance were the Szlachta, or minor gentry, not so wealthy as the great landowners but sharing their rank and privileges, and with an equal voice in the election of the king and the government of the country. Their class was so numerous that at one time in a population of five millions they accounted for over 200,000 people. Like the great nobles they discharged their obligations to the Crown by giving military service and were practically exempt from paying taxes. Their condition varied. Some owned hundreds of acres; others only a couple of fields and a cottage, but the status of each was the same. However poor he might be he could claim equality with the greatest noble in the kingdom. The one might attend elections to the monarchy splendidly apparelled and followed by a long train of retainers, the other mounted on his own horse with his sword (the emblem and privilege of nobility) attached to his waist by a threadbare girdle. But the vote of each was of the same value.

It was this system which earned for Poland the rather paradoxical title of "a republic of nobles," which in fact it was, a genuine democracy based on freedom and equality, scorning mercenary considerations. And that at a time when bribery and corruption were rife in practically every government in Europe. It had, however, the disadvantage of applying to only two sections of the nation. The all-powerful great landowners and their companion body the Szlachta shaped the destiny of Poland. Behind them millions of peasants toiled in the fields, thousands of citizens and humble artisans plodded patiently to carry on the industries of the country in whose government they had no voice.

Centuries passed. The kingdom of Poland disappeared. But the nobility who had bolstered it up and pulled the strings controlling the puppet kings did not disappear with it. The Partitioning Powers split up their estates into German, Russian and Austrian territories, levied enormous taxes on them, but they remained fundamentally unchanged. The aristocracy of any country is naturally conservative, reactionary, prone to follow the lines of least resistance, and the great Polish landowners were no exception. The fetters which weighed so heavily on the rest of the stricken nation were in their case only silken bands. Before the partition they had attended the Courts of Vienna, St. Petersburg and Berlin, they continued to attend them. Many of them had lands and interests abroad. They were thus only too vulnerable to the external influence which has always proved so disastrous to Poland. At the same time the intrigues of the Czar's agents in the districts under Russian rule and the Austrian agents in Galicia fermented trouble between them and the peasantry so that the majority of them took no part in revolutionary efforts. The Szlachta, who had adapted themselves to the new conditions, founded the middle class and produced many of Poland's most famous men . . . artists, scientists, poets and musicians . . . proved their patriotism time and again. They gave their sons unsparingly to every endeavour of the nation to shake off its chains, to Kosciuszko's army, and again in later generations to the Insurrections of 1830 and 1863. But the great land-owners, with certain exceptions, remained aloof.

To this, the most conservative caste in Poland, Joseph Pilsudski belonged by birth, but he had few of its tastes and still less of its mentality. His sympathies were with the peasants and working men of whom he had an instinctive knowledge and understanding. He was bitterly opposed to the reactionary attitude of the nobility and wrote from Siberia to his cousin urging him to stir up among the neighbouring landowners some interest in the question of national independence. . . .

"No class, however powerful it may be," . . . he wrote, "can carry through a successful insurrection. It must be the work of the entire nation. Let us set aside these barriers of class and unite the people only as men and women. . . ."

The labour conditions which he saw in Wilno made him burn with indignation even in his student days. In describing them he wrote . . .

"According to the law enforced throughout Russian Poland the trade institutions with a few exceptions are obliged to remain closed until 2 P.M. on Sundays. So the pious Catholics shut the front doors of their shops and go to church, but leave their wretched hirelings at work in the back part of the premises. The police, who are well paid by these slave-driving employers, are careful to confine their inspection to the front of the house and turn a blind eye to what goes on in the back.

"There are no limits to this exploitation of shop assistants and the working classes in general. In most institutions work lasts from 8 A.M. till 10 P.M.—a fourteen-hour day with only a short break for lunch! Many of those who work under these conditions are boys and girls from twelve to fifteen years old."

The plight of these inarticulate thousands too crushed to take the initiative of fighting for themselves roused him to fierce rebellion.

At that time he made his first contact with Socialism. . . .
"I began to call myself a Socialist in 1884" . . . he wrote.
. . . "I say 'call myself' with emphasis because that is all it
was. To say that I had any very clear and definite ideas regarding the principles of Socialism would be quite another
thing. The Socialism which I professed then came to us in
Wilno from St. Petersburg, and it was quite different from
that of later days. It was a curious mixture of Socialist criticism
of bourgeois society with an anarchist ideal of self-governing
communes, and a somewhat reactionary faith in the Russian
nation in which, in contrast to the bourgeois West, Communist
elements were in full bloom. This Socialism was hypercritical
as regards Europe, but flattered Russia and was then in process
of transformation into the most commonplace doctrinaire
radicalism which used Russian messianism as a screen to hide
the lack of effort to raise the consciousness of the Russian
working people. . . ."

He began to study Socialism. The only books he could
procure were those on which every Russian Socialist pinned
his faith . . . the works of Michailovski, Pesarev, Lavelaye
and Iwaninkow, but their vague, misty talk and confused
theories bored him. With difficulty he got hold of a volume
of Karl Marx's *Das Kapital,* but although he studied it carefully
he rejected its abstract logic and the dominion of goods over
man. He was still unsettled in his ideas in 1885 when he entered on a course of medicine at the University of Kharkov.

He left the University at the end of his first year.

It was not a great disappointment to him. He had never felt
any vocation for medicine and had only agreed to study it after
long and heated arguments with his father who had insisted
on having a doctor in the family. All his own inclinations were
towards engineering and mathematics.

He returned to Wilno with the intention of going abroad
to continue his studies. In the meantime he formed a secret
society whose members were for the most part University
students and young men of the middle class. They drew up
their own program, a compound of Socialism and Polish na-
tionalism, and brought out a publication consisting of one
or two typewritten sheets, which was circulated among them-

selves and their friends. This little circle which used to meet in the attic of his father's house was his beginning both as a journalist and as a political organizer.

Even in those early years he was opposed to all acts of political terrorism and violence, and it was therefore an irony of Fate that he should have been arrested in consequence of one in which he was not even remotely concerned. His elder brother, Bronislas, who was a student at St. Petersburg, had become involved in a circle which included among its members several of the men responsible for the attempted assassination of the Czar Alexander III in 1887.

Bronislas, knowing nothing of the plot until after it was exposed, had in all innocence given Joseph's address in Wilno to one of these men who intended to take refuge in that city until the affair had blown over. Instead, he was arrested and the card was found on him. The Russian police, determined to establish widespread complicity, seized upon this fresh "evidence" and both the Pilsudskis were convicted. Bronislas was sentenced to the Katorga and afterwards to exile for life. Joseph was given five years in Siberia.

Five years can seem a lifetime at twenty and he rebelled fiercely at the injustice of his sentence, as he set out on the long march across the frozen plains of Siberia. At Irkutsk, one stage of the journey, he took part in a mutiny among the prisoners and received a blow on the mouth from the butt of a guard's rifle which knocked out most of his teeth, and injured the jawbone. His mouth was his one vanity, he was proud of its fine curves and full sensitive lower lip and always regretted when he was obliged to let his moustache and beard grow.

After the first few months in Siberia his mother's unquenchable spirit asserted itself in him . . . "Endure, remember, and wait. . . ." He repeated the words to himself many times as he lay awake at night in his lonely hut on the edge of the forest. But he would do more than wait. He would plan. Plan for a day which drew nearer with every dawn and sunset. . . . "It was only there in Siberia, where I could peacefully think over everything I had gone through in the past and everything I wished to do in the future, that I became what I am" . . . he wrote later.

Physically he owed much to those years of exile. After a year in desolate Lena he was sent to the region of Tunka, and the purity of the climate there rid him of an hereditary tendency to weakness of the lungs. He spent hours in the open every day, fishing the limpid mountain streams, roaming the forest, hunting the wolves and the fierce brown Siberian bears. The love of the country which he had known in his childhood awoke once more in him. He became conscious of his own affinity with the earth; the grandeur of the mountains brought him peace and consolation, the beauty of the sunrise over the forest was a message of home. He was never to lose this sense of kinship with nature. In the later stormy years of his life, when he wrestled not with his own personal problems but with those of a nation, he would always seek the solitude of the woods and fields when he could.

The Russian Government allowed its exiles in Siberia unlimited freedom within a certain broad radius, knowing that they would not attempt to escape because they had nowhere to escape to. The wilderness and the wolves barred their way more effectively than a whole regiment of soldiers. So he was able not only to hunt in the forest but to go into the neighbouring village.

He became friendly with other Polish political prisoners, among them Bronislaw Szwarce, who had played a prominent part in the Insurrection of 1863. They used to sit over the fire in Szwarce's little cabin talking for hours, the old patriot, white-haired after twenty years in exile, defeated but still unbroken in spirit, full of his dreams of another armed insurrection that should free Poland. And the young man listening to him, fired by his enthusiasm, registering a vow that one day he would lead that insurrection and that when the time came it should not fail.

He met among these exiles men of all types: Poles, Russians and Jews. Followers of Tolstoy, anarchists, disciples of various religious sects whose doctrine had aroused the resentment of the Czarist authorities, and Socialists of different parties. He listened to all their theories, learned to distinguish between the true and the false. Those years in Siberia changed him from a youth, ardent, romantic, full of half-defined ideals to a man, practical, calculating, confirmed in his convictions.

His exile ended in 1892 and he went back to Wilno where he found that a number of political parties had come into being. Only one of them united in its program the two aims which were to him inseparable . . . national independence and Socialism . . . the new Polish Socialist party which had been formed in Paris. Two of its founders, Mendelssohn and Alexander Sulkiewicz, were then in Wilno and they invited him to join them. They organized a branch of the party and held their first congress in Wilno in the summer of 1893. Among the resolutions passed was a plan for the publication of a party newspaper. Joseph Pilsudski was given an imposing appointment of editor-in-chief. What he actually became was editor, business manager, compositor and printer. The name of the paper was chosen, the *Robotnik* (Workman) and the first number was printed in February 1894 in London.

He spent the next few years in building up the party, in organizing its campaign and recruiting new members. He was on the Russian Government's Black List now; his photograph and description were issued to every police station with orders for his arrest. He dropped his own name and became known as "Comrade Victor," or "Misezyslaw," changed his appearance by shaving off his beard and cutting the heavy eyebrows which were characteristic of him. He travelled incessantly all over the country, availing himself of the facilities of the different territories. When Russian Poland grew too unsafe for him he would cross over into the Austrian provinces and remain there in hiding. He became in those years "a specialist in frontier breaking," as he described himself.

He went into the country districts addressing himself to the peasants, enrolling hundreds of them in the party, and to the great industrial towns to circulate his pamphlets and canvass the workers in their dinner hour. He even carried his propaganda into the Russian universities, rallied the students to his cause. One month he would be in London, where a Polish Socialist Committee had been established, making contact with the English Socialists and securing contributors to his paper. And the next he would be in Zürich attending an international congress. He used to sit up half the night writing his articles, or printing them with Wojciechowski on their little press.

It was a hand-to-mouth existence for him in those days, for the party had scarcely any funds behind it and his political activities had estranged him from his family. He was constantly in flight from the Russian authorities; he could rarely remain in the same place longer than a few days. When he was in Wilno he slept out in the forest night after night because none of his acquaintances dared to take him into their houses for fear of a search by the secret police. He used to spend such leisure as he had sitting in some church, since he could not walk in the streets without running the risk of being recognized and arrested.

In 1896 he attended the International Congress of Socialism in London. The question of Poland's claim to independence was discussed. The Russian Socialists were opposed to it on the usual contention that a separation of Polish and Russian commercial interests would have unfavourable repercussions among the workers, and also that Polish cultural development and Polish capital were needed to further the Socialist movement in Russia.

Joseph Pilsudski stated the cause for his country with such passionate eloquence that he carried the day. The Congress passed a resolution "that the Independence of Poland was necessary both in the interest of the international workers and the Polish proletariat." Later the formula was amended to one proclaiming the right of every people to determine its own nationality and government. It was his first victory.

He spent many months in London, for he was bringing out a brochure which was to be smuggled into Poland and circulated there. He called it "In Remembrance of May," and among the English contributors were Tom Mann, E. Aveling and H. Quelch. It was edited in his lodgings at Leytonstone. There he could work in peace, free of the shadow of the secret police. During the next few years he spent much of his time in England and some numbers of the *Robotnik* were printed there.

Those days in London were happy ones for him although he lived in the simplest fashion, spending money only on the barest necessities. He used to go for walks on Leytonstone

Common with the children of the young Polish couple with whom he lodged, sailing their toy boats on the pond for them, getting them to teach him English, which they spoke fluently. Years later one of these same children, now grown into an attractive young lady, came to visit us at the Belvedere, and I remember how my husband laughed when she reminded him that he had never been able to get the correct pronunciation of the word "ceiling," even when she had stamped her feet at him until he threatened to throw her in the pond. He had a great affection for children and an instinctive understanding of them so that they were always drawn to him.

He spent as much time as he could spare in exploring London. He avoided the usual program of the average tourist from the Continent, preferring to wander in the peaceful courts of the Temple, or the crowded markets of Soho. On Sundays he used to listen to the Hyde Park orators or mingle with the groups round the Serpentine, a quiet, rather lonely young man, one of London's thousands of foreigners but with plans that were to change the destiny of a nation germinating in his brain.

He was fond of London for all it represented to him, for the freedom of its people, for its political tolerance and centuries-old tradition. Although he was a Socialist and a revolutionary there was much of the conservative in him, and an ingrained liking for law and order. The solid structure of Victorian England founded on the unchanging character of the nation appealed to this.

The English craze for sport first puzzled and then intrigued him . . . "I came to the conclusion that the average Englishman could not even see a stone lying in the road without wanting to kick it" . . . he told me in those days at Kiev . . . "And then I saw that this kicking of stones and pursuit of balls appeared to have a favourable effect on the young men of the nation and that therefore we Poles ought to copy it." So he included in his plan for the future of Poland a scheme for establishing sports and physical training centres which would be within the scope of all classes. He carried it out to the letter and in the twenty-one years of our existence as a separate state our youth attained a surprising standard of efficiency in sports.

PART FOUR

★

THE WHITE EAGLE

CHAPTER XIII

"THE ROBOTNIK," the official organ of the P.P.S. for workmen, had a chequered career. Two consecutive numbers were
rarely edited in the same place. It was printed in secret in a
variety of dingy houses and damp cellars, smuggled over
frontiers and circulated among labourers who hid it under
their overalls, and students who pasted cuttings from it between the leaves of their exercise books. But the demand for
it steadily increased. When affairs began to improve slightly
Joseph Pilsudski took an apartment which he shared with
his friend Stanislas Wojciechowski, who later became President of Poland. It was a very small apartment and most of
the space was taken up by the printing press and its acces-
sories. They would not employ a servant or charwoman for
fear of being spied upon, so the housework was done by
Wojciechowski who was a practical young man and even
managed to do all the cooking on their one little stove. Joseph,
who was incapable of so much as boiling an egg, told me that
he was most grateful to his friend, who not only kept the
ménage running smoothly but looked after him like a mother,
though he used to complain that his most ambitious culinary
efforts were generally spoilt by his being called away at the most
critical moment to help with setting up type. On those days
they used to sit down to charred meat and sodden vegetables.

As the success of the paper among the working classes
became established it was decided to publish it on a more
extensive scale, and to make the busy industrial city of Lodz
(our Polish Manchester) its headquarters. Pilsudski wanted to
reach the thousands of mill hands and textile workers who
slaved amid the noise and heat of the looms for 12 hours a
day. They were the fertile soil in which he could sow the
seeds of an armed rebellion that would free not only themselves but the whole nation.

He went to Lodz in 1899 with his first wife, Maria Juszkiewez, to whom he was now married and a young man, Carol Rosnowski, an ex-student of the Moscow University, who was to help with the printing. They took a first-floor apartment in one of the busiest quarters of the city. The largest of the rooms was given over to the press and almost every article of furniture in it served a double purpose. The printing machine and boxes of type were kept in a wardrobe, the paper was concealed in the hollow back of a sofa, manuscript and reference books were locked away in a chest of drawers, and the key of the press was hidden in a space scooped out in the base of an Eastern idol. In that room they worked ten and eleven hours a day with scarcely a break, editing and cutting the articles and setting up the type. The actual printing could only be done in the busiest hours of the day when there was sufficient noise coming from the neighbouring warehouses and offices to drown the sound of the machinery but they often sat up all night writing. A twelve-page number generally took fifteen to sixteen days for the little machine was intended to be used only for small advertisements and visiting cards, and could never turn off more than one page at a time. As each monthly issue consisted of 1,900 copies, one page therefore needed at least eight hours' work, and more if there were frequent interruptions or special care had to be taken in the matter of noise. All the editorial work had to be done in scraps between the four or five-hour shifts at the machine and there were moments of crisis when it was discovered that the leading article was ten or twelve lines too long or that there was not another letter "r" left. Then the harassed editor-manager-compositor had to make hasty adjustments, cut down the offending leader without sacrificing its sense, substitute words containing no "r."

At the end of the first year in Lodz the circulation of the paper was sufficient to trouble the sleep of the Russian authorities and set them searching for the secret press. There were frequent alarms when the apartment was visited by strangers, but the press was always dismantled and hidden in the nick of time and they saw nothing of a suspicious nature. Then on February 22nd, 1900, sheer chance put all the cards into their hands.

A young man named Malinsky, who had been imprisoned, managed to escape and went to Lodz to see Pilsudski. In the street he was recognized by two police agents who followed him at a discreet distance to the apartment.

At a late hour that same evening Joseph Pilsudski was toiling over the thirty-sixth number of the *Robotnik* when the door was flung open and several policemen headed by a lieutenant-colonel burst into the room. There was no time to hide anything from them; the press stood there before their eyes with a page of the newspaper whose origin they had so long sought to discover lying upon it. The lieutenant-colonel picked it up, pointed an accusing finger at the leading article . . . "Triumph of Freedom of the Press" . . .

"For my part" . . . he remarked dryly as his men took the prisoners into custody . . . "I think there is something to be said against the value of the printing press."

Pilsudski could only stand by in silence while they dismantled the machine. . . .

"I confess that in spite of the many cheerless moments I had spent over it" . . . he wrote later . . . "and although I had often lost my temper with it and called it 'an old rattler' and 'a stupid beast,' yet my heart ached to see it in the hands of the police agents as they moved it from its stand to a basket. When the basket was sealed I stood by as if the coffin lid had closed on some one near and very dear to me. So many hopes, so much love, so much devotion were bound up with this scrap of iron, now condemned to silence and inactivity."

After a couple of months in the local prison at Lodz he was transferred to the Warsaw Citadel, that name of fate engraved on the history of Poland by generations of her patriots who have passed within its damp and gloomy walls. There he remained for the best part of a year, in solitary confinement in a narrow whitewashed cell containing only a battered iron bedstead, a dirty table, and a wooden stool.

Yet he was not altogether unhappy. Many years later he wrote of his experiences there. . . .

"As far as I am concerned I always held that I was born a prisoner, because it was easy for me to reconstruct the charm of life. This is perhaps the hardest part of imprisonment, the necessity to create for oneself something independent of any outsider, to create a prison life out of one's own resources. To create it under abnormal conditions, alone and without assistance, seeking to find by some means or other what I might call 'the luxury of prison.' When a man seeks for material to achieve this end he finds that he is so limited in means, so restricted in methods, that he almost gives up the attempt. His hands can find nothing to do. There are no tools available with which to make anything. Material objects are so limited and so insignificant that the mind gropes with difficulty for something to cling to.

"And what is there in prison? Only walls and a small number of articles designed for the prisoner's use. One makes various attempts to imitate the life which is teeming elsewhere. In the prison cells there are flies and other creatures which have got there. There have even been prisoners who have grown to have a great affection for bugs, and thus satisfied their need for independence. To seek a life outside prison conditions, to create a luxury for oneself alone, that is the prisoner's psychological need.

"I was thankful in those days in the Citadel for the natural gift which enabled me to evoke in my soul dreams and ideas with great facility. I did not become attached to any material things, but, when I look back on my experience in many prisons, I remember one particular pleasure—my great joy in being able to move things about in my cell. There are many prisons where nothing can be moved because everything is fixed and screwed down. That is why I look back with pleasant emotion upon my confinement in the Warsaw Citadel. In other prisons, you had nothing for yourself, but there everything belonged to you, because you had the right to move it.

"When I was brought into cell number twenty-six of the Tenth Pavilion of Warsaw Citadel it seemed to have all the charms of a hotel room, though a very poor one; my suitcase was lying there, and I could move my things freely from one corner to another; when I kicked the table it moved obediently.

"If I represent prison life in this manner it is because I do not consider it to be totally without pleasure. I could fight against prison conditions with my lively and vivid imagination; I was able to create my own life of thought and dreams, a life of illusions in which I had freer rein than was possible in everyday life, when so many eyes are watching with suspicion. You are conscious of no restraint once you ignore the jailer's watchful gaze. Once I had reached this stage I was able to create in myself everything I required, for time was no consideration.

"If you believe that with my vivid imagination, which grasped at everything and covered all the domains of human thought, I differed from other prisoners, who lacked my freedom of thought, you are mistaken, for I have found that all the other prisoners whom I questioned acted as I did. In how many prisons have I not seen this desire to create their own independent luxury!

"They start the study of languages though they never studied them in their lives before. They toil over strange words and queer expressions, in which they vainly endeavour to find some sense, and which they do not know how to pronounce, so that they acquire faults of pronunciation of which they are never able to free themselves afterwards. I, myself, had this experience over the English language, which I studied while in prison, and in which I became so used to faulty and incorrect pronunciation that I have never been able to speak it properly since. Never having had a particular fondness for the study of languages I should not have had the courage to learn them while I was at liberty, and yet I committed this crime against myself in moiling and toiling at the English language while I was in prison.

"I used to be passionately fond of chess, although, unfortunately, this is a game which requires a partner. I tried to make a tiny chessboard, and I managed to make one on the back of a book which lay in every cell, the Bible.

With the help of matches, which I had, since luckily I was allowed to smoke, I was able to make the black squares of the board. The chessmen I fashioned so clumsily that I would be ashamed for any one to see the miserable rooks and bishops which I produced. I concealed this with cunning and skill during the daily cell inspection, so as to retain as long as possible the treasure by which I outwitted my merciless oppressors. It is absolutely essential thus to seek for resources in oneself, to seek to fashion from the crumbs which one has brought into prison from the scraps which fall into one's hands, a new spiritual prison life" . . .

Prison to him was sweetened by the thought of the patriots who had walked that same road before him, a long and unbroken chain stretching back to the days of the First Partition. In imagination he could feel their presence. In the lonely evenings the cell seemed full of the ghosts of men who had fought for freedom. Their efforts became identified with his, in him they lived again. . . .

"For a long time prisons have formed a part of Polish civilization" . . . he wrote later . . . "During the last hundred-and-fifty years there was hardly a man who did not come in contact with prison in some way. There has not been a single prominent movement in which prison has not been the companion of Poles from the cradle to the grave. Every one spoke of prison as of a living part of his soul.

"I have frequently asked myself whether all those prison experiences of Poland, with all their sacrifices and terror, with all the beauty of the human soul tormented in abnormal conditions, garrotted, beaten, tired out, and yet prompt to rebel, whether this beauty is not one of the traits peculiar to our generation. When I think of this and gaze on the eyes of children and young people living under happier conditions than we did, I ask myself if the time is not approaching when those verses, which caused our hearts to beat in the past, will not be read and recited in schools as something strange and distant, to be passed over in the same manner as we passed over and disregarded the beauties of Greek poetry when they were forced upon us.

"Then a great sadness comes to those who have passed through prison life with rebellion and fight in their souls, and who created from themselves, and their greater or lesser sufferings a Polish culture, which is now passing. There is strength in prison and a charm of forgetfulness, too. We, the people of the prison era, are fading into the past. A new generation is arising, a new generation which will soon be alien to us, for its lips have never quaffed the cup of mingled bitterness and delight that we tasted. I see the eyes of children open wide with surprise that there could have been times when prison, that is to say, a humiliation that crushes a man to the ground, could awaken in us a spark of enthusiasm, light fire in our eyes, and bring smiles to our lips. And then I think of those who are coming after us without anxiety. May they forget us, the prison generation, may they forget our struggles and sufferings, may they advance to a new life, where the charm of prisons will not bring a smile to the lips nor poison to the heart. . . ."

So Joseph Pilsudski wrote in those tranquil days of 1925. But alas, since then that new generation whose untroubled eyes inspired him with hope for the future has in its turn become "a prison generation." To-day the jails of Poland are once more full of those who have known how to resist aggression and tyranny even as their fathers resisted it, and who have, like them, "quaffed the cup of mingled bitterness and delight."

.   .   .   .   .

The prison system of Russian Poland was a curious compound of brutality and indulgence. It was unbelievably harsh in many respects and ridiculously lax in others. Above all it was incompetent, like all Russian Government institutions.

"In the prisons of Russia proper" . . . wrote Joseph Pilsudski . . . "the chief aim of the prison regime was to

create a condition of fear in the prisoner, the whole
prison system being based on the principle of correct-
ing naughty children by hurting them. Relations with the
prisoner were to a certain extent based on law, but only
on a law of jailer and prisoners. The standard of conduct
was not merely one of violence and force, but there was
an almost scientific search for ways of inflicting pain and
suffering on the prisoner, of systematically intimidating
him.

"The Russian prisons in Poland were quite different.
A typical specimen of these was the Tenth Pavilion of the
Warsaw Citadel, which was for political prisoners only.
Those who locked us up in these prisons were supremely
indifferent. Force and violence were used frankly, without
any effort to justify them by arguments of 'morality' . . .
It was simply that all undesirables were confined there.
For this reason I have never encountered a more cheerful
prison than the Tenth Pavilion, almost everything which
was strictly forbidden elsewhere was admissible there. Every
generation of prisoners used to dig tunnels under the walls,
and these were calmly filled up, so that the next generation had the task of reconstructing them. The rule forbidding us to dig tunnels might have been a mere formality, for no one cared in the least whether the prisoner did
so. A prison cell in which everything could be moved,
where we could change all the furniture around, move the
bed from place to place, such an hotel of a prison in fact,
I have never met anywhere else. . . ."

It was this very incompetence which facilitated his escape.
From the day of his arrest members of the party had been
working energetically on his behalf. The first necessity was
to find a means of communicating with him, but for some
time this appeared impossible since he was not allowed to see
visitors and no parcels containing clothes or anything else
could be sent into the prison without special permission, which
was only rarely accorded. In any case they would have been
too thoroughly examined by the prison officials to hold out
any hope of concealing a message. Several weeks passed before

the problem was solved by one of the women members of the P.P.S. who prevailed on a warder to act as go-between.

This warder, Alexel Siedielnikow, was a Russian representing all that is best in the Russian character, simple, kindly, deeply religious, a man who would have been after the heart of Tolstoy. Resident in Poland for many years and married to a Polish wife he was in sympathy with the political prisoners of whom he had charge, and made their lot more bearable in many ways. With very little persuasion he consented to take notes to "Comrade Victor," as Joseph Pilsudski was known. This difficulty having been overcome the next step was to devise a means of escape.

In the case of a political offence of such magnitude in the eyes of the Russian Government as publishing a revolutionary newspaper no leniency could be expected. After a few years of solitary confinement while awaiting trial the minimum sentence would be ten years in the North-East of Siberia where the worst prisoners were sent since they were not likely to survive the climate long enough to give much trouble.

Escape would be utterly impossible from Siberia and almost as difficult from the Citadel, so the only solution was to compel the authorities to transfer Pilsudski to another prison. This was rarely done except in the case of illness too severe to be dealt with in the Citadel Infirmary, or else insanity. It was decided that the latter could be most successfully feigned. The plan was outlined in a letter which the friendly warder smuggled into the prison. Pilsudski immediately agreed to it and a well-known mental specialist who was in sympathy with the P.P.S. supplied him with detailed instructions. Acting on them he changed his whole demeanour, became morose and melancholy and refused to speak to the officials who visited his cell. After a week or two he began to evince symptoms of persecution mania and refused to eat any food lest it had been poisoned. The kindly warder tried to tempt him with first one delicacy and then another, but he rejected them all and would touch nothing but boiled eggs, which he said could not be tampered with by his enemies. At night he used to hold conversations with imaginary visitors, playing his part so realistically that some of the more ignorant and superstitious jailers spread the report that the cell was haunted by the ghosts of former prisoners and began to avoid it. He had always had a natural gift for acting and mimicry and he utilized it and the medical knowledge he had gained at the University so successfully that he deceived even the prison doctor. But at the end of several months the strain of his self-imposed starvation had told so severely upon his health that he was obliged to abandon this part of his pose. Finally one of his relatives wrote to the Governor of the prison asking that a mental specialist should be permitted to visit him and offering to pay the necessary fee. The request was granted on the condition that the specialist should not be a Pole and therefore Dr. Ivan Sabashnikov, director of the Russian Lunatic Asylum of St. John the Divine, was called in.

The moment that the doctor entered the cell he knew that he was dealing with a sane man. He sat down and began to talk to him, not about his health but about Siberia, his own native place. They chatted for an hour or more of the forest and the hunting without any reference to the real purpose of the visit. But that apparently irrelevant conversation, based on a mutual interest, did more for the prisoner than any eloquent plea for aid, for the doctor who was passionately devoted to his native country was drawn to him. When he left the cell he signed a report to the prison authorities in which he stated that in his opinion Joseph Pilsudski's mental state was being seriously affected by his solitary confinement and that with a return to more normal conditions he would be restored to complete sanity.

The authorities responded to this by transferring the prisoner to the lunatic asylum of St. Nicholas in Petersburg.

The months which followed were, as he afterwards told me, the hardest ordeal in his life. To leave the world of sanity, to let himself be branded as a madman, and enclosed within high stone walls in the company of madmen, with only the slender chance of one day recovering his liberty, demanded his utmost reserves of courage. There were times when he longed to find himself back in his cell at the Citadel, when he cursed his folly in consenting to the daring scheme.

He was put into a dormitory which housed over fifty

lunatics, men suffering from every type of delusion from
religious obsessions to homicidal mania. Their ravings kept
him awake at night. The system of supervision at the asylum
was lax in the extreme and terrible fights broke out between
the inmates which were only quelled when the attendants burst
in upon them, striking out brutally with their truncheons.

As the weeks passed by he grew more and more despondent,
thinking that his friends' plan had miscarried, that they had
not been able to communicate with him and that he would be
left to his fate, condemned to live a sane man among madmen, until he too went mad in reality. Then at last a message
reached him. All was well. Only patience was needed.

Among the members of the P.P.S. was a young doctor
named Wladyslaw Mazurkiewicz, who undertook to carry out
the principal part in the escape, though it meant the sacrifice
of his own career. The decision was a hard one, for he was
ambitious and on the threshold of success, and he had not
even met the man for whom he was asked to risk so much.
Yet he did not hesitate. He applied for a post as house surgeon
at the St. Nicholas and obtained it.

Once on the staff of the asylum the rest was comparatively
easy. He brought in, piece by piece in order to avoid carrying
too bulky a parcel, a suit of clothes for Pilsudski to wear when
he went out into the world again, and secreted them in one
of the medicine chests. This having been done he waited his
opportunity. It came on the first of May, when a fair was
held in the city and discipline was relaxed even at the asylum.
Fortunately, the head physician was absent at a conference
and Mazurkiewicz was therefore in charge. The staff were
delighted at the generosity of the new house surgeon in giving
them leave to visit the fair. No sooner were most of them out
of the way than Mazurkiewicz asked for the records of the
different cases to be brought to him in his study. He went
through them with the assistant, taking notes and making
comments. Presently he came to that of Pilsudski, remarked that it appeared interesting and decided to visit the
patient.

An attendant took him to the room where Pilsudski was
sitting, sullen and indifferent. Both played their parts to

perfection. The house surgeon was calm and impersonal, humouring the patient. Pilsudski was sullen and morose.

Mazurkiewicz gave orders that the patient was to be brought down to his office, and left the room.

Half an hour later Pilsudski was led in by an attendant . . .

"I shall have to spend some time examining this man" . . . said the house surgeon. "You need not wait. I will ring when I want you."

The next few minutes were tense with drama. Mazurkiewicz got out the suit of clothes, gave it to Pilsudski who changed into it. Then the two of them walked out boldly and crossed the courtyard. The great outer gates were locked, but the porter recognizing the new house surgeon, unfastened a side door and let them both out. A droshky was just passing. They hailed the driver and got into it. The doctor remembered afterwards that while he had been all impatience at the slow speed of the old horse, Pilsudski was calm and untroubled, talking of the beauty of the avenue of chestnut trees through which they were passing and of the scent of spring in the air.

After twice changing their droshky as a means of precaution they arrived at the house of a member of the P.P.S. They stopped there that night and on the next day Pilsudski set out on his flight. After a fortnight in the country he arrived in Kiev, where in spite of the danger he remained twenty-four hours for the *Robotnik* was being printed there now and he was aching to set the worn press in motion again. He spent the whole night working on it and the next day set off for Galicia.

The next few years were years of storm and struggle. There were lean times when he lived only on the proceeds of his journalism and contributed articles to the Cracow newspapers, whose editors were willing enough to publish them since they attacked the Russian system and there was no love lost between Austria and Russia. There were strenuous times when he fled from one town to another, crossed and recrossed the frontier, marked down by the authorities as a dangerous revolutionary, constantly expecting to be rearrested. Only in the friendly peace of Zakopane could he know any rest. He used to climb the winding paths up to the tops of the mountains where the eagles had their nests and look down upon the lake of Czarny Staw, lying spread out beneath him, with the sun turning its ripples to shimmering silver . . . "like the mantle of a knight in armour" . . . he used to say. In the silence there he could' dream and make plans.

One of these dreams was realized in the creation of the Bojowka, the first resort to arms since the Insurrection of 1863. To him one step along the road which would lead to Poland's freedom.

. . . . .

That was Joseph Pilsudski's story as he told it to me in the gardens of Kiev. And when he had come to the end of it he told me that he loved me, and that he had loved me since those first days when we worked together at Zakopane. I remember how surprised I was because he had seemed so impersonal, only the perfect comrade. But afterwards I learnt that perfect comradeship is the best of all foundations for love. In the years that followed we had none of the things which are considered the essentials for a happy marriage . . . peace, ease, security, a home. Instead we had unrest and danger, ceaseless work, and often poverty and hardship. Yet our love survived them all, survived too in later years the still harder test of success.

But many years passed before we could know the happiness of marriage, because Joseph's first wife, from whom he was separated, refused to divorce him. We had to wait until her death released him.

CHAPTER XIV

DURING THE years between 1905 and 1912 the Bojowka waged an incessant guerilla warfare against the Czarist Government. Armed demonstrations were carried out all over the provinces; Government convoys were attacked to provide funds for the release of Polish political prisoners, the upkeep of the Military Training Schools and the purchase of arms and ammunition.

This form of campaign, which the party was forced to adopt, since at that time it was not strong enough to raise an open insurrection, has been criticized by Joseph Pilsudski's enemies both during his lifetime and afterwards. It must, however, always be borne in mind that we considered ourselves at war with Russia and that we had to wage that war with any and every means at our disposal. Every operation against the Government was prompted by a purely political motive and a scrupulous record was kept of all money which came into the hands of our organization and of the purpose to which it was relegated. No one ever made even a fraction of personal profit from it. (Incidentally, these account books are still in existence, or were before the German occupation of Warsaw.)

In 1908 there was urgent need of funds to equip the venture which Casimir Sosnkowski was organizing at Lwow . . . "The Association of Active Struggle," a group of young men who would be trained on more advanced military lines. It was a project near to Pilsudski's heart since it offered the chance of preparing for the European war which he was convinced was only a question of time. The money must therefore be obtained and the best way of obtaining it was to take from the Russian Government what they had extorted from Poland, to force them to disgorge at least a portion of the vast sum that had been amassed by exorbitant taxation and so-called "fines" which had not even a shadow of justice behind them. So he planned the hold-up of the mail train at Bezdany on

September 26th, 1908, the Bojowka's most ambitious attack
on the Russian Government. It was carried out by sixteen
men and four women, of whom I was one. Now the Bezdany
affair has been widely discussed and seldom, if ever, presented
in its true light. Some of those who have written of it have
contented themselves with touching upon it briefly, leaving
the impression that it was a regrettable episode in my husband's
career, which was afterwards redeemed. Others have represented it as an act of banditry ranking with the exploits of
William Tell, or the English Robin Hood. I have often been
amused at the way people have spoken to me of it, with a
rather scandalized admiration. At the back of their minds was
obviously the thought that had Pilsudski not chosen to be a
soldier and a statesman he might have become a highly successful gangster.

Actually Joseph Pilsudski and the men of the Bojowka
were neither would-be martyrs nor adventurers. They were
sane and practical people who would have been, in ordinary
circumstances, law-abiding. From a material point of view
they had nothing to gain from their activities against the
Russian Government, and everything to lose. One or two
of them were members of the nobility, several were wealthy
landowners, the rest were men of the professional and working classes . . . doctors, university professors and students,
engineers, artisans and clerks. There was no distinction between them in the party; those who had titles dropped them,
and those who had money pooled it whenever there was need
for it. They all had the same end in view; they all ran the
same risks, death, the Katorga and Siberia. They were called
upon to make frequent sacrifices, to give up their own careers
for the success of the party.

From these men then were drawn all those who took part
in the attack at Bezdany. Their fares and the actual expenses
which they incurred were reimbursed out of the party funds
but that was all. Out of the proceeds of the attack they had
nothing. The 200,000 roubles of which we took possession
that day, money which had been wrung by force from the
Polish people to pay for the extravagant follies of the Imperial
Grand Dukes, went to the purchase of arms and the training

of officers who were later to lead the Polish Army to victory.

Bezdany, a little railway station some miles from Wilno, was the halt for the mail trains on which at certain fixed times in the year large sums of Government money were transferred from Russian Poland to St. Petersburg. Certain members of the Bojowka who had entrée into Russian official circles were able to furnish us with the approximate date of these transfers and we made our preparations accordingly.

Early in the summer several of us settled in Wilno or the neighbourhood, travelling there one or two at a time. One of the men took a cottage on the banks of the river and posed as an ardent fisherman. Thus he had an excuse not only for travelling frequently between Bezdany station and Wilno but for mooring a boat outside his cottage. Madame Hellman, an old lady whose son was taking part in the attack, and who was herself an intrepid patriot and the wife of a veteran of the '63, then installed herself in a small apartment in Wilno which we used as our headquarters. We were all very fond of her and she mothered us, particularly Joseph Pilsudski, who had a special place in her heart. She used to spoil him by cooking his favourite dishes every time we were invited to dinner with her, which was often. The remaining women, besides myself, were Madame Prystor, who had not long been married and refused to be separated from her husband although he wished her to remain safely at home, and Madame Kosakiewicz, who was, unfortunately, one of the three people arrested after the attack.

We had decided that I would stay in Wilno since Bezdany was so small a place that the presence of strangers would cause comment. I travelled down from Kiev in the month of April taking with me the arms which would be used, revolvers and dynamite. I carried them in a suitcase which I was careful not to let out of my own hands. There was no one else in my compartment, so I put it on the luggage rack just over my head and settled down to read. Just as the train was starting two men got in and sat down opposite me. They had several pieces of luggage but as we had the carriage to ourselves there was plenty of space and to my relief there was no need to move my suitcase.

The day was warm and with the motion of the train I grew more and more drowsy until I fell asleep.

I woke with a start as we drew up at a station to find myself alone in the compartment. Instinctively I glanced up at the luggage rack above me. My suitcase was gone!

My heart missed a beat at the thought that the men who had sat opposite me must have been secret police agents and that they had probably followed me on to the train and taken possession of my case while I slept. Even now they might be examining its contents in some other compartment. The train was still standing at the platform and for a moment I had a wild impulse to get out and run anywhere so long as it was out of the station. But then I realized that if my worst suspicions were true and the men meant to arrest me I should only be followed and caught a few minutes later. I was slightly reassured too by the sight of another suitcase on the opposite rack, larger than mine but of the same colour. Perhaps after all they had only been ordinary travellers and had made a genuine mistake.

Just then the attendant walked along the corridor. I called him in and, speaking as casually as I could, explained what had happened. . . .

"I know where the two gentlemen are" . . . he said helpfully . . . "They asked me to find them seats in a smoking compartment and I helped to take their luggage along. But you will have to hurry because they were getting out at this station. . . ."

He grabbed the alien suitcase and sped along the corridor. I followed him, hoping fervently that we should not be too late. Perhaps the strangers had by now discovered their mistake and were already examining my case in the hope of finding some clue to the owner. And the first thing they would come upon would be an assortment of revolvers and explosives!

We reached the carriage to find it empty. A glance out of the window showed me the two men standing on the platform collecting their suitcases. To my joy I saw my own among them. I seized the other case from the attendant and ran for the door. Just then the train gave a lurch and started to move. It was now or never. Disregarding the attendant's warning shout, I jumped and by sheer luck made a clear landing on the platform. A few minutes later I was in possession of my own suitcase, with its incriminating contents still undetected, waiting for the next train to take me to Wilno.

On my arrival I set out to look for a room. Seeing a card in a window advertising apartments I went in to investigate and found that it was the house of a Russian policeman whose wife let lodgings. The room they showed me though plainly furnished was clean and airy and I decided to take it partly because it appealed to my sense of the ridiculous, and also for the more serious reason that it was the last place in which any one would think of looking for a revolutionary. The policeman was a friendly giant with a bushy black beard and the Russian's love of gossip. He was full of sympathetic interest when I told him that I had come to Wilno to look for work in an office, and in order to give colour to my role I went round the next day and got taken on at a library. It was a rather vague arrangement under which I was to work only at certain hours during the day, for a very small salary, but with the understanding that I might read as many books as I wanted. The owner of the library was a pleasant young woman who had a great sympathy for revolutionaries.

By the end of July the provisional date for the attack on the mail train had been fixed and the plan was nearing completion. Nothing was left to chance. We had all memorized the country around Bezdany so thoroughly, particularly the forest through which the escape would have to be made after the attack, that we could have followed any path blindfold.

It was originally arranged that at the time of the attack, which was to be made at night, I would be waiting with a boat on the river and that we would row downstream under cover of the darkness, but later it was decided that this would be too risky and that horses would afford an easier means of escape. There were winding bridle paths through the forest which would make pursuit almost impossible, especially if the men separated. So horses were purchased and stabled with a veterinary surgeon who was secretly in sympathy with the party, and a young student of the Polytechnic at Lwow who had recently joined the organization was given the task of looking after them. Some years later he fought with great gallantry in the Legions and finally became a colonel in the Polish Army.

Among the men who took part in the attack were Colonel Prystor and Walery Slaweck, both of whom later became Prime Ministers of Poland, Count Swirski and several workmen, members of the Bojowka. These last were pioneers of the new type of labouring class which was beginning to arise in Poland as in other countries, men who were intelligent, capable and responsible. All of them afterwards became officers in the Polish Army.

Count Swirski, who was a student at the Warsaw École des Beaux Arts when he joined the Bojowka, was the son of an ancient Polish family having large estates in the country. His patriotism was inherited, his Socialism came from his own convictions. For these two ideals he was willing to sacrifice everything. The Bezdany was his first undertaking of any importance in the Bojowka and he paid a terrible price for it, for he was one of those arrested. He was originally condemned to death but the sentence was commuted to the Katorga for life. The tragedy of his arrest was that there was no necessity for it. He was betrayed.

There was in the Bojowka a young labourer, a man of limited education but of exceptional character. He read widely, played the violin beautifully, and spent all his spare time in art galleries. He was sensitive, imaginative, and highly strung, a sincere patriot and a brave man, but, unfortunately, the worst type to fall into the hands of the Russian police. After the Bezdany affair he was arrested and interrogated. He was given the usual promise of a light sentence provided he would reveal the names of those associated with him in the attack. For several days he refused to speak. Then the Chief of Police directed that he should be flogged. Under the ordeal of the knout he gave way. He disclosed the name of Count Swirski.

The Count was immediately arrested and confronted with the man who had accused him, but he did not reproach him. He, too, was interrogated but without success although he was several times threatened with torture. In the end the police realized that there was no hope of securing a confession from him and gave up the attempt.

The two men were tried. The labourer was sent to Siberia, Swirski to the Katorga with fetters on his wrists and ankles and a ten-pound weight of iron attached to his waist.

Years passed. The Great War ended. The Russians released their political prisoners. From Siberia there came back a stream of men, white-haired, young in face, rather bewildered still from having lost touch with the world. Count Swirski was one of them. He went to Warsaw; found that Joseph Pilsudski was now Chief of State. Pilsudski made him his adjutant.

Some years later the labourer too went back to Warsaw. Unemployment was at its worst in Poland at that time, and he could not get work of any description. He tried to appeal for help to the men who had been his comrades in the old days. They shut their doors in his face. He had done the one unpardonable thing. Betrayed a member of his party. There was only one among them who did not condemn him. The man whom he had wronged. Swirski on hearing of his misfortunes immediately sent for him and gave him a post on his own staff.

Walery Slaweck was one of Pilsudski's lieutenants in the attack on Bezdany but he was unable to remain longer than a few hours in the neighbourhood on account of the facial disfigurement which rendered him easy to identify. He had been an exceptionally handsome man until two years previously when he had been terribly injured by the accidental explosion of a bomb. He recovered but grew so morbidly sensitive over his appearance that he shunned all contact with his former friends and shut himself up in his house, morose, a prey to despair. He had lost all interest in life when Joseph Pilsudski, with his unfailing instinct for touching the right chord in people, told him of his plans of Bezdany and said how much he needed his help in carrying them out. Slaweck answered the appeal at once and the difficulty and danger of the project before him called up all his reserves of courage. He returned to work in the party, developed great skill in organization and later played a prominent role in the reconstruction of the new Polish state.

Pilsudski, who always made his plans calmly and dispassionately, organized the Bezdany affair with the attention to detail which he gave later to his big military campaigns. He led it in person and he was under no illusions as to the penalty of failure. A few hours before it he wrote the following letter to his friend Perl . . .

"My dear friend,

"Some time ago you promised to write my obituary when the Devil takes me.

"Now when I am starting on an expedition from which I may not return, I am sending you these few words for the obituary, with a little prayer. Of course, I am not going to dictate to you what you should write about my life and work. Oh, no! I leave you a free hand. I only ask of you not to make of me a 'whiner or sentimentalist.' In other words, a self-sacrificing martyr who has allowed himself to be nailed to the cross for love of humanity or some such humbug. I used to be somewhat like that, but only in the days of my proud youth. Not now, however. That is over irrevocably. These whinings and this desire for the self-sacrifice have grown insufferable to me. I have seen too much of it in our 'intellectuals'—helpless and hopeless as they are. I fight and I am ready to die simply because I cannot bear to live in this latrine which is what our life amounts to. It is insulting to a man with a dignity above that of a slave! Let others play at throwing bouquets to Socialism or Polonism or anything they like in this atmosphere of a latrine (not even of a water-closet!)—I can't. This is not sentimentality on my part, nor whining, nor clap-trap about social evolution, or anything of that sort. It is simply being a man. I want to conquer, and without a fight, and a fight with the gloves off. I am not even a wrestler but an animal submitting to knout or stick. I hope you understand me. It is not despair, not self-sacrifice that guides me, but the will to conquer.

"My latest idea, which I have not yet fully developed, is to create in all parties, and most of all in our own an organization of physical force, of brute force, to use an expression which is insupportable to the ears of humanitarians. It has been my intention to carry out this idea during the last few years and I have promised myself to realize it or perish. I have already done much towards its fulfilment but not enough to be able to rest on my laurels. So now I am staking everything on this last card.

"Just a few words more. You know that my only hesitation is that I may die in this 'expropriation' and I want to explain why I am leading it myself. First for sentimentality. I have sent so many men to the gallows that if I too perish it will give these unknown and obscure heroes a certain natural moral satisfaction that their leader had not despised their work and has not regarded them merely as tools to do the dirty work while he reserved nobler tasks for himself. That is one reason. The other—is the dire necessity. Money! May the Devil take it! How I despise it! I prefer to win it in a fight than to beg for it from the Polish public which has become infantile through being chicken-hearted. I haven't. I haven't got money and I must have it for the ends which I pursue. What I want, I who have been called 'The Knight of Socialism,' who after all have been of some little service to the cause of national culture, is to stress, in my own person, this very bitter truth that in a nation which does not know how to fight for itself, which withdraws every time some one strikes it in the face, men must die even in actions which are not lofty, beautiful or great.

"Well, that is all. And now good-bye, my boy, to you and to all of you my old comrades with whom I have dreamt so much, lived through still more, and loved so well.

"Yours—and theirs,
"Ziuk."

On Friday, September 18th, eight days before the attack, we held a counsel of war at Madame Hellman's little apartment in Wilno. The preparations had taken longer than we expected and some of the men who had been obliged to leave their work were coming to the end of their resources. Joseph Pilsudski suggested that we should pool our money, and set the example by emptying out the contents of his pocket. When every one else had done the same he divided the small pile of roubles into equal shares, taking nothing himself and giving nothing to me. Wilno was his home town and he had friends with whom he could stay, while I had a gold watch which I could sell.

On the evening of September 26th, six of the men, including Slaweck, travelled on the mail train. They were to deal with the soldiers and police who would be guarding the postal wagon. In the meantime the rest arrived at the quiet little wayside station singly or in pairs. One of them was apparently absorbed in a flirtation with a Jewish girl, another sprawled over a bench pretending to be uproariously drunk. Pilsudski and Prystor got ready petards to create a smoke screen. Sawicki, another member of the party, who afterwards held the rank of Colonel in the Polish Army, was outside the station with a carriage and horses. I and the other women waited in a cottage on the edge of the forest.

As soon as the train drew into the station the attackers surrounded it. There was one sharp exchange of fire in which a soldier was killed and five wounded but the police and military escort on the train were so taken by surprise that Slaweck and his men disarmed them before they even realized what was happening. Those who did not take flight were ordered into the station with the railway employees and the passengers. There three of Pilsudski's men mounted guard over them with their revolvers while a fourth blocked the signals, and cut the telephone and telegraph wires. While this was being done, Pilsudski and Prystor burst into the mail wagon, dynamited the iron coffers and took possession of the bank-notes. They stuffed them into mailbags and sacks, filling as many as they could before the sound of other trains approaching in the distance warned them that they had barely time to escape. Then they fled to the carriage and Sawicki whipped up his horses. After a long and perilous drive in the darkness through unfrequented tracks and by-roads of the forest they arrived at the cottage where we were waiting.

It had been decided that immediately after the attack we would disperse in different directions. So Slaweck and two others travelled by an indirect route to Cracow; Luce-Birk, a young engineer, and the three or four men from the Warsaw branch took a small rowing-boat and rowed down the river to Riga. Pilsudski and I, after remaining in the neighbourhood for a day or two, took the train to Kiev. These separate departures had to be made calmly and openly under the very eyes of the police, for we knew that once the hue-and-cry had been raised there would be guards at every station and patrols all along the road. Any appearance of undue haste would only draw suspicion on us. The disposal of the money was another problem. Some of it was to be taken straight to the Central Committee to be spent on bribes to secure the release of members of the party who were in prison under sentence of death. The rest was to be left in the neighbourhood until such time as it could be moved in safety. Joseph Pilsudski and I and another member of the party buried it in the forest next day. We were afraid to trust it all to one place and dug several holes, making some sort of landmark near each one so that we should know where to look for it again.

Pilsudski tied up the sacks of silver with firm fingers and shovelled the earth over them. . . .

"It must be a lot of money," I said. "They are so heavy."

"It is not money" . . . he answered slowly. . . . "It is the books on tactics and the guns that will give us power. It is the freedom of those who are slaves now, and the country that our children will inherit. . . ."

The next day we went to Kiev. Before we left we divided the money which had not been buried into two parts. One of these was taken by Prystor into Russia, where the notes could more easily be changed. The other Joseph Pilsudski and I were to take to Kiev. We hid the banknotes and the packets of roubles in our clothing, devoutly hoping that we would not be searched at the station. In case we were we had our remedy with us. A dose of cyanide of potassium. Death would have been a hundred times preferable to the sort of punishment the

Russian Government would have given us. I could almost hear the beating of my heart when we walked on to the station, but looking at Joseph Pilsudski I saw that he was perfectly calm. There was not a shadow of emotion on his face as we passed through the barrier. All around us we heard people talking of Bezdany; the station was full of soldiers and police. Every few minutes a police officer would pick out at random some man or woman in the crowds of travellers and give orders for them to be searched. We fully expected to be stopped but fortunately no one took any notice of us, and we reached our destination without misadventure.

Two months later I returned to Bezdany to recover the buried money. I broke my journey at Suvalki so that I could see Aunt Maria, who had been ill. It was strange to find myself back in the little town again for so many things had happened since I had left it. It looked just as I remembered it. There were the same ruts in the main street. The crystal cross over the Russian Church still sparkled in the pale November sunshine.

Aunt Maria seemed much older but she was as thoughtful and affectionate as ever, ordering my favourite dishes, worrying whether my underclothes were warm enough, and wanting to hear all that I had done since she had last seen me. She was distressed when I told her about Bezdany, not that she disapproved of the attack . . . she was too firm a patriot to condemn any action against the Russian Government . . . but because she feared that I might grow unfeminine. . . . "Leave things like that to the men," she urged. "You have your profession and you can earn money and give it to the party to help in the fight. The other way is unladylike. . . ."

She was quite unhappy over it until I thought of a way to set her mind at rest. . . . "You know very well that Grandmother would have done it when she was younger," I said.

She digested the words for a moment and then a smile broke over her face. . . . "Yes, I suppose she would," she said with a little sigh of relief. The argument had ended, as every argument had ended for her all through her life, with Grandmother having the last word.

She was quite comforted and gave me her blessing when I
went on to Bezdany the next morning. I never saw her again,
for she died suddenly a few weeks afterwards.

I took the train to Wilno, where I was met by Joseph Pilsudski's brother, who warned me that the police were looking
for me. So avoiding the vicinity of Bezdany I went by another
route to a village at some little distance where a certain Madame A., who was a member of the party, had a farm. When I
explained the reason of my return to Bezdany she at once
agreed to help me and suggested that she should drive me to
the forest. We then got into communication with Sawicki.
The next morning the three of us set out in a rickety trap
drawn by an old and decrepit horse. Under the rugs we hid
a spade and a big suitcase which was to contain the money.

It was a twenty-mile drive to the forest and it took us the
whole day to get there, for the horse was in such wretched
condition that we had to walk most of the way. When at
length we reached our goal the November evening had already
closed in. We tethered the horse to a tree and began to grope
our way down the silent avenues. After some difficulty we
found the right place and began our digging operations. The
earth was frozen so hard that it was almost impossible to get
our spades into it. When after working till the perspiration
streamed down our faces we succeeded in laying bare the holes,
we had to grope for the bags of roubles in the dark, for we
did not dare to show a light. After two hours we had only un-
earthed about two-thirds of the money and Madame A. and
I were so exhausted that we could not go on digging. Sawicki
suggested that we should drive home with the money we
had recovered and leave him to spend the night at a peasant's cottage, return to the digging next morning and follow
us later in the day with the remainder. So we packed the
heavy bags of silver into the suitcase and started on the home-
ward journey. At the end of the first mile the poor old horse
was almost dropping between the shafts and we realized that
our only chance of getting home at all was to walk. So we
trudged beside it all through the night along the dark and
lonely road over the plain, buffeted by the cold east wind and
so tired that we could scarcely drag our feet along. I remember

that just before dawn I realized to my horror that I was getting hallucinations. I clutched Madame A.'s arm and pointed out to her an imaginary pack of wolf hounds sweeping down on us. She, of course, assured me that there was nothing though she was in reality terrified, thinking that my brain had given way. Her quiet voice dispelled the vision of the hounds and a moment later I was laughing at myself, but that and other similar delusions kept returning to me before we arrived home. For many years afterwards I worried over that queer experience and never liked to speak of it to any one, fearing that it might be a prelude to madness. Then by chance I met a famous mental specialist who told me that such hallucinations, coming from extreme fatigue, are by no means rare.

We were some two miles from Madame A.'s house when the horse fell down and as we could not possibly get it on its feet again we were obliged to leave it lying there until we arrived home and could send help. Fortunately it recovered from its adventures. But I shall never forget that last lap of the road when we stumbled along, carrying the heavy suitcase between us, too tired even to speak. We did not reach home until 8 A.M.

The next day Sawicki joined us, bringing the rest of the silver. To my great relief he undertook to travel to Cracow with all the money and deliver it over to the Central Committee. It meant that he had to run the gauntlet of several police barriers, but he was successful.

CHAPTER XV

Despite the success of Bezdany, the year 1908 ended in discouragement and setback. The Bojowka was broken up; nearly all its members were in prison or in flight across the Austrian frontier. It was obvious that the struggle against the Russian Government was too unequal to continue.

The Polish horizon had never seemed more darkly overcast. The revolution which had fostered the brief illusion of a united nation shaking off its fetters had failed. The fight for independence had been lost once again; the fight for Socialism had only resulted in a stalemate. What little improvement in working conditions had been achieved by the strikes had been countered by a series of lock-outs.

In the Prussian-ruled provinces of Poland the iron hand of Von Bülow was tightening its grip. Alarmed at the increasing Polish population, he adopted a new policy which was, he explained, designed "to protect, maintain and strengthen the German nationality among the Poles; in fact, to fight for the German nationality." . . . So in the spring of 1908 his Expropriation Bill came into force, authorizing the forcible dispossession of estates owned by Poles and their transfer to German settlers. Thousands of Poles were turned out of their farms and holdings, left to tramp the roads, homeless and penniless, or seek work at starvation wages from German masters in the industrial cities. There were shocked protests in the Press of many countries, but trouble was seething in the Balkans and Europe had other things to think of. The plight of the Kaiser's Polish subjects was soon forgotten.

In Russian Poland the Party of National Democracy, under Roman Dmowski, was in the ascendancy, pursuing its policy of conciliation with Russia, sending its representatives to the Duma to advocate a united Slav front against the ever-increasing menace of Germany. The masses drifted uncertainly in its wake. A dreary fatalism spread over the country.

Only Pilsudski's voice was raised urging resistance, pleading the need for an armed force. . . . "I wanted Poland who had forgotten the sword so completely since '63 to see it flashing in the air in the hands of her own soldiers," he wrote later. It was his ceaseless prayer. It met with varying response. . . .

"I am working now for two things," he wrote to a friend in 1908. "First, to raise enough money to constitute a capital for the future. Secondly, to extend what I call this Military Propaganda. I was afraid in the beginning that the bare suggestion would appear ridiculous but to my great surprise I have found many ready to listen to me. If I can succeed in creating a new current of thought and awakening the interest of the youth of the nation I shall be more than satisfied. I have at least taken a step in that direction." . . .

The "step" was the new-born Association for Active Struggle which had been established by Sosnkowski at Lwow. At its first meeting in June 1908 it was decided that . . . (a) it was to operate in Galicia as the most suitable place; (b) its purpose was the preparation of a future legion of insurrectionary soldiers trained in accordance with military discipline.

There was violent opposition to the project from a large section of the party, and Pilsudski, who supported it with his usual dynamic energy, lost the sympathy of all the older members, one and all of whom pronounced the scheme as madness. I remember him pacing up and down the floor. as he always did in moments of crisis, smoking cigarette after cigarette, in a fury of impatience at what he described as "this dead weight of years and caution." The entire youth of the party stood solidly behind him. He had faith in their judgment. . . . "The so-called youthful hot-headedness is far less dangerous in leadership than the timorous indecision of old age," he used to say. . . . "Experience is no asset to a man if it means that he keeps his eyes on the past instead of towards the future. . . ."

So he resisted the attempts of the greybeards to throw cold water on his scheme. . . .

"Some of my comrades came to see me yesterday," he wrote in one of his letters to me. "We discussed many things, principally of course this question of the Association. I am in despair. Imagine. On one side I have the young who believe in me, but who have need to lean on older men with experience and judgment. On the other side I have the older men whose point of view goes only as far as what has been done before. New questions, new ways and new opinions are to them a closed book. When they feel this new current of thought beating upon them they make no effort to adapt themselves to it."

The older men carried the day with the Central Committee of the P.P.S. and attempted to put an effective spoke in his wheel by refusing to make any grant from the party funds for the organization. It was a hard blow for the whole scheme was threatened with collapse, but he was not defeated. . . . "Very well. We shall have to begin without arms," he said. "We can buy them later. We will make a fund of our own. . . ."

So the rich sold their shares, university students went without cigarettes, and the young farm labourers gave up their pocket money to buy books on military tactics. Pilsudski took over the organization into his own hands. It was a task after his heart. At least he could put to practical test the military science which he had studied for years. Hundreds of volunteers joined the movement within the first eighteen months. He drilled them in backyards and in orchards, when he could do so without interruption, instructed them, as far as the limited space permitted, in manœuvres and in the use of the few out-dated rifles and revolvers which represented the entire resources of the Association. The townspeople of Lwow got wind of the "secret army" and came to stare and laugh at the rows of earnest young men, bank clerks and shop assistants, factory hands, students and peasants, who paraded after work on summer evenings and Sunday afternoons. Pilsudski came in for a great deal of ridicule, but it made no impression on him.

At the end of two years the number of the organization had swelled from hundreds to thousands, and the isolated groups of raw recruits had given place to well-drilled and efficient companies who assembled in the fields outside the city to go through the regulation military exercises and manœuvres of the Austrian infantry. The older section of the P.P.S. had given way before the success of the scheme and one after another of them had gone over to Pilsudski's standard, until they were backing him as unitedly as they had formerly opposed him. But now a fresh obstacle had to be faced. The Austrian authorities suddenly awoke to the fact that the Association was something more than a group of impetuous young Poles playing at soldiers and their tolerant amusement changed to suspicion. Pilsudski was sent for by the Chief of Police and asked for explanations. The interview began on a hostile note, turned to a discussion on military history, in which both men were absorbingly interested, and ended with a promise that the Association should not only continue its activities but that it should be legalized and officially recognized by the Austrian Government.

It was an important step for the scope of the organization was widely increased. Its name was changed to the Strzelcy (Union of Riflemen). Branches were formed at Cracow, in Russian Poland and even outside the country, in Paris, Geneva, Liège, Brussels and other European cities where there were Polish colonies. The program of instruction was amplified. Pilsudski instituted special courses at the Cracow School of Economics and Social Sciences, and gave lectures on tactics, military history and the technique of warfare; summer camps were formed, and classes held for the training of officers and N.C.O.'s. A few Polish officers on the Austrian General Staff began to take an interest in the organization, and even in Russian Poland the scheme gained support, though necessarily in the strictest secrecy. I shall always remember Pilsudski's joy when two Polish officers holding high rank in the Russian army, sought him out when they were on leave in Cracow and offered their aid.

His success encouraged others. The military spirit which he had long dreamt of awakening began to stir through Austrian Poland. More and more young men of all classes started drilling and studying tactics. The Conservative youth, not to be outdone by the Socialists, launched their own organization, the Druzyny Strzeleckie. These two forces of the Left and Right were later to drop their political differences and merge into the Polish Legions.

In the meantime the Austrian Government was not the only one which was taking an interest in Pilsudski's activities. Rumour of them had already penetrated to St. Petersburg, where the Minister of Foreign Affairs warned the Minister of Home Affairs that according to reports received from his Ambassador in Vienna an impudent Pole had had the audacity to form in Galicia an armed force with the avowed purpose of preparing for an insurrection in Russian Poland. After the months of delay incidental to any Russian departmental action the Minister of Home Affairs wrote in his turn to a Russian official in Poland communicating to him the information he had received and asking whether he could throw any light on the subject. . . . "The political centre of the Polish question is not now in Russian Poland" . . . replied the official . . . "it is in Galicia. In Russian Poland there is complete calm; in Galicia a whirlwind. There, openly and in perfect security, armed detachments are being organized under the command of our Pilsudski, whom we so light-heartedly suffered to escape from prison. . . ."

He was right. "The Polish question" had indeed passed into Galicia.

●   ●   ●   ●   ●

Pilsudski's dream had at last been realized. He had his military force, a force of nearly 15,000 men, divided into local groups extending over the great part of Austrian Poland. It was not merely sanctioned by the Government but actually encouraged, for Austria's policy at that date was one of conciliation with the Poles. For a period of several years her relations with Russia had been growing increasingly strained. The clash of their interests in the Balkans, resulting in the Bosnian crisis of 1908, had cast over Europe the shadow of the forthcoming war. It served her purpose then to extend her patronage to this embryo Polish force, whose co-operation might prove of use.

So the Riflemen trained in the open instead of in secret, and with a show of generosity the Government presented them with a stock of obsolete rifles discarded by the Austrian regular troops. As the proportion was an average of one to twenty men their distribution among the different companies was something of a problem. Yet many of these same ancient rifles played their part in routing the Czar's picked troops.

One of my most vivid memories of my husband is of his holding the first parade of his Riflemen outside the House of Parliament in Lwow. He stood on the flight of steps leading up to the building to take the salute as they marched past him, several hundreds of them. Only the officers were in uniform, the simple blue tunic and trousers afterwards adopted by the Legion, for shortage of money had made it impossible to equip the ranks, but they all wore their new Maciejowka caps and swung past with a fine military bearing. In later years when Poland was free I saw many parades of Polish troops, but I always remember that first march past and the pride and joy in the eyes of Joseph Pilsudski as he watched it.

Those pre-war years were crowded for him with lectures and reviews of his troops, with the organization of new branches and the study of military tactics and history. With the changed conditions other qualities in his character came to the surface. He was no longer the revolutionary in flight from the police, but the commander-in-chief of an army, even though that army was an irregular one. He developed the capacity for leadership and for overcoming obstacles by that inflexible will which carried him through so many crises. He worked incessantly, often allowing himself only three or four hours' sleep in a night. Even his short summer vacations were given up to organizing the military schools and camps. His heart gave him trouble more than once, and frequent attacks of asthma worried him. He was always afraid of dying before Poland was free. . . . "If I could only be sure of living another three years!!!" he used to say . . . "or perhaps even five. I think that by that time I may have done something. . . ." And he was always glad when the cold winter months were over. He was at his best in the mountains at Zakopane, and

much of his writing was done there. I have still letters which he
sent me telling me of his work. In one of them he writes . . .

"I have been interrupted in my scribbling because of
dinner. The windows are open and the fresh cool wind of
the autumn is blowing over me. The mountains in the distance are thickly covered with snow. That is the picture
which lies in front of me. The table is littered with maps
and books and scraps of paper, some of it covered with
writing; the rest blank. In fact it is in its usual perfect order.
And if you must know it, you who are the very soul of
order, I very much like this disorder of my table. I do not
pretend to be tidy, and on the very rare occasions when I
make the effort to be I find that the most necessary things
have hidden themselves away whilst other quite unnecessary things are in a prominent place. Perhaps this disorder
with which I am surrounded is an outward sign of the disorder within my own mind. For instance, this passion of
mine for working in fragments, without any method in
what I do, concentrating on the things which interest me
heart and soul. Here is an example. Instead of having practically finished this work (the preface to his book on Military Tactics), if I work at all I study the different phases
of the battle under Mukden and examine the maps of Poland
and Lithuania, tracing with my finger across the new rail-
ways and roads, and imagining what I should do if Poland
were free and I had been asked to undertake the strategic
defence of the frontiers. A nice amusement, isn't it, for a
man as much of a realist as I?

"I have started on something else, the review of a military book. It is work which I detest and although I have
as yet done only the introductory chapters I have found
so many deficiencies . . . all of which I must explain
or point out . . . that I have grown sick of it and put
it aside. As for Langiewicz (the Dictator of 1863) I have
decided to write this during the holidays. I am afraid of
the subject although I have studied it for so long. But
lecturing on a subject is one thing, and writing of it is
another. I feel that I am not fully prepared, that I have

too little material at hand. Yet I want to finish my military history of '63 with a monograph on the dictatorship of Langiewicz. So you see how overwhelmed with work I am, work that is not yet finished and work which is only just begun. And then you must add to it all the work which I must undertake for the organization and lectures to the Riflemen after the holidays. You can imagine that my time is fully occupied. . . ."

There were moments of acute discouragement, when the walls of prejudice seemed unsurmountable and he was oppressed by the sense of failure. He still maintained contact with many of his former friends in the P.P.S. but their uncompromising attitude was a bar to any real exchange of opinion. After a visit to one of them he wrote to me. . . .

"How much it rests me to be with you or with my boys (Riflemen), with them I never have to go into futile arguments. They are convinced and confident without having to be shown this and given the formula for that. They too have perplexities, doubts and uncertainties, but they have faith that everything is being decided for the best for them. They are so different from these old politicians with their long futile discussions in which one has to gloss over all irritating questions. It is absolutely maddening sometimes" . . .

Then, as in his political life years later, he detested haggling over details. Accustomed to make his own decisions quickly and to stand by them he was impatient of vacillation in others.

For me too those years before the outbreak of the European War were eventful. The greater part of my day was spent in earning my living as secretary to a big firm in Lwow, but my hardest work began when I left the office. There was an enormous amount of correspondence, propaganda and keeping of accounts in connection with the Strzelcy organization and most of this was done by me. I was also responsible for the maintenance of the library of books on military tactics and history. This began as a small collection occupying a couple of shelves in my wardrobe but before very long it had reached a total of hundreds of volumes and had to be transferred to an office which we opened in the city. In addition to the usual routine of the library I had to supplement the stock from time to time. There were practically no works on strategy or any branch of military science published in the Polish language and therefore we had to fall back on those in Russian. As the majority of the members of the Strzelcy, who were Galician Poles, knew little or no Russian I had to prepare translations. I used to sit up hour after hour at night poring over technical terms and diagrams until I fell asleep. After a while I became quite an expert and used to translate not only from Russian but from French and German as well.

I had plenty of work to do in connection with a scheme which we called "The Prisoners' Aid Society," which was not quite what its name probably suggests to English and American readers. We were not a charitable organization concerned with the welfare of ex-prisoners but a much more lawless institution, supplying not offers of employment and good advice but files for cutting through iron bars, false passports and plans of escape. We dealt, of course, only with political prisoners whose crimes ranged from being in possession of banned literature to persistent agitation against the Government and smuggling arms, but as every jail in Russia had its quota of these we had a long list of cases. The headquarters of the Society recorded every arrest and a visitor was sent to the prison to get in touch with the prisoner and smuggle in letters or messages. In cases where a long exile in Siberia was anticipated and an escape seemed feasible, the society would call upon its members, every one of whom was pledged to furnish the utmost aid in his or her power, and make all arrangements. Escapes planned and carefully organized in this way had naturally a much better chance of success than isolated attempts.

In 1912 I began to take a more active part in the organization of the Strzelcy.

Pilsudski had always promised that when he succeeded in creating his military force he would include a companion organization for women. The feminist movement was beginning to spread through Europe. In England the Suffragettes were chaining themselves to benches in the House of Commons and setting fire to country mansions in an endeavour to gain the vote; feminist groups were being formed in France. But at that time only Socialism had accorded any real measure of freedom to women. The program of the Socialist parties in Poland and Russia had stressed the equality of the sexes in work and in working conditions.

The Strzelcy being largely a Socialist organization must include a women's section. It came into existence in 1912 as a small offshoot of the main League, but it played an important role during the war for it carried on most of the Intelligence Service of the Legions.

I was at the head of a section of the women's branch. Pilsudski drew up our program and arranged that our training should be as comprehensive in our own sphere as that of the Riflemen. We were to work in front of and behind the lines, that is to say that in event of war or insurrection we were to take over the Intelligence Section and also all clerical work, cooking, first aid, etc., so that every man could be released for the actual fighting.

As a preliminary step we attended the lectures on military tactics which were given to the Riflemen by Pilsudski, for it was considered necessary that we should learn something of the defence of cities and also know enough of the technique of war to be able to furnish useful information of troop movements and enemy concentration. We made a special study of the Russian Army and familiarized ourselves with the organization and characteristics of every regiment. All of us received instruction in signalling and attended regular rifle and revolver practice. We used to take part in manœuvres with the Riflemen and soon grew as proficient as they in the reading of charts and the planning of campaigns. Since there was never any intention of utilizing us as a fighting unit these studies may sound a waste of time and energy; actually, in view of the roles we were called upon to play later, they were a vital necessity. More than once important military operations depended on the accuracy of our observation and reports.

We were, I believe, the first women's army auxiliary

organization to be formed in any country. There were originally some sixty of us in Lwow alone, women of all types
. . . students, shop girls, school teachers and clerks . . . and
of all ages. One I remember was an old lady of over sixty,
who was enrolled in the organization rather as an acknowl-
edgment of her patriotism than for any other reason. No one
expected her to take any active part in the work, but she
became so absorbed in the study of military tactics that she
borrowed every book we possessed on the subject. During
the war she was able to supply valuable information to our
headquarters, for the Russians, not suspecting so aged and apparently harmless a woman, let her go about freely in their
lines selling fruit and vegetables.

The whole framework of this Intelligence Section, which
was to collaborate later with the Army, was built up long before the war became a certainty. I and the other woman engaged in it were assigned the task of collecting information
relating to the different towns and country districts, compiling
lists of those who could be counted upon in the event of war
or insurrection, and the different types of service which each
could be expected to render. Some would offer shelter and
hospitality, others horses, many would undertake to convey
letters and act as couriers between one town and the next.
Then in addition to this we made careful surveys of the various
localities, noted the disposition of the railway lines, the state
of the roads and facilities for moving troops, etc. All these
records, which were set down in code, were kept at the Central
Office of the Strzelcy in Lwow. Later they were put to good
use in the war.

During those years all my spare time was spent in travelling
up and down the country. The building company was generous
in the matter of holidays and fête days, and I was able to
cover a surprising amount of ground. I had some curious adventures and only narrowly escaped arrest on several occasions.

I shall always remember a journey to Wilno in 1911 when
I was one of the delegates to the P.P.S. (Revolutionary Fraction) Congress which was being held there. Although it was
the month of April there had been an exceptionally heavy

fall of snow and all the trains were held up. We had to wait
hours at some of the junctions. When we arrived eventually
at Wilno I saw police agents posted all over the station. They
had evidently got wind of the Congress and intended to arrest
as many members of the party as they could. My first thought
was one of profound relief that Pilsudski had decided at the
last moment not to run the gauntlet of the Russian frontier
and had remained behind in Lwow. My second was to wonder
whether I had already been noticed. I feared so. To make sure
on this point I went into the station telegraph office, took a
postcard out of my bag and began to write on it. At once a
man who had followed me unobtrusively into the office came
up behind me and began reading it over my shoulder. Having
had my doubts thus confirmed I could only try to evolve some
plan of escape. I walked out of the office as nonchalantly as
I could, bought a newspaper and went into the station waiting-
room. There I sat for the best part of an hour, apparently
reading, in reality wondering what to do. It was out of the
question, I realized, for me to go to the little hotel where I
was expected. I should only be followed and arrested, and in
all probability other delegates to the Congress would be staying there and would share my fate.

Finally I decided to go to another hotel, where I had not
stayed before, and from there to get into touch with friends
who would convey a warning to other members of the party.

I got into a carriage, told the driver to take me to a good
hotel and on arriving there engaged a room. I remained upstairs for a while, fully expecting to hear a knock at my door,
but there was none and as everything seemed quiet I went
out into the street again and walked to the house of a friend
who was also a member of the party. There I heard that nearly
all the delegates from the Strzelcy had been arrested and a
number of other members of the P.P.S. with them. The Congress had been cancelled. All I could do, therefore, was to
return to Galicia. But it was not going to be so easy. By some
stroke of good luck I had given the slip to the agent at the
railway station. I did not care for the prospect of facing them
again so soon, so I decided that I would remain in Wilno for
at least that night.

It was about 5 P.M. when I returned to the hotel to be accosted at the entrance by the proprietor who asked me, with profuse apologies, to take round my passport to the police station. It was a new regulation, he explained. Previously he had been accustomed to attend to all registration formalities for his guests, but now no visitors might remain in the city unless they had received an official permit for which they must apply in person.

That settled the question. I must leave Wilno before nightfall. I decided to go to Minsk where I was unknown to the police. There I might be able to get a permit authorizing me to cross the frontier into Galicia.

It was late when I arrived at the railway station and I blessed the laziness of the Russian authorities. The army of agents had disappeared. The one sleepy-eyed policeman on duty took no notice of me or any of the other passengers.

Once safely ensconced in the train I could apply my mind to the problem of crossing the Galician frontier. I should have to find a suitable pretext for getting the necessary permit, and if the police were in a suspicious mood, which seemed more than probable, they would need a good deal of convincing. I was no nearer a solution when the train drew up at a station.

A fat woman with a lot of parcels got into my compartment. She was seen off by a friend who stood on the platform shouting through the window the vague, disjointed remarks people always exchange in farewell moments . . . "Now don't forget to write" . . . said the woman on the platform for at least the sixth time. . . .

"No, I shan't" . . . rejoined the other . . . "And I will send you some smoked ham when I get to Minsk. You know it is celebrated. I have heard they supply to all the best Russian restaurants" . . .

Of course! Inspiration had come to me. On arriving in Minsk I went straight to a hotel and slept soundly. Early the next morning I made a tour of all the factories which turned out smoked hams and tongues, and salted pork and sausages of every description, collecting from each samples of its specialities. Then I bought a bag of the type favoured by travelling salesmen and arranged my packages inside it. Armed

with this I went to the police station, where I gave another
name and address and asked for a permit to cross the frontier
into Galicia. As I expected, I was asked my reason. I opened
my bag and displayed the tempting array explaining that I
was travelling in smoked meats and hoped to establish a connection in Galicia. . . .

"I shouldn't think you will have any difficulty in doing
that" . . . said the police inspector sniffing appreciatively . . .
"Those sausages look good."

"They taste better still" . . . I said . . . "Try one and
see."

He took one and munched it with relish while he signed all
the necessary papers without even a question.

I walked out of the police station with an imposing permit
authorizing me to leave the realm of His Imperial Majesty the
Czar of Russia for the purpose of transacting my lawful business in Galicia. But even so I did not dare to risk crossing
the frontier at one of the main stations for fear of being recognized, in spite of my assumed name and passport by the
police on duty there. So I decided to cross at a tiny frontier
post in the heart of the country. The only means of getting
there was in a hired carriage drawn by two horses, which took
hours to cover thirty odd miles along roads which were
frozen at some stages and knee-deep in snow at others. Several
times the horses could scarcely keep their feet and I and the
old coachman had to get down and lead them. It was nearly
midnight when we reached the station and by that time I was
so cold that my teeth were chattering in my head and so
stiff that I could hardly walk.

Several other travellers were already there and the police
officers in charge began to examine passports and permits,
calling out the names of the owners in turn. The sudden contrast of the warmth of the station after the bitter cold of the
drive made me sleepy, and I sat in the row with the rest of
the people half dozing not noticing what was going on until
suddenly I heard the policeman shouting loudly and saw that
he was trying to attract my attention. He was asking me my
name and to my horror I realized that I had quite forgotten
the one on my passport!

There was a dreadful moment of silence while every one looked at me in surprise. Still I could not remember. Then the man shouted again . . . "Don't you know your own name?"

With disaster staring me in the face I made a desperate effort. The mists of fatigue cleared from my brain. I managed to remember my assumed surname, which apparently satisfied him for he stamped my permit without a word.

A few minutes later I had crossed the frontier into friendly Galician territory.

CHAPTER XVI

In the spring of 1914 Joseph Pilsudski stated in a lecture to the Geographical Society in Paris . . .

"The problem of the independence of Poland will only be solved when Russia is beaten by Germany and Germany by France. It is our duty to lend our help for that aim; otherwise we shall have to pursue a very long, very hard and almost desperate struggle. . . ."

Months before the assassination of the Archduke Franz Ferdinand at Sarajevo had set a match to the conflagration which was to spread throughout Europe he had foreseen the outcome of the inevitable war and was coolly and dispassionately weighing up the chances of Poland's Partitioning Powers and laying his plans. He described the situation as "infinitely rich in possibilities." . . .

"The war will have unexpected results" . . . he predicted . . . "Russia is far weaker than she is supposed to be, a Colossus with feet of wax. She will be the first to crumple up under the blows of the Central Powers. England and France will eventually beat Germany. Poland's hour of destiny is approaching and we must be ready for it." . . .

By mid-July war had become not a possibility but a certainty. He cancelled the summer school at Cracow and instead prepared to mobilize his troops. In the meantime he took stock of the position.

He was a realist, uninfluenced by any considerations of sentiment. The issue of the war meant nothing to him except in that it concerned the future of the Poles. He was for Poland alone and Poland owed loyalty neither to Russia, Germany nor Austria, since all were her enemies. It remained therefore to decide which of the three was the most likely to prove amenable. Of the three Partitioning Powers Austria alone had shown any intention of conciliating her Polish subjects or of affording them even a measure of autonomy and liberty of action. Further she knew her own weakness. She would offer the best terms for Polish support. He explained his reasoning in a speech which he delivered at Cracow in 1922. . . .

"I knew that Poland would be the theatre of war, and that the Partitioning Powers would have much greater power and authority among my countrymen than I should. But even at the beginning of the war I calculated that, contrary to the general opinion of the moment, war would not only exhaust and weaken the conquered, but would adversely affect the conqueror also. I knew that none of the Partitioning Powers thought of Poland, that she was not only not their object, but on the contrary their obstacle. When I came to the conclusion that no one wanted to fight over Poland and that political factors could play no part, I had to calculate on the hard basis of 'Do ut des.' I could either give soldiers or, let us use the term, a spy service. I had to say to myself that I could not provide the latter, because my character made it impossible, so I decided to give what appeared to be most difficult in this case, the trained arm of a soldier who must acquire for himself the title of soldier among his own people as well as among foreigners, by his hard toil. Then I asked myself which partition offered the possibility of creating an armed force which would count when all, both conquerors and conquered, were weakened under the tyranny of war. At once I saw that the only country where it was possible to begin and carry through such a scheme was Austria. I reckoned that Germany, with her iron state organization and her military machine would immediately throw in every one capable of fighting. Russia was no use; she was too confident in her own strength and her policy of force in dealing with her subjects. Austria remained the weakest state, maintaining herself alive as a type of political tight-rope walker, dependent on her subjects, easiest to talk to, even if it was 'Austrian talk.' "

The Austrian authorities received the offer of this arrogant Pole to supply them with an armed legion for use against Russia with no great enthusiasm. With his usual directness and scorn of subterfuge, even when the most vital issues were at stake, he made no attempt to disguise his motive. He let it be apparent that he was acting in the sole interest of Poland and that he was prepared to make no concessions in the matter of Polish independence.

"I asked Austria only for arms and would accept no political conditions" . . . he said in describing his negotiations with the Government . . . "I was threatened with the arrest of all the Strzelcy organization and with internment for myself. I would not move from my position and that was why we had such miserable arms and such miserable equipment. I did not accept humiliating conditions because I wished to preserve my moral strength."

The Austrian statesmen were in a dilemma. The Polish force which was prepared to take the field at the bidding of this extraordinary man already numbered several thousands, the nucleus of an army. An independent Polish army might prove a dangerous asset. On the other hand, no good purpose could be served by antagonizing the Poles at the very outset of a war which was obviously going to tax Austria's resources to the uttermost. The Strzelcy were well-trained and disciplined in spite of their lack of arms and equipment; their leader Pilsudski had already gained some renown as the author of articles on military tactics; with tactful handling he might gain the support of many Russian Poles. They decided on a compromise. He obtained a somewhat grudging acceptance of his offer and a promise of equipment which was the reverse of generous. It was discouraging but he had hoped for no more and it gave him at least a basis. He ordered his Riflemen to mobilize on August 2nd.

They answered the call joyfully. Clerks and University students cancelled their vocations, peasants left their farms and workmen their benches. The rival organization of the Right, the Druzyny Strzeleckie (Non-Socialist Youth), on hearing of the mobilization called a meeting, decided unanimously to drop their political differences of opinion and put themselves under Pilsudski's leadership. The two assembled at Oleandry, outside Cracow, and drew up in lines facing one another. Then Pilsudski and Burkhardt-Bukacki, leader of the Druzyny, advanced and exchanged their respective badges.

Henceforth there would no longer be two organizations but only one: The Polish Army. The forbidden White Eagle that had floated victoriously over many a battlefield in the days of Poland's greatness was unfurled. Pilsudski addressed the massed troops.

"Soldiers. You have the great honour of being the first to enter the Realm and to cross the frontier of the provinces annexed by Russia, as the head of a column of Polish troops marching to fight for the deliverance of the country. You are all equal in the face of the sacrifices which you will be called upon to make. You are all soldiers. I do not confer any ranks. I only appoint the most experienced among you to carry out the duties of leaders. You will win your own promotion on the battlefield. Each one of you can become an officer, and each officer can be reduced to the ranks, which may God forbid. I look to you as the frame for the future Polish Army and·I salute in you the first company of that frame."

They mustered on the first day some four thousand strong, out of whom 140 men were chosen as officers. Pilsudski had planned an immediate invasion of Russia, but he had counted without the dilatoriness of the Austrian Government. He and his men were forced to hang about for three days waiting for the promised equipment. When at length it materialized there were not enough rifles to arm even half their numbers and therefore only three companies were able to march.

In the meantime Pilsudski had realized that a Polish army without a Polish Government behind it would not carry much weight. He must create a Government. He did so. Within twelve hours its first proclamation appeared.

"Poles,

"A National Government has been constituted in Warsaw. It is the duty of the Polish people to close their ranks under its authority. The citizen Joseph Pilsudski has been appointed Commander-in-Chief of the Polish Military Forces and he must be obeyed.

By Order of the National Government."
Warsaw, August 3rd.

In the early morning of August 6th, Pilsudski gave the order to march and the army set out in the direction of the Russian frontier, preceded by an advance guard composed of the entire cavalry, three men on horses and some half-dozen optimists carrying saddles in preparation for the mounts they were going to capture from the enemy. They found the frontier deserted; the Russian patrols had retreated.

The three companies of Strzelcy broke down the barriers and swept into the territory that had once been Poland's, singing the old insurrectionary songs; the songs that the army of Kosciuszko had sung. It had been arranged that Pilsudski would proceed with his force to Jedrzejow where he would co-operate with Austrian cavalry in the neighbourhood of Kielce. Franz Joseph's officers, resplendent in their smart uniforms with centuries of military tradition behind them, had been contemptuously tolerant of their raw, untidy guerilla allies when the plan was discussed in Cracow. Yet the Poles were in Kielce before them, having driven back the Russians on the way . . . "They are great fighters these Polish troops" . . . reported the Austrian General in Command . . . "irregular certainly, but one could not wish for better soldiers. . . ."

It was indeed "irregular," this Polish Army. An army miserably armed and miserably equipped, without machine-guns or artillery, without even field kitchens or telephones, shouldering the antiquated Werndel rifles which were the only weapons which the Austrians had troubled to issue to them, carrying their cartridges in their pockets in default of ammunition pouches. A motley army dressed anyhow. In the plain blue breeches, short tunic and Maciejowka caps of the Strzelcy, in a variety of discarded Austrian uniforms, misfits from regimental stores, thrown out at random to equip the Polish volunteers, in city suits and in workmen's overalls. An unorthodox army for any country to send forth. But an army great in fighting spirit, a young, gay army that laughed and sang as it marched.

The Russians retreated from Michow and the Strzelcy occupied the town. Pilsudski issued a proclamation to the National Government.

"The decisive hour has struck. Poland is no longer en-slaved. She will henceforth determine her own destiny, and carve out her own future, throwing into the scale the force of her armies. The First Companies of the Polish Army have penetrated the territory of the realm, and are occupying it in the name of its true and sole owners, the Polish people who have enriched and fertilized its soil with their blood. We bring to the whole nation freedom from its chains." . . .

He signed it . . . "Pilsudski, Commander-in-Chief of the Polish Troops."

It was one of the best moments in his life. At last, at the age of forty-seven, he saw the realization of the dream of his boyhood, the creation of a Polish army to fight against Russia. And he was the leader of that army. "That first fight, that first contact with war" . . . he wrote a few years later . . . "I do not know what it held for others, but to me it had as much poetry as my first youthful love affair, my first kisses" . . .

He was profoundly happy for he was serving the two ideals which had dominated his whole life. His love of Poland and his love of the army. He had so long been a voice crying in the wilderness, a soldier in theory only, a mere writer on military strategy. Now the sword was in his own hand.

Yet the road ahead of him was by no means smooth. There were many problems to be faced in this task of moulding an army. He had excellent raw material to work upon, his troops were well-trained and full of fighting spirit, but that was not enough for him. He wanted to create not merely a victorious fighting force but an army that was to be the nucleus of a national standing army. Poland had had no regular army of her own within living memory and therefore her soldiers could only acquire slowly through personal experience the discipline and military traditions which were ingrained in other nations.

The necessity for organization was critical. It took some time to get into working order a military machine which had been manufactured overnight. There was constant friction over the ordinary details of army routine, questions of seniority and discipline among the officers and so forth. When, for instance, the providential capture of a number of Russian horses enabled a Cavalry Corps to be formed nearly every man in the army, with the Pole's characteristic love of a good horse, wanted to be in it, and there was such bitter jealousy that the Commander-in-Chief had to affirm loudly on every suitable occasion that the heart of an army was always held to be its Infantry!

The fact that his relations with the Austrian Government were not clearly defined made incessant demands both on his diplomacy and on his qualities of leadership. . . .

"From the beginning I had to realize that the attitude of the Austrian and German troops, standing armies with centuries-old traditions, would be one of profound scepticism as to the military value of our volunteer formation," he wrote in describing those first difficult weeks of the campaign. "I was prepared for this attitude, and knowing well the lofty ambition of the Strzelcy I was very much afraid that I might not only wound this ambition of theirs at the first reverse, but even worse, destroy their faith in themselves as soldiers. And a reverse was more than likely in the extremely poor state of our technical armament and equipment. I had then to defend my soldiers not only from external humiliation but also from the internal humiliation to which the consciousness of being less efficient than the troops around them might well give rise."

He arrived with his small force at Jedrzejow, found no sign of the Austrian cavalry and decided on his own responsibility to march on Kielce. It was a daring move and one which might well have resulted in a signal defeat. .

"I was quite aware that in the depths of their hearts all my soldiers were afraid of their mad undertaking," he wrote later. "And afraid of the test which we should shortly have to pass both in the eyes of our allies and in our own. When I considered the state of our armament and thought of this test I told myself that I must be cautious and not give rein to my fancy. But then all the will, pride and ambition in me rebelled against these 'prudent' reflections. Besides, there was no escape. We could only win what we needed above all to win, self-confidence and the military respect of those associated with us by taking big risks. I staked a great deal on a single card. . . ."

The game was in his favour. On August 12th he entered Kielce at the head of an army composed of 141 officers and 2,257 men. Among their ranks were members of the aristocracy, students of the Strzelcy Military School, professional men, doctors, artists and musicians, labourers and artisans from Russian Poland and peasants recruited from the farms and villages along the road. The cavalry numbered five officers and forty-seven men under the command of Belina.

"They effected nothing short of miracles," wrote Pilsudski. "Untrained to long marches, on saddles made for hack-riding, on worn-out horses, they blistered themselves raw. Armed with long rifles unsuitable for use on horseback, they tore their backs till they bled to carry out patrols of seventy to eighty kilometres a day." . . .

Among these men was Sieroszewski, the famous writer, who although he was approaching his sixtieth year, served throughout the war as a trooper in the cavalry.

In the meantime there was considerable agitation in the political circles of both Austrian and Russian Poland. Pilsudski had marched off to war, created a National Government and occupied several towns before any one else had decided as to what attitude was to be adopted.

The war between the Partitioning Powers had forced upon Poles the alternative of either defying their respective rulers or else fighting in opposing armies. The unhappy nation was see-sawed this way and that, threatened and cajoled in turn by the belligerent governments. Roman Dmowski and the National Democrat Party urged complete support of Russia, an alliance of the Slav race against the Teuton. The Grand Duke Nicholas, Commander-in-Chief of the Russian Armies, issued a proclamation promising that Poland should be "re-born, free in faith, in language, in self-government." It met with a mixed reception. Four of the political parties, headed by the National Democrats, hailed it with enthusiasm and issued a manifesto pledging the wholehearted loyalty of the nation to Russia's cause regardless of the fact that only a fraction of the nation was behind them. There was strife and dissatisfaction everywhere.

In Austrian Poland the position was no less complicated. The Government had intended to take refuge in a negative policy, making no compromising pledges, leaving the Galician Poles to serve in the Austrian Army. But this turbulent Pilsudski had forced their hands. Although they were constrained to treat him as an ally, they remained more than a little doubtful of his intentions, since he still made no secret of his dream of an independent Poland tied neither to Austria, Germany nor Russia. Moreover, he had upset their mobilization plans. There had been complaints from the War Office in Vienna that Poles who would normally have been called up for Galician regiments were serving under the banner of Pilsudski. The situation was somewhat strained.

For him there was no going back. He had indeed "staked a great deal on a single card." When he gave the order to march upon Kielce he risked not only the military setback which he dreaded but the collapse of his whole enterprise. Those first few weeks called upon all his courage and faith in himself. The Austrophil Poles in Cracow, true to their invariable custom of underrating one of their own countrymen, wavered and hedged, unwilling to risk their privileges and their good relations with the Austrian Government by giving him unqualified support. After a great deal of argument the N.K.N. (Chief National Committee) was formed, a quarrelsome, unwieldy body containing representatives of nearly all the Galician parties. Under its auspices an agreement was reached with the Austro-Hungarian Monarchy for the creation of Polish Legions to fight under the supreme command of Austria. Pilsudski was to be at the head of the First Brigade, and the small force which was already serving under him was to be its nucleus. Subsequently a Second and Third Brigade were formed, but the three were not united until 1916 on the Volhynian Front.

Within the first few weeks thousands of Polish recruits flocked to the Legions; modern rifles and new equipment were hastily issued. The Austrian Government drew up a manifesto urging the Russian Poles to throw in their lot with their own countrymen and fight against the Czar, promising them in return a Polish Kingdom. Objections from Hungary, who feared too strong a Poland, prevented its being signed.

Fighting discouragement, Pilsudski entered Kielce. There, he proceeded to consolidate his position, to open up lines of communication and supply. The Austrian and German troops who came up to reinforce him found everything running smoothly.

In the meantime I and the other women who formed a unit of this new army had our own part to play. We crossed the frontier into Russian territory on the same day as the Legions, several hours after we had seen them go, and in some trepidation for we could get no news of them. However, we could only obey orders so we set forth, a struggling little procession of civilians in rickety country carts, with our baggage piled up around us. I remember that the cart in which I rode was overloaded with all our books and papers and a printing press. However, we had the good fortune to come up with the troops that first night and we took over our duties immediately. The cooks set about preparing the meals, the clerks and store-keepers took over such supplies as were available and the Intelligence Section went out to reconnoitre. When the troops occupied Kielce we followed after them and set up our headquarters in the town. M. Danilovski, a young writer, and I opened an office in what had been a Russian Government bureau, and began to turn out propaganda. The Russians had departed in such haste that drawers and cupboards were in wild disorder, papers lay strewn all over the floor and one of the officials had even left his cap with its badge of office hanging on a peg. M. Danilovski wanted to throw it out but I said that we must keep it for luck. Events more than justified my superstition for we owed our escape to it a few days later.

For the first few days there was complete calm in the town. Not a sign of any Russian troops. The small Austrian and German detachments moved in and took up their quarters. There seemed so little prospect of an enemy attack that Pilsudski decided to go to Cracow, where the N.K.N. were being organized. There were various formalities to be discussed with the Chief National Committee and the Austrian High Command—the training of recruits and the issue of additional equipment, etc., and his presence was necessary. He went by car, leaving Sosnkowski in command.

Within twenty-four hours of his departure the situation took a new turn. For no apparent reason not only Kielce itself but the whole region rang with rumours of large Russian forces of cavalry advancing.

The Austrian and German commanders, whose troops consisted only of a few cavalry patrols, decided to retire. Without a word of warning or explanation to Sosnkowski they withdrew their detachments overnight, leaving the small Polish force with its inadequate arms and equipment to defend the city or not as it chose.

The Russians attacked almost immediately. Their numbers had been greatly exaggerated, but even so the odds were enormously in their favour. Belina and his handful of cavalry put up a gallant resistance but their defeat was a foregone conclusion.

The first tidings of disaster reached me when the porter came running into the office where I was working with M. Danilovski crying out that the Cossacks were in the town. As he spoke we heard a volley of shots and the sound of horses charging through the streets.

We had two alternatives: to try to escape to the railway station which our troops would be defending, or stay where we were until we were arrested by the Russian officials who would come to recover possession of their bureau. In a common impulse we decided to run for it. M. Danilovski snatched up the Russian official's cap which was still hanging on its peg and put it on his head. Then with an air of as much unconcern as we could achieve we walked out into the street arm in arm. We met numbers of Russian soldiers but those who took any

notice of us at all glanced at M. Danilovski's cap and let us
pass without question.

Fierce fighting was going on in many of the streets and
we had to make several detours before we reached the station.
There we saw our own troops occupying the trenches which
they had dug when they entered the city, while Belina's cavalry was meeting the Cossack charges. We were debating how
to join up with the Polish troops without being caught between the two lines of fire when we saw a group of our soldiers bearing down upon us. They were shouting at Danilovski
and I snatched the Russian cap from his head just in time!

The fighting lasted for some hours but our force was too
heavily outnumbered to have even a chance of success. Sosnkowski had no alternative but to withdraw. His troops fell
back in good order in the direction of Jedrzejow.

I remained in Kielce with the civilians and I think that
the ensuing few days were some of the worst I have ever lived
through. Hour after hour went by without news, for we could
not establish communication either with Pilsudski or Sosnkowski. The blank was filled with the wildest rumours and
conjectures which seemed to sweep like a breath over the
town, for no one could trace their origin. On all sides, among
all types of people stories began to circulate of a desperate
battle in which the Poles and Austrians had been defeated. I
remember going out one morning and buying cheese from a
peasant woman who turned my heart to lead by telling me
with many tears that the Russian cavalry had met the Polish
Legions and had practically annihilated them. Pilsudski, who
had returned from Cracow and rejoined his troops on the road
had been killed, she said. She had heard it from her cousin's
son who was serving in the Legions and had been one of the
few to escape after the battle.

A little farther on I heard the same story, with a few
additions, from an old crossing-sweeper. He too claimed first-
hand information from one of the Legionaries. A priest, whom
I knew to be a most truthful man and a sincere patriot, also
confirmed it. In his version Pilsudski had not been killed but
had been taken prisoner . . . the country priest who had
given him the news had actually seen the motor-car in which

he had been returning from Cracow lying abandoned by the roadside. A variation which brought no comfort to me for I knew that of the two fates he would have preferred death a hundred times.

Nearly a week passed while the Russians occupied the town and we waited in vain for news. Then one morning the little servant at the house where I was staying ran in to tell me that the Cossacks had gone. They had departed silently in the dawn, leaving all their baggage and a quantity of guns and ammunition. A few hours later I stood at my window and watched Pilsudski ride into the town at the head of his Legions. There had been no battle. He had not been taken prisoner, though his car had certainly been left at the roadside, for the unromantic reason that it had broken down. So much for war rumours!

He remained in Kielce for several weeks and during that time he set the whole machinery of the new army in motion. The commanders of the German and Austrian detachments assigned to him by common consent the former palace of the Russian Governor. He established his headquarters there and began with his usual untiring energy the task of organizing and equipping his troops. A regular service of baggage trains was instituted, workshops were set up . . . tailors', carpenters', and saddle-makers'. A medical department was created to attend to the sick; the Intelligence Section was extended.

The role played by the women in the Intelligence, the "Couriers," as we were known, was an important one, for since the war zone stretched between Russian and Austrian Poland we alone could serve as links between the two regions. We fulfilled a double function, conveying news and propaganda from the army to its supporters in Russian Poland and returning to headquarters with the information which we had collected on our way. This was generally of a twofold nature, strategic, concerning the progress of the party organizations, and military, gleaned during our passage through the enemy's lines. Very often this last was of considerable value, for the Russian system of surveillance was as slow-moving as the rest of its military machine, and we were able to slip between the lines time after time without incurring suspicion. It was a dangerous experiment, naturally, but it was chiefly a question of keeping a cool head and getting to know the various gaps in the lines through which we could pass. We evolved a number of ingenious pretexts for our journeys to and fro. Some of the women dressed themselves as peasants and sold fruit and vegetables to the Russian troops, others pretended to be seeking news of husbands or brothers. From our conversations with the soldiers we would often learn important details of troop movements, expected reinforcements, and so forth. I have still a letter from Pilsudski in which he gives me my instructions for collecting this information.

"Remember that all your work amounts to the gathering of raw material" . . . he writes . . . "Afterwards it can be sifted methodically and used in developing a plan. Do not be discouraged because the results appear to be small. Every detail may have great importance in the future. . . ."

In the autumn of 1914 Pilsudski formed the P.O.W. (Polish Military Organization). He was jealous of his original program of the independence of Poland, afraid lest it should be overlooked in the alliance with Austria, which he never looked on as anything other than a temporary expedient. The idea that the nation should be sundered in spirit, as it had already been sundered in territory, by the Partitioning Powers was to him intolerable. The P.O.W. was therefore created to reach the populace of Russian Poland and unite it in the military effort which was still confined only to a section of the nation. As it could only exist in the strictest secrecy it depended on the women of the Intelligence Section for its contact with Pilsudski's headquarters. Branches were as far-flung as Moscow, Kiev and Odessa, and we travelled constantly between them and the army carrying news and propaganda. Some fifty women took part in this work; not one of them received any money for it, over and above their bare expenses. . . .

"Your work must necessarily be much harder than that of the soldiers" . . . Pilsudski used to tell us . . . "They are sustained by fighting side by side, while you are alone and can only rely on your own strength, and that requires much more courage. . . ."

At a later date he wrote, in describing his Intelligence Section . . . "The women fulfilled their duties with heroic self-sacrifice. They jolted along in carts over every road, covering greater areas than the cavalry."

We did indeed cover thousands of miles in a month, sometimes by train, sometimes in rough peasants' carts, often on foot. Several were arrested and sent to Russian prisons, one, a young student whose brother was serving in the Legions, was afterwards shot as a spy. Her mother who was forced to witness the execution heroically overcame her grief and went on to deliver to headquarters the information which her daughter had obtained at the cost of her life.

CHAPTER XVII

THE EARLY autumn of 1914 brought Pilsudski disappointments and setbacks both military and political. The campaign went badly for the Austrians who were already beginning to show signs of weakening morale. The German force sent to bolster them up was inadequate and their joint offensive was repulsed with heavy losses. The Russians, who had flung the whole weight of their vast military machine into the war, continued the inexorable "steam-roller" advance which caused their allies and enemies alike to over-estimate their strength in those early days. The Austrian Commander in Kielce, disheartened by reports of enemy concentration, gave orders for retreat. Pilsudski fumed in secret that the town should be thus abandoned without a single shot. It was all very well for the Austrians and Prussians, who got all they wanted from Vienna or Berlin. His small army depended for its equipment on the workshops he had set up in Kielce, the tailors and carpenters and saddlers. Many of his men had not even overcoats or boots for the long marches. He was distressed too at the prospect of leaving at the mercy of the enemy the civilians who had worked for him. Yet he had no course but to obey orders.

He was hampered on all sides both by his own people and by the Austrians. The majority of the Poles showed no disposition to support him. In Galicia the Chief National Committee (N.K.N.) adhered slavishly to the dictates of the Austrian High Command. The Poles in Russian Poland were disputing among themselves and divided by party politics. The National Democrats would not fight Russia. The Social Democrats would not fight at all.

There was friction with the Austrian army under whose command he was serving. Those in high authority distrusted him. When he wanted to march on Sosnowiec and Czestochowa, important industrial centres in Russian Poland where he had a large following among the workmen who would have rallied to him, he met with a blunt refusal. It was perfectly obvious that while Austria was content enough to avail herself of the services of the Polish Legions she would steadfastly discourage any attempt at creating a united Poland.

The Austrian officers did not trouble to conceal their scorn of their allies. . . . "By high and low we were regarded with disdainful hostility or at the best with patronizing contempt" . . . wrote Pilsudski. "This caused a great number of disputes and unpleasant incidents which were generally humiliating. After a few quarrels with the High Command it became the rule to treat me as a *bête noire*."

From one quarter he received unqualified trust and support: his Legions. There was not one among them who would not have died willingly for him. They had no army tradition behind them, no experienced N.C.O.'s to lead them, and many of them were only boys under twenty, yet they performed deeds of sheer heroism. Again and again they achieved the apparently impossible, took and held positions which defied the well-trained, well-disciplined Austrian and German troops. Their relations with him may have lacked the conventional military formality, but they were warm, personal and friendly. He called them "My boys"; they treated him like a father rather than a Brigadier. Though he could be as exacting as any Prussian officer where duty was concerned, and expected a high standard in courage and initiative from his men, he spared them whenever he could. He visited them when they were in hospital, helped them in their individual problems and stood between them and the criticisms of the supercilious, overbearing Austrian officers. He was always accessible to them, went among them in the trenches and listened to their opinions, for he regarded the whole campaign as an experiment in which all shared. Between them they evolved a sort of military democracy, an *esprit de corps* that was something more than mere army discipline.

He loved his men and he understood them. He was as sensitive to their moods as he was to those of Kasztanka, the beautiful Arab mare who carried him through the war. He knew instinctively when they were discouraged, and when

they were confident, when he could demand their utmost efforts and when he would have to be lenient if he was to obtain
that complete co-operation of which he wrote:

> "War is an art. Art is creative, and the whole object
> and art of war is victory. The general seeks in victory the
> fruit of his work in command, the product of his brain,
> nerves and will power. The work of the troops under his
> orders is the materialization of what he has thought, ex-
> perienced and contrived. . . ."

His reactions to the war were twofold. At one moment
he was the soldier, the strategist, devoted from his boyhood
to the whole "art of war." At another he was the idealist
appalled at the carnage around him, tortured by a too-vivid
imagination. Thus he could write at different times:

> "What a curious impression it is to be physically unaware
> of the enemy! How happy our ancestors were at war,
> when they had fewer exhausting problems to solve, and
> on account of the short range of their weapons, were often
> not only aware of their enemies' presence, but could actu-
> ally count them. To-day this physical proximity to one's
> opponent has become relatively rare, and is generally the
> final incident of a long episode." . . .

And again . . .

> "Somewhere in the distance boomed the quiet hollow noise
> of firing, which I had learnt to recognize as that of heavy
> artillery. Immediately afterwards I heard the slow, twist-
> ing flight of a shell in the air. That noise somewhere above
> one approaches so slowly that one's eye searches for it
> in the air instinctively, and yet it whistles and lisps with
> such hostility and so pitilessly, as if it said . . . 'You won't
> escape. I am coming to you; certain death; but I am com-
> ing slowly, unhurrying, because I wish to see how your
> face blanches before you die.' In this hostile whistle of heavy
> shells there is a shade of mockery, of malicious, self-assured
> power slowly advancing and scoffing at helpless man. There
> is nothing of the hurry, fever and clamorousness of the shells
> of the field artillery. . . ."

All through the autumn of 1914 the Austrian army met
with one reverse after another. After the withdrawal from
Kielce the Polish army, as the rearguard, put up a determined
fight along the left bank of the Vistula and although heavily
outnumbered succeeded in holding back the pursuing Russians
for several days. It was their first action of any importance
and it won them laurels in the eyes of the Austrians and confidence in their own.

Early in October the Austrians launched another offensive
northwards in the direction of Warsaw. Pilsudski gave useful
collaboration by calling upon the P.O.W. (Polish Military
Organization) to enter the conflict and take arms against
Russia. Under the command of one of his own men, a student
named Fadeusz Zulinski, hundreds of young apprentices, students, and artisans of Warsaw banded themselves together and
conducted a guerilla warfare against the Russians. Pilsudski
himself with six battalions of infantry and a squadron of
cavalry held important positions near Demblin in spite of a
terrific bombardment from the guns of the fortress. However,
General Dankiel, who was in command of the Austrian Army,
gave orders for a retreat.

To Pilsudski the decision was a bitter disappointment. For
him so far the campaign had been nothing but a series of
withdrawals and rearguard actions fought against heavy odds.
As usual, the Austrian staff did not honour him with their
confidence and he was left to suppose that they were retreating to Cracow. He even sent on all his baggage and heavy
equipment there . . . "I thought that there, collected together with all our casualties, convalescents and stragglers of
all sorts, we would halt in defence of the city from which
we had gone to the wars" . . . he wrote afterwards . . .
"There, even an unhappy end to our attempt to create a Polish soldier would have the right historical background. . . ."

But the columns of retreating troops swung away from
Cracow, away westwards to the Dombrowa Basin. The road
became blocked with baggage trains withdrawing in confusion; the artillery coming up behind tried to clear a way
through by sheer weight and ruthlessness; the infantry and
machine guns piled themselves on top. The retreat which had

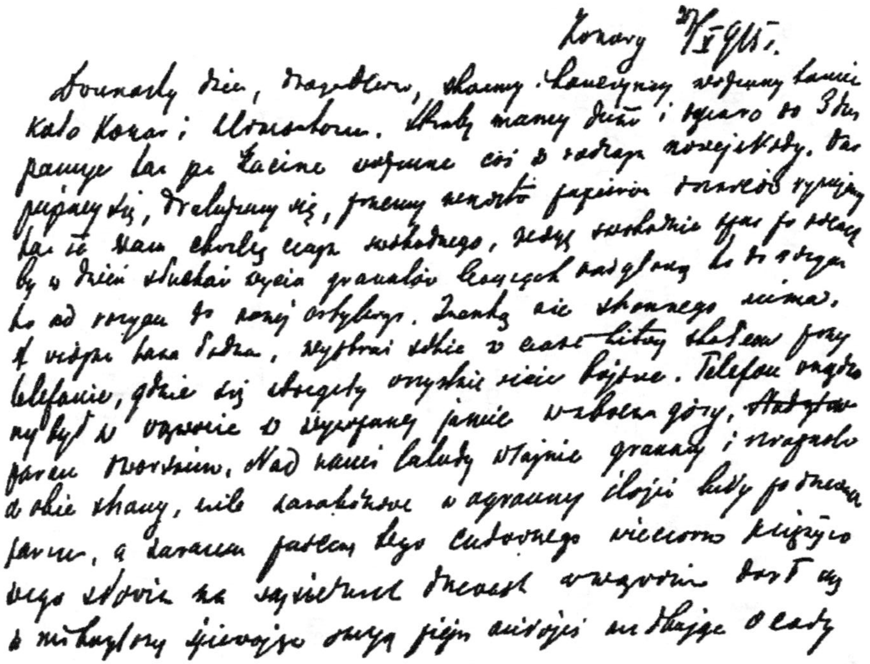

Letter written to me from the battlefield of Konary

started methodically was turned into a disorderly flight, in which each man thought only of himself. Pilsudski strove to keep his soldiers together. The commander of the Austrian brigade behind him cursed him for impeding delay and threatened to complain to headquarters. The Czechs in front, who despised the Polish Legions as an irregular gang, almost came to blows with his men. Outside the little town of Wolbrom the retreat developed into a stampede, a pandemonium of shouting, struggling, quarrelling men. Determined at all costs to get his Legionaries clear of it he halted them before the edge of the town and let the fleeing Austrians sweep past him.

The November evening closed in. His men laughed and sang over their smoky camp fires as they made tea and cooked potatoes, but for once he had little heart to join them. He was facing the realization of where this retreat would end. When the Austrians rallied sufficiently to make a stand against the enemy it would not be upon Polish soil. Poland would be delivered over to the advancing hordes of Russia, while the Polish army fought for Austria!

The thought was intolerable to him . . . "The Austrians might defend Breslau, Vienna or Berlin" . . . he wrote later . . . "But we free Polish Strzelcy would not do that. We would try to die with honour but we would die in our own land." . . .

There rose before his eyes the vision of the walls of Cracow, that beloved city of Cracow whence he had set out to the war, and suddenly his mind was made up. Cracow was a fortress: it had stood many a siege in the past: he and his men with the Austrians could hold it for days, maybe for weeks. Between the Russian forces which were closing up behind the retreating Austrians was still a corridor wide enough to permit a small detachment to pass through to the south. It was a desperate risk but he would take it, even though it meant acting in direct defiance of his orders.

Leaving three battalions of his Legions to continue with General Dankiel's army he marched southwards with the remaining three. In spite of the gravity of the step he was taking he was relieved, almost gay, for he had thrown off the shackles of the Austrian Command! His troops shared his elation though they were haggard from the strain of a heavy rearguard action, long marches and lack of sleep. They had been obliged to leave all transport and supplies behind them, and had only as much ammunition as they could carry. Their food depended on what they could get at the villages through which they passed. In one they ate hot bread baked for the Russians, in another a farm supplied them with milk and kascha. They marched over miles of ploughed fields and through straggling woods. It was a mad adventure, but its very madness and audacity made it successful. They passed right through the midst of one enemy corps and through the advance guard of another without losing a single man. At Ulina Mala they rested calmly for a whole day while Russian troops and transports marched only a few kilometres away on either side of them.

They entered Cracow in triumph. The townspeople acclaimed Pilsudski; the women showered flowers upon him. But the Commander of the handful of Austrians garrisoning the fortress received him coldly and refused at first even to give him billets for his men. It was only one more official snub and he did not care. He had avoided fighting for Austria on foreign soil: that was all that mattered to him. But he had also gained something else. . . .

> "I confess that it was only after Ulina that I began to have confidence in myself and belief in my powers" . . . he wrote at a later date . . . "And perhaps just because of that I so often heard my soldiers say . . . 'Now we can follow our Commandant anywhere. If he could get us out of Ulina we need not worry!' It was like an examination that I passed both before myself and before my men. . . ."

Cracow did not fall. The tide of war turned again. The Germans launched a fresh offensive towards Lodz which broke the force of the Russian advance. In the South the Austrians made a stand, sent reinforcements to Cracow and held the city and the surrounding country. Pilsudski and his Legions took Kamienica from the Russians and guarded the Austrian right wing during the great battle of Limanowa which drove the Russians back beyond the Dunajec.

By the end of December the Polish First Brigade had become famous. The Austrian General had written in glowing terms of its courage and efficiency at Limanowa. Pilsudski's prestige had increased enormously. The Austrian High Command had begun to respect him as a military leader though they distrusted his political influence: he was steadily gaining the confidence of his own countrymen. When he entered Nowy Soncz on December 12th at the head of his victorious troops the townspeople lined the streets to greet him and cheered themselves hoarse. I can still remember how that welcome delighted him, not because he set any personal value on it, but because he was happy that at last, after so many years, Poland had an army of her own, an army in which her people could take pride.

At the end of December he went to Vienna for a conference of the N.K.N., which was still obstinately Austrophil and critical in its attitude to him. At the banquet which was held afterwards he pleaded for unity. . . .

"We are our country's knights going out to war, but we must have not only the strength of the mailed fist but the strength of mind and heart behind it. The union of our people behind the N.K.N. can give us this. The spirit of the nation must complete our victories in the field, and justify the sacrifice of our blood." . . .

When one of his Legionaries, Danilovski, the writer, who was another of the speakers, upbraided him laughingly for not valuing his own safety and taking unnecessary risks in the trenches, Pilsudski interrupted him by striking the table with his fist and calling him to attention. . . . "If you want to criticize your superior officer in public you must take off your uniform" . . . he said: "If I were really the Commander-in-Chief of my army instead of a mere colonel I should have to behave like a Commander-in-Chief. As it is I can remember that a colonel's place is with his troops, not behind them. . . ."

.   .   .   .   .

The year 1915 saw the continuation of the Austro-German campaign with rising fortunes. Russia, as Pilsudski had predicted, was already beginning to totter on her "feet of wax":

her ponderous military machine was slowing down through lack of organization and general inefficiency. The temperamental Austrians, encouraged by the victory of Limanowa, rallied and drove the enemy still farther back along the Vistula; the Germans won a decisive battle at Gorlice in May. All through the summer months success followed success for the Central Powers. In June they regained the city of Lwow; in August the Russians evacuated Warsaw and were driven out in the key fortresses of Kovno and Modlin.

On August 6th, the anniversary of the day they had gone out to war, Pilsudski could look back upon a year which, while it held no spectacular triumphs, had at least not been a failure. His First Brigade had acquitted themselves with honour and fought well. Since the previous Christmas they had been almost continuously in action, held positions on the Nida and taken part in the great offensive following on the German victory of Gorlice. In an order to his troops he said:

"Soldiers and comrades-in-arms. A year has passed, a year of heavy toil hampered by so many difficulties that it is a wonder that we find ourselves still in existence as an army; a wonder too that our native forests have not long ago murmured a funeral song over us, the Polish soldiers of the Great War. Now after a year of war we are still only Poland's vanguard in arms, as we are also her moral vanguard in knowing how to risk everything when risk is necessary. . . ."

In a letter to me written during that autumn he said:

"We are staying here for a short rest which all of us, myself included, need and deserve. I have had influenza again which always seems to leave traces after it, either weakness or just cold. So rest, physical, and above all mental, will be welcome because our success has been bought with hard mental toil, much suffering and many painful and bitter moments, which I have had to live through while steering the course of that queer vessel, my army. After our crazy and dangerous adventures, not so much the actual fighting as our relations with our whole

military entourage, we need a breathing space! And so
we are resting, sometimes being ill, sometimes trying to
keep ourselves from being ill, learning much and organizing
a little, and amusing ourselves when we can.

"I have been wondering for a long time what to give
you for a birthday present. Until now I have only been
able to find my own photograph. You can see from it
that I have a beard no longer, which will please you as
you never liked it. I must tell you that I was thinking
of you when I shaved it off. It was nearly on the date of
your birthday, so you have another present in the form
of my beard! . . ."

He wrote me many letters in those years of the war, whenever he had a moment to spare and there was any means of
sending mail. His letters were vivid, characteristic, reflecting
every mood, whether he wrote of the war and of the difficulties
that beset his path, or of the trivial things of every day. Here is
one written during the battle of Konary in October 1915:

"This is the twelfth day that we have stood facing one
another, dancing a military dance, around Konary and
Klimontow. Our losses have been heavy but during the
last three days quiet has reigned. We are entrenching ourselves again and putting up more barbed wire entangle-
ments. I sleep undisturbed at night now and during the
day I listen to the scream of the shells over our heads as
they fly backwards and forwards between the Russian
artillery and ours. Otherwise there is nothing sinister and
war might be almost a pretty thing. Imagine: during the
battle I was standing by the telephone where all the
different lines are linked up. The telephone was in a
valley, hidden in a cave hollowed out in the slope of the
mountain. The shells went screeching past overhead and
a hail of shrapnel and rifle bullets pattered against the
trees on either side of us, and yet during a few seconds'
lull in the fighting a nightingale in the trees in the valley
burst full-throated into his song of love, heedless of the din
of battle and the massacre of humanity going on around him
on this beautiful moonlit night. It was an impression I shall

never forget to the end of my days. That force of life in presence of the force of death was profoundly moving."

Those years in the trenches developed that sensitive, creative imagination of his which was so at variance with the realism and the concentrated energy of his daily life. At night in his dug-out or in his billet behind the lines he formed many of the impressions which served later as foundations for his articles and lectures. He wrote, for instance, of that companionship with death which every fighting man must, consciously or unconsciously, experience. . . .

"A soldier's profession means work in abnormal conditions. It creates in him a special attitude to death. Every one must die, of course, but when a soldier goes to death, Death takes him by the hand and walks with him on to the field of battle. Death and the thought of dissolution surround him constantly; the spectre of death stands beside him every day. The effort to grow used to this brotherhood with death, which is the duty of a soldier, imprints deep grooves on his soul and changes his character. The man who is going to die to-morrow sees things from a different angle. He does not value his comforts, because by to-morrow all comforts may have disappeared. He does not appreciate other people's comforts overmuch, and his own count for nothing with him. In this long contact, this perpetual brotherhood with Death material comforts become cheap and valueless, things with which one easily dispenses. The life of a good soldier must be a continual lottery and therefore material wealth is of much less importance in his eyes than in the eyes of most people." . . .

The year 1915 was a year of victories for him, that is to say, of victories in the field. Politically the situation grew no less complicated. There was still the same friction with the Austrian High Command who treated him and his First Brigade "like a disorderly rabble." There was the same half-hearted support and constant criticism from the N.K.N., whose lack of confidence was the more galling to bear since it came from his own countrymen. . . .

"Our national psychology makes the majority of Poles have no faith in the birth of a Polish soldier and a Polish army" . . . he wrote bitterly . . . "They prefer to trust to the good graces of the Austrian Government, and to influences at the court of Vienna to obtain benefits for Poland rather than that we should rely on ourselves. That is the psychological wall that stands between our First Brigade and the rest of the nation. . . ." More than a year had passed since the Polish Army had gone to war, yet the hope of establishing a free and united Poland in Galicia seemed fainter than ever.

In Russian Poland, too, the situation was discouraging. By the end of 1915 the Russians had been driven inch by inch out of the country, but the heavy hand of Russian overlordship had only exchanged for the no less heavy hand of German occupation. The people were too inert and too divided among themselves by party politics to offer any effective resistance. The influence of the National Democrats had waned with the Russian reverses and Roman Dmowski had fled to St. Petersburg, but numbers of Poles were still serving with the Russian forces. Pilsudski, casting about for a means of uniting the nation in a fight for independence, found everywhere the signs of disunity. They were even brought home to him on the battlefield.

One day he was taken to interview a wounded prisoner and found a handsome boy of eighteen, from the same district as himself, lying in a cart evidently very badly wounded. On questioning him he discovered that he was related to one of his old schoolfellows at Wilno. . . .

"It was terribly painful to me" . . . he wrote later . . . "And still more so when I read through the papers found on him. There was a letter from his mother which breathed deep love and anxiety for her son. But at the same time there were things in it that were new to my ideas of Lithuania. She wrote that she knew from the newspapers that he was already near Cracow, and that therefore he was probably under the command of either General Ruzzski or General Brusilov, both of them heroes for whom prayers were offered daily in church, as defenders of Lithuania. I flung the letter on the table in a passion. I had not yet seen the pious of Lithuania praying for Russians! But the young face of my fellow-countryman, shot by my soldiers, is still before my eyes as a living witness to the moral burden which fell upon Poland and the Poles when war broke out. A cursed consequence of slavery!"

He must at all costs build up a military organization sufficiently powerful and united to carry the claim for independence to a successful issue. He was well aware that nothing but vague promises could be expected from the conservative and Austrophil N.K.N. With his usual custom of "looking truth in the face," to use one of his favourite expressions, he had never considered it as anything but an intermediary in his relations with the Austrian Government. He began to suspend recruiting for the Legions and instead concentrated all his energies on his own organization of the P.O.W. (Polish Military Organization) which offered him a wider scope since it was tied neither to Austria nor Russia. Since its first guerilla campaign against the Russians in the early months of the war it had developed into a powerful instrument with branches all over Poland and many thousands of members, drawn from all classes of the nation. Statistics collected from the various local centres showed roughly a composition of 31% intellectuals, 33% workmen, artisans and employees, and 36% peasants. They were the very spirit of independence in the nation; between them they built up a bulwark of resistance to German and Austrian designs. In an order to them Pilsudski wrote:

"Yours is the hardest post which the Polish soldier can hold. Without banners and without the moral satisfaction of a hand-to-hand fight with the enemy you bear yourselves gallantly, threatened by an invisible army, like a soldier who makes his stand at a post which appears to be lost. If you had failed in this you would have failed in the whole spirit which is making of our national struggle a united struggle, one with the tradition of our fathers. Your courage reconciles me to the heavy lot which has been my part of this war . . . if in this short time I have created what I believed to be an impossibility, the First Brigade, a brave and efficient army without one professional soldier in its ranks, I believe that I can make of you another 'impossibility' . . . a military force under the conditions of secrecy and conspiracy. . . ."

In order to raise the money for training and equipping these thousands of recruits Pilsudski and the officers of his First Brigade voluntarily cut down their pay to 100 crowns a month. They had their reward in the autumn of 1915 when the P.O.W. was able to send its battalion to join the Legions in the field. The new troops went into action for the first time on the Volhynian front and fought gallantly and with success although their young commander Thaddeus Zulinski was killed.

The German occupation of Warsaw in August 1915 made Pilsudski decide to press for a definite answer concerning the independence of Poland. He hurried to Warsaw and took political soundings. The result was unsatisfactory. He had opened up the very question which the Central Powers wished to avoid. Both Germany and Austria had their own reasons for postponing a settlement of the Polish claim. They were agreed on one point, that the fullest use must be made of Poland's man power. In spite of their success the war was already taking toll of their armies, and they could not afford to lose the opportunity of recruiting millions of Poles. But before they could do this they must emancipate them and enlist them as allies. Therein lay the difficulty. Austria would have been willing enough to add the former Russian provinces to Galicia and establish an Austro-Polish-Hungarian empire, but neither Hungary nor Germany would agree to this solution. The Hungarian Government was jealous of its own powers and privileges which might be lessened in a Triple Monarchy; Germany realized that a strong Polish state would upset the Germanization of Prussian Poles. So the Central Powers hedged and prevaricated and Pilsudski could get no answer to his question either one way or the other. In disgust he told the N.K.N. that he considered the political role of the Legions was at an end and that he intended to sign on no more recruits although he would continue to fight at the head of his First Brigade. He returned to the Front and remained there during the latter months of 1915 and the early part of 1916 with the brief intervals for hurried journeys to Lublin, Vienna and Cracow for political interviews and discussions which led to nothing.

.   .   .   .   .

During the year 1915 I was one of the women couriers in the Legion and travelled continually to and fro between the different local centres carrying propaganda and aiding recruiting. It was inevitable therefore that sooner or later I should come under the ban of the German police.

The attitude of the German authorities towards Pilsudski at that time was a compound of surface cordiality and suspicion. With their hide-bound conception of military etiquette they looked upon his First Brigade as an irregular guerilla troop led by a revolutionary, and distrusted his political activities. But as allies of Austria they could not show open hostility to the Legions and were constrained to accept, or at least tolerate, the man who commanded them. On the other hand, they could, and did, use every effort to suppress the P.O.W. on the ground that it was a secret military organization acting against the Government.

At the close of 1915 two-thirds of the country was under German occupation. In Warsaw the Prussian Governor-General, von Beseler, ruled with an iron hand. The Kaiser's secret police poked long inquisitive fingers into every crevice and corner of the city, searching for agitators, as those of the Czar had done before them; the jails were occupied once again by a new batch of political prisoners. Thus it happened that one afternoon in November I arrived at the house where I was staying in the city to find two German police agents waiting to arrest me on a charge of "inciting citizens to join an illegal organization known as the P.O.W."

I was taken to the Paviak prison, now under German administration. It appeared to have changed little since I had last seen it eight years before, except that the jailers wore different uniforms and the corridors were slightly cleaner. I was put into a cell with two other women, both of whom were classified as criminals, although there was no evidence against them. They were, I discovered, victims of the iron system of German justice. Having the misfortune to be married to men charged with various crimes they had been automatically arrested with their husbands and would probably be detained in the prison for an indefinite period. For the first ten days I remained with them locked in a damp cell which was generally in semi-darkness, for the light filtered in through one small grille which took the place of a window. After nightfall we had not even a candle and we used to sit huddled together round the little stove which was our sole means of heating, telling stories to pass the time. Later I was removed to a separate cell which I occupied with one other woman, Madame Klempinska, a political prisoner like myself, and a member of the P.P.S.

The conditions of the prison were much the same as they had been under the Russian regime; the food was little better. Breakfast consisted of a cup of weak tea and a slice of bread without butter; dinner was a plate of kascha; in the evening there was nothing but a cup of boiling water. After my trial, however, I was allowed to have a parcel of provisions sent in by my lawyer, Mr. Pazchalski, and I and my companion in misfortune lived on it for a couple of days. Never did food taste so delicious!

The German court found me guilty of political agitation and ordered me to be put in a detention camp. At the end of a further fortnight in the Paviak I was taken to Szczypiorno, near Kalisz, one of the biggest camps for prisoners of war in Poland.

CHAPTER XVIII

My FIRST impressions of Szczypiorno were discouraging to say the least.

Imagine a windswept, desolate field, knee-deep in mud in many places, crossed and re-crossed by lines of dug-outs in which some four thousand prisoners of war and a hundred civilians were herded together. That was the picture which greeted me when I arrived in the gloom of a bleak December afternoon with Madame Klempinska and four men, Polish civilians, who were also to be interned. Wooden-faced Bavarian soldiers received us from the police who had accompanied us from Warsaw; a young lieutenant ran his finger down a list setting forth our names, occupations and sentences, reeled off a perfunctory warning on the folly of trying to escape and then handed us over to the guards. The four men were marched off in one direction, Madame Klempinska and I in another.

The camp had been originally planned in the form of huts, but at the last moment timber had apparently run short, and there had been a compromise resulting in dug-outs, sunk deep into the earth and topped by a flimsy structure of wood about three feet in height and containing small windows. Seen from the front the effect was rather like rows of doll's-houses.

Madame Klempinska and I crossed the field in a thin drizzle of rain which our guard cheerfully informed us fell nearly every day during the winter months, and descended a flight of wooden steps into a sort of cave. It reminded us irresistibly of a vault and had the same musty, earthy smell. When our eyes grew accustomed to the dim light we saw that it was a comparatively large apartment, divided into two by a trench which was spanned by duckboards, a necessary measure for after days of heavy rain it became like a moat. This primitive accommodation was designed for eighty men but as we were the only women in the camp we had it to ourselves until we were joined by a

young servant girl. It was bitterly cold in those winter days
for the one small stove in the centre only gave out heat within
a limited radius and the icy winds of December curled through
the doors and windows. In one corner were two heaps of sacks
filled with sawdust and covered with army blankets. Our
beds. There was no furniture of any description, not even
a table. For the first few minutes we were too stunned even
to give voice to our dismay, but when the guard returned with
some papers which we were to sign I asked for an interview
with the Commandant of the camp. At first he refused even
to pass on the request, saying that it was against the regulations at that hour of the day, but I was so persistent that
at length he departed, very reluctantly, to consult the officer
on duty. Half an hour later he returned with the message
that the Commandant would see me, after I had been disinfected. He stared at me in blank astonishment when I burst
out laughing and then explained that the process of disinfection was part of the routine of arrival at the camp. A few
minutes later Madame Klempinska and I were initiated
into it.

We were taken into a room where a tall grim-looking German woman divested us of our clothes which she rolled up in
bundles. Then she led us to two small bath tubs which she
proceeded to fill with a very small quantity of water and a
great deal of strong disinfectant. After telling us to get into
them she departed carrying our clothes, and leaving the door
open so that the wind whistled round our naked forms until
I ran shivering to shut it. The process of bathing was the
reverse of pleasant. The atmosphere in the room was almost
glacial, for there were no panes in the windows, and the water
in the baths was almost boiling. Consequently we were alternately chilled and scalded, while the disinfectant stung our
skins until we were the colour of lobsters. After we had endured about fifteen minutes of this the German woman returned bringing two wraps of coarse towelling in which we
were bidden to clothe ourselves until our own garments were
dry. In the meantime she washed our hair in a strong carbolic
lotion which left it as hard and as brittle as straw and so sticky
and unmanageable that it took weeks to recover.

The next process was a hasty examination by the German army doctor attached to the camp, who pronounced us in good health and gave us each a couple of injections for typhus. Evidently the theory of disinfection did not extend to this, for he plunged the hypodermic needle first into me and then into Madame Klempinska without even troubling to wipe it.

While we were undergoing all this our clothes were being disinfected in another room with Germanic thoroughness. Apparently they were dealt with even more drastically than we were for when they were returned to us my blue dress had turned green while poor Madame Klempinska's gloves had shrunk so much that she could not get them on.

The rite of purification having thus been accomplished I was taken to see the Commandant, an elderly man, a Prussian officer of the old school with charming manners. He received me courteously and listened sympathetically to my complaint regarding the quarters which had been allotted to me. The camp, he explained, had not been intended for the accommodation of women prisoners, and we were in fact the first whom he had received there. He had already sent in a request to headquarters for beds and mattresses for us and hoped that they would be forthcoming before long. In the meantime he suggested that I should go round with him next morning and see whether I could find among the unoccupied huts one better than our present one.

With this I was forced to be content, but the night that followed was one of the most unpleasant I have ever lived through. I lay awake hour after hour in the darkness listening to the rats scurrying up and down the planks. The trenches were infested with them, and they grew so bold that they used to run over us as we lay on our sacks. I still shudder at the remembrance of those wet, hairy bodies crawling over my arms and neck! After the first few nights I got into the habit of wrapping my blankets round me so tightly that not even my head was left uncovered. Although the Commandant kept his word and moved us to another hut which was slightly less damp and in time even secured camp beds for us the rats continued to be one of our worst trials.

The days passed slowly for us and we had no means of killing time and no contract with the outside world. In theory we were allowed to receive letters but for some reason or other they never seemed to reach us. During the greater part of a year I only heard once from Pilsudski, yet he wrote to me many times. The absence of news was one of the hardest things to bear. One tortured oneself wondering what was happening. Occasionally one of the guards brought in a German newspaper, which was passed round from hut to hut until it almost fell to pieces. We had only one book, the life of Julius Cæsar. We read it over and over again, from cover to cover.

The prisoners of war were divided into two camps, French and Russian. They had their separate cookhouses and were responsible for cooking their own meals. Although the food which was supplied to them was the same—exceedingly good and in enormous quantities—their manner of preparing it was entirely different, characteristic of the two races. The French, although there were no professional cooks among them, expended time and care on their meals and managed to achieve a very creditable example of the cuisine française. The Russians, fatalistic and indifferent, used to heap everything that was given to them—fish, meat, potatoes, cucumber, or anything else that happened to be going—into one stewpan, put it on the fire and then ladle it out in vast platefuls. Madame Klempinska and I and the little servant used to eat in our own hut but we had to fetch our food from the Russian canteen, and we were so disgusted at the unappetizing mess that was served out to us that we petitioned to be allowed to share the food of the French prisoners. However, official red tape would not stretch so far.

The last weeks of December were inexpressibly dreary. The rain poured down in torrents, filling the trenches and turning the field into a bog. Christmas Eve dawned in an atmosphere of gloom for guards and prisoners alike. Madame Klempinska and I sat crouched over the stove and talked of past Christmases, which is a foolish thing for any one, except the very happy, to do. And so my thoughts went back along the years to Suvalki, and I saw myself as a child again, standing at the window watching the snowflakes spreading a soft, glistening blanket over Grandmother's garden, and searching the sky for the first pale star; the Star of Bethlehem, Aunt Maria had said. Only after it had appeared could the Christmas feast begin, and I was hungry for I had fasted since the night before. In imagination I could hear the laughter and chatter in the kitchen where Anusia and Rosalia were putting the finishing touches to the dishes they had been preparing all day, the twelve symbolical dishes of fish and the sweet cakes filled with honey and spices and poppy seeds. My sisters and I had helped too, strewn fragrant herbs and grasses on the tablecloth in remembrance of the first Christmas that had dawned in a stable, and hung the Christmas tree with sweets and red apples from the garden.

"No, not apples" . . . said Madame Klempinska . . . "Paper dolls. I used to make them for a full month before Christmas, and we had cakes on our tree instead of sweets."

"Toys are the best" . . . said a deep bass voice from the doorway . . . "My father used to carve them out of wood for us in the winter evenings." . . .

It was the tall German sentry who could speak a little Polish and wanted to join in the conversation. So he told us stories of Christmas in his peasant home in Bavaria where he and his brothers had gone out into the forest and cut down a young fir tree to be brought and decorated by the mother with toys and gingerbread and little almond cakes made in the shape of crowns for the Kingdom of the Babe of Bethlehem.

Then we talked of the war and he asked me why the Polish Legions were in it . . . "We hear that they were not mobilized as we were, but that they volunteered of their own free will" . . . he said . . . "My comrades and I have often wondered why. Do you Poles love the Emperor Franz Josef so much then that you would shed your blood for him?"

I explained that we loved our freedom and were fighting for that.

"Ah, that is what the whole world would fight for if we knew how" . . . he answered . . . "The Socialists promised it to us, but I do not believe that we shall get it although I am a Socialist. . . ."

Of the war he seemed to know nothing except where it directly concerned him. For him it was narrowed down to his own officers, his own battalion, the strip of Front on which he had fought the Russians. Of the wider issues he had scarcely even heard. He said in his soft Bavarian German . . .

"Gnädige Frau, I see that you have had much more education than I or any of the men in my regiment, so perhaps you can answer for me a question I have often asked myself. Why precisely are we fighting this War?"

Remembering the Russian prisoners from whom I had so often heard the same words, I thought how heavy was the moral responsibility of the rulers who had sent out those vast masses of men, in blind obedience to destroy one another.

Madame Klempinska and I remained at Szczypiorno until the middle of February, and then we were sent for by the Commandant who told us that he had arranged for us to be transferred to another camp at Lauban, where he believed we should be much more comfortable. Then he said good-bye to us as courteously as though we had been his guests instead of his prisoners. I have nothing but pleasant recollections of this man who was the best type of German—cultured, kind and considerate.

Lauban was a pretty little town in Silesia, surrounded with woods which were carpeted with wild flowers later in the year. In February, however, it was intensely cold and we shivered as we walked between guards across the quadrangle to the women's quarters. It was a mixed camp, consisting of a number of enormous wooden huts holding thousands of prisoners of war and civilians, all separated from one another by wooden palisades. Civilians were in one section, French prisoners of war in another, Russians in a third and two Englishmen had one all to themselves in solitary state. A great many of the civilians were Lithuanians who had been evacuated from villages in the firing line. The women and children, who numbered several hundred, were next to us and to pass the time I gave lessons in Polish to many of them. Our hut housed a curious assortment of types and nationalities: Madame Klempinska and myself, a French governess who had been unable to escape from Warsaw before the German occupation of the city, a beautiful Polish girl, who had been the mistress of a well-known Russian spy and was suspected of being herself an international agent, and another woman who owned a large estate behind the firing line and was married to a Polish officer.

The camp life at Lauban was far more pleasant than at Szczypiorno. We were allowed a certain amount of liberty and could even go to the town to buy what we could get (which was not much) at the local store. It was soon sold out of such luxuries as tinned meat, chocolates, and soap. As the months passed the shortage of food grew serious and rations were cut down more and more drastically both for us and for the soldiers who guarded us. The French prisoners of war suffered the least for nearly all of them had "marraines," under the French war charities scheme, who sent them parcels of food. The German officers were glad to buy chocolate from them, although they were too proud to deal with them directly, and one of the women in our hut, the wife of the Polish officer, used to act as go-between. She was an exceedingly pretty woman, very popular with the gallant Frenchmen. The long conversations which she used to hold with them over the palisade kept the occupants of our hut supplied with news both of the camp and of the outside world. The latter was generally either inaccurate, founded on the gossip of sentries, or stale, taken from newspapers weeks old, but we welcomed it and passed it round among ourselves.

In a community like ours national characteristics asserted themselves strongly. The two Englishmen, true to the proverbial reserve of their race, kept rigidly to their own society, bowed and smiled amiably at their fellow prisoners when they encountered them on their way to town, but resisted all attempts at closer acquaintance. The Russians, almost without exception simple, uneducated peasants, accepted their lot with dreary fatalism but made no effort to get the best out of it. The Frenchmen, many of whom were professional men, lawyers, doctors and clerks, were, on the other hand, philosophical and good-humoured, organized concerts and provided the entire social life of the camp.

The concerts which were held every week were very popular and revealed a surprising amount of talent, although after many months the program grew rather stale. A Polish girl from Lithuania who was well-known on the professional stage used to sing, and the French usually contributed a sketch. But personally I got more amusement out of the grouping of the audience than from the actual program.

This was arranged with the German love of etiquette and social procedure which could even extend to a prison camp. We were all rigidly graded. In the front row were the German officers, in the second the "Bessere Dame" (Better Women) as the occupants of our hut and a few of the Lithuanians were classified. Then came the "bessere" French, which meant French prisoners of war who had been professional men in civilian life. With these were the Russian doctors. (The two Englishmen were conveniently disposed of in a corner which eliminated the problem of their social status.) Behind the "bessere" French were the "ordinary" French, and last of all the "ordinary" Russians, who were a picturesque assembly . . . Cossacks, Kalmuks, tall slender Sartes, handsome Caucasians.

In one hut were several women who were kept apart from the rest, classified, with true Germanic directness, as "prostitutes." Actually only one of them merited the name as a professional. The rest had been forced by starvation to sell themselves in the streets of Warsaw. Two of them had been teachers in private schools which had closed because of the war, another had been a saleswoman in an exclusive dressmaker's shop which had also put up its shutters, a fourth had been secretary to a rich foreign woman who had hurried back to her own country at the first threat of war. Behind each one was an individual tragedy.

Their lot at the camp was unspeakably wretched. They were subjected to countless humiliating restrictions, and were openly insulted by the guards when they went out for exercise. Yet at night the young soldiers used to climb over the palisade into their huts and force them to accede to them. One of them, a girl of seventeen who had been sent for detention with her mother, cried so bitterly when she told me of this nightly degradation that I protested to the German doctor attached to the camp. He seemed surprised at what he evidently thought a most unreasonable complaint, reminded me that the women were prisoners, and that it was wartime. He flatly refused to do anything in the matter. Eventually matters were brought to a head by an open scandal.

We were sitting in our hut one evening when a Lithuanian woman burst in screaming that all the women in Hut Number X were dying. "Number X" was what was officially known as "The Prostitutes' Quarters."

We hurried there and found some of the women writhing in agony while others sat on their mattresses crying. In the extremity of their misery they had broken up the contents of several packets of needles and swallowed them.

We sent one of the guards for the doctor but he came back with the report that he could not be found and that the dispensary was locked. The nearest hospital was miles away and time was precious. We had no medicine or any means of treating the poor women, and we could think of only one remedy. Fortunately the kascha for our evening meal had just been cooked. We fetched great bowls of it and forced it down their throats. It saved their lives for although some of them were very ill they recovered.

Their tragic attempt at suicide was reported to the Commandant of the camp and an inquiry was instituted. As a result the youngest of the girls was, at our request, allowed to come to our hut.

The spring days lengthened into summer and the summer into autumn and still we remained at Lauban. The news from the outer world grew more and more confused. We heard of the collapse of Russia and of German victories on the Western Front. Yet the guards at the camp were withdrawn and replaced by men too old for the firing line; we shivered in the intense cold of September and October because there was no fuel for heating the camp, and every day the food got less. At length our daily ration was a tiny slice of bread made of a mixture of coarse flour and potatoes, and a plateful of turnips boiled in ox blood. We could only bring ourselves to eat it by holding our noses and swallowing it like medicine.

I remember almost weeping with gratitude when one of the prisoners of war who had been working on a neighbouring farm gave me some potatoes which he had secreted in his pocket.

It was difficult to keep one's morale. Even the French lost their cheerful optimism; the German guards were as depressed as the prisoners. But worse than the actual hardships, to me at least, was the continued absence of news. The year 1916 was drawing to its close and month after month had gone by without a letter from Joseph Pilsudski. I had heard, more or less vaguely, from the German soldiers at the camp that he was with his Legions behind the Styr and that the fighting had been very heavy there during the summer. I tried to comfort myself with the thought that if he had been killed or taken prisoner I should have seen it in the German newspapers which reached the camp fairly regularly. I wrote to him many times, but my letters were unanswered. Afterwards I discovered that none of them had reached him. I tried to get in touch with other friends and to obtain news of the different organizations for which I had worked, but with no better success. I could only wait.

Then one evening during the first week of November I was stopped as I was leaving the camp concert by a German officer, a young lawyer who had often shown me small kindnesses. . . .

"I think that this will be your last concert here," he said with a smile.

"Why should it be?" I asked.

"Because you will be free in a day or two. Germany has proclaimed the independence of Poland."

In less than a week I was on my way back to Warsaw.

. . . . .

The year 1916 had been critical for the Central Powers. In July the Russians had rallied unexpectedly and under General Brusilov launched a tremendous offensive which broke the Austrian front. Germany, who needed every man she could conscript for the Western front, had grown alarmed at the demands made upon her to hold up her weak-kneed ally and turned envious eyes on the teeming population of Poland. By some means or other these millions of recruits, fresh fodder for the Russian guns, must be annexed, said Ludendorff. If the price was Poland's independence then it must be paid. No doubt it would cause political complications with Hungary and prove a hindrance to the Germanization of Prussian Poles, but these things could be dealt with after the war. For the present the one essential was victory and it could only be achieved with the aid of more man-power. So German opposition to a free Poland was withdrawn. Austria was urged to participate in a joint policy of conciliation.

Pilsudski in the meantime was waging two wars, one at the front where the Legions were bearing the brunt of the fiercest fighting during the Russian offensive, the other in the political field where he was stubbornly resisting the attempt by the Austrians and the N.K.N. to shelve the question of Poland's independence and absorb the Legions into the Landsturm. He summoned a Council of Colonels at which it was unanimously decided to press once again for a definite answer from Austria and to demand that all the Legions should be united with the status of a Polish army.

In July Brusilov's offensive reached its height, broke the Austrian front and launched a heavy attack on the Polish forces at Kostiuchnowka. For three days the three Brigades of Legions withstood the incessant battering of two divisions of Russian infantry and four divisions of cavalry, and then, in obedience to orders from the Austrian Commander-in-Chief, withdrew in perfect order though their losses in both officers and men had been colossal. They took up new positions on the Stochod, and began to fortify their lines.

For Pilsudski, who had led his troops throughout the battle, the moment was one of mingled pride and bitterness. He was proud of the magnificent bearing his men had shown under the pounding of heavy artillery fire which they had been unable to return, and bayonet charges in which they had been outnumbered by three to one. His Legionaries . . . that "army of amateurs," as the Austrian officers had called them, who had left their university desks and their workmen's benches to follow him in pursuit of a dream, had fought with the valour and sang-froid of veteran troops. But he was filled with bitterness at the thought that the men who had died so gloriously had shed their blood in the interests of foreigners. Of what use their heroic sacrifice if it could not buy the freedom of Poland? Two years had passed since the Polish Legions had entered the war. What had they attained? In his order to the First Brigade on August 6th, 1916, their second anniversary, he wrote . . .

"When I led you out from the walls of Cracow and entered with you the towns and townships of the Kingdom I saw always before me a ghost, risen from the grave of our fathers, the ghost of a soldier without a country. The future alone will show whether we too will go down to history as such, whether we shall only leave behind us the short weeping of women, and long tales told by kinsmen at night. . . ."

With that ghost ever present in his mind he sent in his resignation on July 29th. He did not receive notification of its acceptance until September. The Germans had wished to accept it immediately. Von Beseler, the Governor of Warsaw, had all along distrusted his political activities and urged the formation of a Polish state with recruiting for an army independent of the Legions. But the Austrians, more aware of the extent of his influence, hesitated. Already all the officers of the Legions had sent in a memorial to the N.K.N. demanding to be established as a Polish army, fighting under a Polish provisional government for Polish independence. At Cracow a gold medal had been presented to Pilsudski accompanied by an address with 50,000 signatures. If Poland was to be conciliated the conciliation had better be whole-hearted.

So on November 5th, 1916, with a flourish of trumpets and a great show of magnanimity Poland was proclaimed an independent state "united in friendship and in interests" with both Germany and Austria.

Pilsudski, who had retired to Cracow, heard the news and returned to Warsaw.

The effect of the first proclamation was spoilt by the fact that it was followed within a week by another announcing that the Central Powers would continue temporarily to administer the affairs of the new Polish state, and asking for

Polish soldiers. The reaction was immediate. Only a Polish
Government could order Poles to go to war. The celebrations
were cancelled. Indignant protests arose on all hands. Pilsudski in a letter to the Rector of the University of Warsaw
voiced the general opinion when he wrote . . .

"If my own government ordered me in time of war to
clean boots I would do it without hesitation; if it told me to
enlist in an army of Cingalese I would obey. But on the other
hand, since we have no government of our own, I say without reserve that if I were to go to war it would be to obtain
one for us."

The Central Powers, realizing their blunder, made haste
to rectify it and created a Provisional Council of State which
assembled for the first time on January 14th, 1917. Pilsudski
was one of its members and was given the Army portfolio.
He had no illusions as to the difficulties he would have to
encounter in the post. . . .

"I am afraid of it, even though I want it" . . . he says
in a letter written to me at this time . . . "I am afraid because many heavy and unpleasant burdens will be laid upon
me and once more, sword in hand, I shall have to achieve
practical things, which will not always be understood, which
will make me unpopular. But I want it because I shall have
to fight again, and that is what I love. I want to live more
widely, more comprehending than I have done before." . . .

He returned to Warsaw at the end of December 1916 and
took over his new duties in a modest little office in the city.
He rented the apartment of friends, who were absent in the
country and lived in the simplest manner possible, both from
choice and from necessity, for his salary was a merely nominal
one. There was little but barren glory attached to the post
of Minister for the Army. Of that there was sometimes too
much for his liking. He was astounded at the warmth of his
reception whenever he appeared in public. Without realizing
it he had become a legend. In those first difficult months in
his new office he gained the trust of the populace and the
devotion of thousands of simple people, peasants and working
men.

The women too gave him their unswerving confidence and

loyalty. The flower of patriotism had always grown more hardily among them than among the men of Poland, for since the majority of them did not go out to work they had been less susceptible to Russian influence. They had been the first to recognize the awakening of the spirit of freedom and identify themselves with it. To their support in those days of struggle Pilsudski and his Legions owed much. . . .

"They realized the beauty in the life of the Legionary" . . . he wrote of them, "the pride which had defied the world and sent him out sword in hand to win, if not admiration, at least respect for the Polish soldier. Setting their feet in his footprints they marched behind him." . . .

While he rejoiced at the public's recognition of his beloved Legions his personal popularity caused him nothing but dismay. In a letter to me he writes characteristically:

"I fear this new-born adulation, and I am already becoming enslaved by it. Just as in the past I have lived under the ban of the police I dream now of coming under the ban of the public who always torment their elected favourites. There are sometimes funny scenes and situations resulting from this public interest, but sometimes I get furious and then I have to take consolation from the fact that fortunately my photographs have no resemblance to me, and when I am in civilian dress I am not recognized in the streets or in cafés." . . .

For the first time in his life he, who had so often been, as he said, "under the ban of the police," a fugitive, slipping over frontiers, fleeing from place to place, found honours and compliments showered upon him. His speeches were quoted far and wide, journalists waited to interview him, he was deluged with invitations. It was one of the penalties attendant upon success, but it was a source of distress rather than satisfaction to him for he was not deceived by it. He felt the real loneliness of his position then, as he was so often to feel it later. Intensely sensitive to the reactions of those around him he craved the understanding which is almost invariably denied to the man called to the arduous task of leadership. . . .

"I have always been accustomed to solitude" . . . he writes in another letter to me . . . "and to dreaming and ruminating in my own company. But in this war I think that I must attain the summit always alone, always without companions and without shelter, whether in sorrow and weariness, in the ecstasy of pride or the depth of humiliation. It may sound poetical, but sometimes it is sad to outstrip those around you and find yourself without comrades and friends. I am longing at this moment to take off this uniform and be like a child who laughs and is happy because it does not know the meaning of hate, can say as many foolish things as it wishes and amuse itself without a theatre or stilts.

"I have had a foretaste here in Cracow of what I shall have in Warsaw. I am surrounded with meetings, banquets, formalities, speeches and receptions. I think of it all with the utmost dread, as a terrible ordeal which I am obliged to go through. But imagine what it is to me, who have never been accustomed to all these manifestations of national sentiment. Up to the present I have retained my Lithuanian character which cannot bear ostentation and recoils in protest from making a public spectacle. I never know how to act on those occasions, and sometimes I have a mad impulse to put out my tongue at them all, like a child! Just because of this I have to put on a most severe and forbidding expression when I am greeted with a long speech."

CHAPTER XIX

POLAND'S MUCH-PROCLAIMED independence existed in name
only. Germany and Austria kept a firm hold on the helm
of State. The armies of occupation were flung far and wide
over the country. The Temporary Council of State, which
included among its members many sincere patriotic and able
politicians, was bound hand and foot, permitted to pass no
measure until they had received von Beseler's seal of approval.
Those who had cherished high hopes of freedom were speedily
undeceived.

Pilsudski had not shared their illusions. From the first he
recognized the flimsy structure of the newly-created state, and
saw through the fiction of a free people which Germany would
foster for just as long as it suited her own ends. But there was
at least some basis to work upon. The fiction might eventually
become fact. He would accept the existing situation and endeavour to make the best of it. . . .

"I am a realist" . . . he said in an interview which he gave
to one of the newspapers at this time . . . "I take things as
they are, not as I would like to see them. I strive, as I have
always striven, to look at them without illusion. I profess,
whole-heartedly, the principle of the world's greatest man,
Napoleon. The art of overcoming obstacles is the art of not
regarding them as such. We Poles are unfortunately too prone
to create obstacles. Throughout our history we have always
lacked practical achievement. In a narrow sphere we obtain
good results: outside it we shrink back from every obstacle.
Hence the argument that Poles cannot create." . . .

He had indeed many obstacles to overcome in his task of
building up the army. The Council of State, engrossed in
their own struggle against German influence, could give him
little help. The Polish people having had no army of their
own for a century were not particularly interested in the
formation of one, and reacted coldly to recruiting schemes.

More serious was the question of von Beseler's interference.

The German Governor had decided ideas on the subject of the Polish Army for it figured prominently in his plans. It was in fact the one reason which had made him urge the advisability of giving Poland her independence. Millions of young Poles formed into an army modelled on German lines and led by Germans would be a rival asset for the Central Powers. But between him and that roseate dream stood the one man who was capable of realizing it for him, Pilsudski. Pilsudski, who was resolutely determined to keep his army independent at all costs and was therefore using as its frame not the Legions which were still more or less tied to Austria and Austrophil politics, but the wider, freer P.O.W., the very organization which von Beseler intended to suppress.

From the very start then there was friction, although the German Governor, who was a diplomatist as well as a soldier, was too wise to force an issue. He was well aware that Pilsudski held the confidence of the common people, and that he was perhaps the one man who could call the nation to arms. For the present then he was necessary to Germany's schemes and must be tolerated.

As for Pilsudski: he was devoting the full output of that dynamic energy of his to the task in front of him. On January 17th, 1917, in the presence of the Council of State, he held a march past of all the Warsaw branches of the P.O.W., during which an assurance was given pledging the loyal support of the entire organization and placing all its resources at the disposal of the Government. At the meeting of the Council later that day he was acclaimed by the President and the whole assembly rose to do him honour.

A month later hundreds of representatives from all parts of Poland, gathered in Warsaw for the Congress summoned by the Council of State to discuss co-operation between the Government and the populace, cheered him to the echo when he addressed them on the subject of a national army. In his practical way he told them that the army was as necessary to the state as the state was to the army. . . . "The soldier must have a government if he is to be a soldier and the government must have soldiers if it is to be a government." They

promised him full collaboration. Plans were begun on a rising
tide of enthusiasm.

His success of those early months of 1917 was only a flash
in the pan. Even with promising material to work upon and
with all the goodwill in the world he could do little without
the Government, and the unfortunate Temporary Council of
State was crippled by Germany. As the weeks passed its members grew more disheartened and the nation, which had hoped
great things of it and received nothing, more dissatisfied. The
German Commissioner who took his seat at every meeting
vetoed any real measure of progress. Its debates became a mere
farce and the more sincere politicians among its ranks ceased to
attend them, leaving the road still clearer for German influence. Pilsudski entered the lists again and again in an unequal
contest. He had indeed prophesied truly when he had said that
his appointment as Minister for the Army would mean another fight. During his brief term of office the sword was
never out of his hand. At one moment he was stubbornly resisting von Beseler's Germanization plans. At the next he was
arguing with the Council of State, championing the cause of
his Legions who were receiving insufficient supplies of food
and clothing, even while, at the bidding of Germany, an extensive recruiting campaign was being carried on. . . .

"For my brave Legions" . . . he wrote indignantly to a
friend . . . "I deplore the burden placed on their young
shoulders of fighting for the rights and honour of the nation,
amid a passive people. Still more do I deplore the fact that
I cannot be with them to help bear their heavy cross. Fate
has made me turn politician, but every instinct draws me to
my brothers under arms. Of course, when I speak of soldiers
I do not mean those heroes of the rear who are the curse of
the Polish army in the World War. You ask me about the
P.O.W. From the birth of the Council of State it has stood
to arms, like my Riflemen in August 1914. It is happier than
they, for it can answer the call of its own Polish Government."

In the meantime Poland was caught up in the maelstrom
of world changes. Events were moving in the Great War.
President Wilson had demanded a free and independent
Poland. The Russian Revolution of March 1917 had brought

about the defeat of Czarism. The new government in St. Petersburg proclaimed Polish independence. The hammer blows of
the Allies on the Western Front, coupled with the entry of the
United States into the war, were beginning to turn the scales
against Germany. More troops were urgently needed for the
Kaiser's armies on both fronts. Von Beseler, in response to
promptings from Berlin, pressed the Temporary Council of
State to call up the Polish army to fight under the German
High Command wherever it was required.

Pilsudski protested that such a measure was flatly against
international law which forbade any Power in occupation of
another country to recruit troops from that country for use
in war. The Polish army had no political role, he insisted, it
had been formed for the defence of the country. The Legions
had taken their oath of allegiance to Austria, and had fulfilled it, but that in no way bound them to fight for Germany
to whom they owed nothing.

His words fell on stony ground. The Council of State, that
"dead institution built upon a fiction," as he had called it,
would do nothing.

Von Beseler's project produced an immediate reaction. On
June 17th, P.O.W. severed its connection with the Council of
State. The Legions, with the exception of one brigade,* refused to take the oath which would have bound them to obey
as their Commander-in-Chief the German Emperor.

Pilsudski, as the only army representative in the Council of
State, decided that he could no longer bear his responsibilities.
He was heart and soul in agreement with these men who had
been his comrades-in-arms. He would do them the one service
that lay in his power. He sent in his resignation.

Germany's retaliation was swift. The Legions were broken
up. The Legionaries from Russian Poland were sent to concentration camps; the Austrian subjects were drafted to the
Italian front.

Von Beseler invited Pilsudski to visit him at the Belvedere
Palace. His manner was friendly and disarming. It was absurd that they should fall out, he said, when they were in a
position to aid one another. He had only Poland's interests

---

* The Second Brigade commanded by General Haller.

at heart and, unfortunately, the Poles were so often blind to their own interests, so incapable of seeing wherein lay their advantages. He talked in this strain for ten minutes or more until Pilsudski, who loathed hypocrisy and was growing angry, asked him bluntly what he wanted. . . .

The German Governor, looking pained at so crude a question, explained that Poland, always strictly in her own interests, needed a strong army. Pilsudski could create one for her immediately by throwing in his lot with Germany . . .

"You can be one of the greatest military leaders of to-day" . . . he urged . . . "You have never had a scope wide enough. We will give it to you. You shall have the modern armament you have always wished for, and first-class supplies for your men. As for yourself we offer you whatever you wish, fame, power, honours. If you join us it will be to our mutual gain. . . ."

"You are mistaken" . . . answered Pilsudski . . . "You would gain one Pole, perhaps, but I should lose a whole nation!" . . .

A few days later, on July 22nd, 1917, he was arrested with Sosnkowski and taken as a prisoner to Germany.

.   .   .   .   .

The months between my release from the internment camp at Lauban in November 1916 and Pilsudski's arrest in the following July passed quickly, probably because every hour of the day was filled. I went to work in the office of a factory which dried and packed vegetables. But apart from the necessity of earning enough to pay the monthly bills, which was not easy for prices mounted steadily, there was so much to be done in those wartime years. Many parts of the country had been laid waste in the fighting; the constantly changing fronts had put to flight the civilian populace of first one district and then another, and thousands of people had been rendered homeless. The big cities were full of refugees from the war zones, most of them looking in vain for work. Food was growing scarcer every month, and there were outbreaks of typhus. All these problems had to be dealt with by the various voluntary organizations.

Most of my time was absorbed by the Liga Kobiet. This

was an organization which was formed at the same time as the Strzelcy by a little group of women. During the war its membership increased to about 20,000 and branches were opened all over Poland. Its primary object was the welfare of the Legions and most of its work was carried out behind the lines. In the case of a modern, well-organized and well-equipped army there would be no necessity for it, but in these early days of the Polish Army some sort of provision for the physical comfort of the troops was essential. It was responsible for the running of canteens, the supply and distribution of clothing, and for such details as Christmas parcels and entertainments. It also carried out a great deal of propaganda work.

The linking up of the various branches which were scattered all over the country was no small undertaking in view of the limited transport available in wartime. I had to spend every week-end on journeys which would normally have taken a few hours but which then took the greater part of the day. I shall always remember going to organize the first branch in a village buried in the heart of the country. To my dismay I discovered that the only means of getting there and back was by walking, a distance of twenty-five kilometres each way. Fortunately it was early summer so I was able to set out at daybreak, and reached my destination soon after mid-day. After opening the branch and enrolling the first members I rested for an hour or so and then started on the return journey. The road lay through cool forest avenues and fields carpeted with flowers, and the fresh breeze with its faint tang of pine was so welcome after the close, dust-laden air of the factory that I quite enjoyed the walk. But I was so tired when I arrived home that I had to spend most of the next day in bed.

After Pilsudski's imprisonment I was obliged to give up all social and political work, for I was kept under constant supervision by the German Secret Police who visited me every week, opened all my correspondence and observed my movements. I knew that the barest pretext would be sufficient for my arrest and I did not wish to run the risk of an internment camp again.

My daughter Wanda was born while her father was in a German prison. By an irony of fate the knowledge that one of his dearest wishes in life was to be granted came at a bitter moment.

During those winter months I had many doubts and misgivings because my world was not a very happy place into which to bring a child. A country in the throes of war, uncertain of its destiny, and a life which did not seem to hold out much hope of ease or security; this was the only heritage which I could offer. And I worried, too, because I was forced by necessity to live under conditions which were everything science would have most condemned—long hours of work in a factory, insufficient food, and that generally of the wrong kind. The lack of fuel made cooking at home practically impossible, and I had to eat at one of the communal kitchens, where the staple diet was soup, kascha, and occasionally a little horseflesh. Butter was an undreamed-of luxury, and so was almost every other kind of fat. White flour was unobtainable except to a few smart teashops patronized by the German officers, who demanded their usual supplies of rich cakes and pastries though the populace was reduced to bread made from chaff, which was so coarse and unappetizing that I often went hungry because I could not eat it. But I was more fortunate than most people in Warsaw, for I had at least plenty of vegetables. The director of the dried vegetable factory where I worked, a kind and generous man, instituted at my suggestion a wartime garden for his employees and gave each of us an allotment. There we grew our own beetroots, cabbages and beans, and as I have always loved gardening I spent as much time as I could working on mine, with the result that I was soon producing more than I could eat.

In spite of her mother's fears, my Wanda gave the lie to science, for she was the healthiest and most contented of babies. She came into the world one snowy afternoon in February. I worked until within a few hours of driving to the maternity hospital where she was born, and when she was eleven days old I was back at my desk again. I wanted to bring her up myself and as there were small apartments in the building of the factory where I worked I took one of them. There I had to leave her quite alone for the greater part of the day, securely tucked up in bed. But I used to run along the corridor many times to feed her or to see that she was sleeping properly.

It was absurd how helpless I felt at first when I was confronted with the daily needs of this little human being who could so easily be damaged by my inexpert handling, although I expect many mothers have shared the same feeling. However, I primed myself with various books on the management of babies and a woman friend who had successfully brought up a large family of her own initiated me in the mysteries of the evening bath, which was my worst ordeal. After a while I worked out a daily routine which did not clash with office hours. It was probably unorthodox from an expert's point of view, but Wanda seemed to thrive on it, and grew sturdy and self-reliant. I used to carry her out in the park during my lunch hour every day, and in the evenings when the weather was warm, and on Sundays she was taken for airings by relays of volunteers, for we had many friends, and her chief danger came from too much spoiling.

After several weeks of being transferred from one prison to another, Joseph Pilsudski was finally taken to the citadel of Magdeburg, where he was assigned a suite of rooms which had been recently vacated by a Belgian General, a prisoner of war. It amused him to realize that the German reverence for military etiquette was to be duly observed. The orderlies who waited upon him saluted him punctiliously and treated him with deference, resolved never to forget that although he might be a prisoner he was also a Brigadier, and his quarters were made as comfortable as possible. They consisted of three rooms on the first floor, a bedroom, a dining-room and another room which he called "the salon," although he never received any visitors there.

His isolation was complete. The little garden opening out of his apartment in which he used to walk every day was cut off from the world by the great wall of rock which had been part of the old fortress, an armed sentry paced up and down its asphalt walks, and another stood on guard at the palisade separating it from the main courtyard of the citadel. For nearly twelve months, until Sosnkowski was sent to join him, he saw no one but the guards. For this reason we were unable to carry out the plan which we had formed for his escape. Even his brother was refused permission to visit him and we had therefore no means of establishing contact. He was allowed no Polish newspapers and only one or two letters of the hundreds which were written to him ever reached him. Even the telegram telling him of the birth of our daughter was kept from him and she was several weeks old before he learned of her arrival. It was equally difficult for him to communicate with us. Months after he had been set free the Germans sent me over a hundred letters which he had written to me from Magdeburg. Yet only a very few had reached me during the time he was there. Here is one of them; I suppose it was not intercepted because while so many of the others touched on national events, and on things which would seem of importance in German eyes, this is just the simple letter which any husband might write:

"My dearest Ola,
"I was so glad to have all the details of you and of our child. I laughed so much at the idea of 'bringing her up according to the last word in science and progress!' Although I cannot, unfortunately, have a direct hand in this I am relieved to hear that it is being done! For instance, your last card gave me something to think about for weeks. Le bon Dieu had endowed me with a large share of imagination, but even so I cannot imagine this young lady of two months doing gymnastics on the Müller system every morning, poor little thing, and appearing, as you say, to enjoy it. Has she already learned to laugh?
"I was afraid that was not a very good idea of yours to put Wanda's photograph among the cakes you sent me because I have received neither the cakes nor the photograph. So will you send me another photograph in a letter? I am curious to see what my daughter looks like.
"You would be pleased if you knew how little I smoke at present, partly because of my own decision

and partly because of the lack of cigarettes and tobacco.

"Write and tell me more of the baby. I am grateful for even the most trivial details; as I cannot see her they make me imagine that we are all together."

The solitude and monotony of Magdeburg were not unbearable to him although he fretted at the waste of time. He was never afraid of his own company, and his imagination was so vivid and so pliant that it could people even a prison cell. One afternoon, for instance, was spent in planning an imaginary attack on Wilno, another in drawing up a future constitution for Poland. Much of his time was given to writing. He had always wanted to record some of his wartime experiences. This was his first opportunity of doing so. He obtained writing materials from the prison authorities by telling them that he wished to draw up a formal complaint to the German Government on the illegality of his arrest and that he would require a large quantity of paper as owing to his limited knowledge of German he would have to make many rough drafts. On this pretext they supplied him with sufficient to enable him to write his accounts of Ulina Mala and Marcinkowice, although the manuscripts were almost illegible, for he had to reduce his writing to half its normal size.

In August 1918 the monotony of his imprisonment was broken by the arrival of Sosnkowski. In a letter to me, which is dated September 3rd, he describes their daily routine. . . .

"This is to tell you that I have not been alone since last week. They have given me Sosnkowski to share my lot, and the hours seem to pass more quickly. We have managed to have several games of chess, and we have been allowed to go for walks together behind the walls of the citadel. I should like to have some civilian clothes for these walks, a jersey and overcoat if it is possible for you to send them. At present our life is organized in this way: dinner and supper are sent in to us from the town, and breakfast and tea we have to prepare ourselves. We are both getting quite resourceful in this, but we must not let our supply of tea and sugar run out. You will know what we need.

"At last I have received the photograph of Wanda. From what you had told me I had expected her to be more like me. So far I can only trace my high forehead which I fear will not be an advantage to a girl! I am looking forward to seeing the other photograph which you have promised to send me when the young lady is older and has more definite features. This one is all big eyes very wide open, and looking rather afraid of life. You tell me that she has not been well and that you have not yet gone to the country. You must go. I was so happy to think of you with Wanda and our friends in the fresh country air. . . ."

In Warsaw the year 1918 sped by on the wings of unrest. The hand of Germany which had held the tortured country in a vice was beginning to tremble and relax its grip; already the end was in sight. The German troops in occupation were constantly being recalled and replaced by others, generally by men convalescent from wounds received on the Western Front. The officers had lost their élan. They no longer swaggered through the streets, forcing the civilians to step off the sidewalk for them. They sat dejectedly in the cafés instead of in noisy groups drinking to their successes. Their men looked utterly weary and half-starved, which indeed they were.

As the autumn waned a gathering current of revolt began to spread through the country. The peasants getting in the harvest sturdily refused to give up their grain. The soldiers sent to collect it were too dispirited and indifferent to enforce their orders. In the big industrial cities there were clashes between the workers and occupying troops, and many were shot on both sides. Von Beseler and his staff fled before the storm leaving their subordinates to face it and enforce what discipline they could.

October passed into November. The death-knell of Imperial Germany sounded and hope was reborn in Poland. One name began to be on every one's lips. Pilsudski. The handful of Legionaries who had escaped imprisonment flung it backwards and forwards joyously amongst themselves as they came out

Letter written by Pilsudski from Magdeburg Prison

of hiding, put on their uniforms, and paraded the streets . . .
"We shall have our Commandant back again" . . . "Dziadek
(Grandpapa) will put things right for us!" . . . The loyal
P.O.W., the railwaymen and factory workers and students,
echoed it back . . . "We want Pilsudski" . . . The common
people for whom he had worked and fought through many
thankless years caught it up, cried with one voice, "Pilsudski
for Poland. . . ."

The wave of popular opinion reached the Council of Regency which had been set up by the Central Powers and
which was now tottering. The members began to remind one
another that Joseph Pilsudski, whether one had or had not
agreed with his politics, had never feared responsibilities, and
that Poland's urgent need was a strong man to shoulder the
burden of government. Notes were sent to Germany asking
for his release.

Pilsudski used to tell the story of how a grinning orderly
entered the "salon" in Magdeburg where Sosnkowski and he
were playing chess one evening and held out a copy of the
German illustrated newspaper *Die Woche*. In it was a photograph of Pilsudski, "The New Polish Minister of War."
They laughed over it for a moment and then went back to
their game. Neither of them took it seriously. But a few
days later they were taking their usual walk in the garden
when they were approached by two German officers in mufti,
who gave them the astounding news that they were free and
were to start immediately for Berlin whence they would catch
the train to Warsaw. With some embarrassment they explained
that a revolution had broken out in Magdeburg and asked them
to wear civilian clothes and to take as little luggage as possible
to avoid attracting the attention of the crowds who were
demonstrating in the streets.

Bewildered at the sudden turn of events, understanding
only that they were going back to Warsaw they hurriedly got
together a few necessities for the journey. Sosnkowski flung
on an overcoat and packed a small bag; Pilsudski, who had
no civilian clothes with him, was obliged to travel in his uniform of the Legions, and with a comb, toothbrush and cake
of soap wrapped in a newspaper parcel which he stuffed

into his pocket. Even his precious manuscripts representing the toil of so many weeks were left behind to be sent on afterwards by the Germans.

The two officers accompanied them to the bridge spanning the Elbe where a couple of motors were waiting. A few minutes later they were all speeding along the road to Berlin.

Parts of Germany were already in the throes of revolution, but Berlin was comparatively quiet. The train to Warsaw had been cancelled, however, and they were obliged to spend the night in a hotel where they were the guests of their escort. They were awakened next morning by the sounds of shouting in the streets and the waiter who brought their breakfast told them that the Kaiser had abdicated.

To their amazement the two ex-prisoners were invited to lunch by a representative of the Foreign Office, and Pilsudski was amused at the way in which he was addressed as "Your Excellency" and given ministerial honours. His host made it abundantly clear in fact that he was deliberately paving the way towards Germany's future relations with Poland. On their way to the station afterwards they passed through streets almost blocked by crowds of demonstrators waving red flags, but they were allowed to get into the special train which was to take them to Warsaw without any trouble.

Meanwhile in Warsaw the whole city was seething with excitement. The German occupation had cracked like ice, suddenly. The German soldiers, abandoned by most of their senior officers and with no orders, roamed about the streets, dull-eyed and hungry, and surrendered their arms without a fight. One saw the strange spectacle of men in the uniform of the best German regiments handing over their rifles and revolvers to civilians. Fatigue and privations had sapped their morale, the only thing that concerned them was the problem of where they were to go, to which no one seemed to have an answer.

I was living in rooms in one of the suburbs of Warsaw at that time and there Wanda and I waited for her father. I did not want to go to the station to meet him for I knew that the first hour or two must be given over to official business.

He arrived at Warsaw just before noon and was met by Prince Lubomirski, who was one of the members of the Regency, and Commander Koe of the P.O.W. For days there had been crowds at the station watching every train for him, and the news of his coming spread like wildfire through the city. Thousands of people lined the streets to cheer him as he drove to Prince Lubomirski's house for luncheon.

As soon as he could escape he came to me, but the news of his arrival had even reached our suburb, and as it was Sunday afternoon hundreds of factory workers turned out to welcome him. They lined the streets outside the house where I was living and stood waiting patiently in the rain for hours. When at length his carriage drew up at the gate they almost mobbed him.

Knowing that he hated publicity as much as I did, and not wanting our meeting to take place in the sight of so many curious eyes, I remained upstairs, so the door was opened to him by one of our friends, an elderly lady weighing 210 pounds. On seeing him she was so carried away by her emotion that she rushed out on to the step and flinging her arms round him kissed him many times, to the amusement of the crowd who had not expected such an anti-climax. I heard a great roar of laughter, followed by his familiar light step in the hall.

I had been afraid that Wanda would be shy and give him an unfriendly reception, but apparently in the first few seconds of their acquaintance she made up her mind to love her father. She regarded him gravely, head a little on one side, and then held out her arms to him with a radiant smile. The picture of that meeting is one which I shall always keep.

He could not stay long for urgent affairs demanded his presence in Warsaw, so he took a room at a simple little boarding-house in the city which was kept by a member of the P.O.W. and remained there until he moved into his official residence at the Belvedere Palace. It was long after midnight when he retired to his room on that first night, but there were still crowds in the street waiting under his window. They would not disperse until he spoke to them. His heart was too full for speech, but he told them simply of his happiness at being back among them, and then advised them to go home to bed before they caught cold in the rain.

It was indeed an hour of great joy to him. He was back in Warsaw again, in that free Poland for which he had worked since his boyhood, and he knew that at last he held the confidence of his own people. Yet I think that in all that day of triumph no moment was so sweet to him as when he felt Wanda's arms thrown round his neck.

CHAPTER XX

THE INDEPENDENT Polish State had been born, but it was so frail an infant that its survival seemed problematical. Pilsudski, waking on the morning after his return to Warsaw, that fateful morning of Monday, November 11th, 1918, realized that the hardest fight of his life was still in front of him.

In France the echo of the last gun had quivered into silence. The diplomatists were composing their speeches for the conference table. Joyous crowds all over the world were celebrating the end of the war. But to Poland the peace that had come so tardily to Europe was only a mockery. She was free indeed, because the hands that had held her down had lost their strength. They had left her mangled and bleeding, to pick herself up out of the dust and heal her wounds. Her fair fields were laid waste, her cities were in ruins, her people worn down and wearied by a war which had never been their war and which had left them with neither the exaltation of the victor nor the claim to pity of the vanquished. Her boundaries were still undetermined; enemies surrounded her on every side. Thousands of German soldiers, far outnumbering any Polish force that could be opposed to them, were still in the country, unable to return to Germany owing to the lack of transport. Trotsky and his Bolsheviks were waiting the opportunity to strike: step by step, as the Germans withdrew farther from the Russian frontier and in the direction of their own land, the Russians began to advance into Polish territory, loudly proclaiming their intentions of conquering the world and aiding the Socialists in Berlin. The Ukrainians were harassing the Galician frontier. Volunteers were holding them back at Lwow. Silesia and Pomerania were still in the hands of the Germans. The Czechs were preparing to occupy Cieszyn. And the entire force which Pilsudski, who had taken up the burden thankfully laid down by the Regency, could put into the field against all these enemies consisted of three thousand Legionaries and fifty thousand men of the P.O.W.! Afterwards he used to say that he had never dared in those days to look too far ahead into the future! Through the whole of that difficult year he could only walk slowly and patiently, a step at a time.

The most pressing problem confronting him was that of the German soldiers. Deserted by von Beseler and their officers of high rank they had formed their own Soldiers' Council in Warsaw. It was attempting to cope with the situation, but in the meantime the men, demoralized and growing out of hand, were a menace to themselves and to the Poles. So on that day of the eleventh of November when wounds were smarting Pilsudski assembled them, and because he was also a soldier and his heart went out in sympathy to these men who had fought bravely, been defeated, and were now left bewildered, without a leader, he made them an appeal which they could understand. . . .

"German soldiers" . . . he said . . . "I speak to you as a State prisoner of your late Government. That Government drove you to the brink of the abyss, but you have taken the reins into your own hands and have established a Soldiers' Government of your own. You are spent by nearly five years of bloody warfare. Your new Government, your Soldiers' Government, aims at bringing you happily to your homes, to your wives and children, to your fatherland. Remember that this can only be done if you give absolute obedience to your new authority. Around you is a people whom your late Government treated with unqualified brutality. On behalf of the Polish people, I tell you that they would not, and will not, avenge the sins of your Government upon yourselves. Remember that blood enough has flowed; let not another drop be shed. I have heard that German soldiers are selling their carbines and machine-guns to the dregs of the people on the outskirts of the town. Remember that a soldier does not traffic in his arms. I ask you to bear yourselves with perfect calm, to provoke no more the Polish people, and you will return as one man to your fatherland. . . ."

Outside the building hundreds of Poles had gathered, having heard the German Soldiers' Council was meeting. It was a crowd remembering old wrongs, vibrant with emotions that could easily become hostile. But when Pilsudski appeared on the steps the tension was broken and they cheered him enthusiastically. Sensing the atmosphere he spoke to them. . . .

"In this building the German Soldiers' Council is in session. It commands all the German detachments stationed in Warsaw. In the name of the Polish people I have taken it under my protection. You must offer no offence to any of its members. I know the bitterness which this occupation has left amongst us, but I ask of you all not to let yourselves be carried away by anger and vengeance. You must show the calm and the restraint of a nation with a great and glorious destiny. . . ."

The people dispersed contentedly. What might have been an awkward situation was saved. Within a week the German forces had left Warsaw, peacefully and without incident.

Pilsudski next turned his attention to Lwow, which was hard pressed by the Ukrainians. The defenders, a mere handful of Legionaries and a volunteer force, many of whom were only college boys, were putting up an heroic resistance. Almost the entire population of the city was under arms; even the women had mobilized to guard ammunition dumps and bring up supplies, a few of them were actually fighting in the ranks side by side with the men. But the siege had been going on for weeks and it was evident that unless help was forthcoming the exhausted citizens would be compelled to surrender.

With the small force at his command Pilsudski could do little, but that little he did immediately. He sent one of his old Legionaries with a couple of regiments and three batteries of heavy artillery to the relief of the city. The plan succeeded. The Ukrainians, believing the Polish troops to be the vanguard of a much larger force, withdrew, and although they returned to the attack the respite allowed the defenders, who were now reinforced by some two thousand fresh troops and a quantity of supplies, to strengthen their fortifications in preparation for a long siege.

In the meantime Pilsudski, in Warsaw, was concentrating all his energies on the political situation. The Council of Regency, despairing of reconciling the different parties, had decided on November 11th to dissolve and had invited him to form a National Government and take over the organization of the army. He accepted the invitation, although with reluctance, for he was at heart no politician. Only the fear that the frail structure of the new State would be rent by hopeless wrangling and indecision made him take over the responsibility. A few days later he issued a decree declaring himself temporary Chief of State, accountable for the government of the country until a Diet assembled. It was a position calling for the utmost delicacy of touch. If he held the reins too lightly they would drop from his hands and Poland would be delivered over to quarrelling factions: if he pulled them with too much force the people themselves would rebel. The nation was widely divided in politics. There were three separate governing bodies: one which had been set up in Posen, another in Lublin, formed on November 7th, and a third in Cracow. Not one of these Governments could be considered the voice of the country, but collectively they might produce a basis of unity. Pilsudski, realizing the danger and folly of party strife at a moment when the very existence of the State was threatened by foes from without, when an army must be formed with all possible speed and an economic system created, summoned representatives of all the different parties and endeavoured to reconcile them. The attempt was a failure. . . .

"I listened to them for two nights and a day" . . . he wrote later . . . "It was terrible. Each one had his own views on the question of government, which were entirely different from those of the rest, and clung resolutely to them. None would make any concessions to the rest, or lend themselves to the formation of a Cabinet. . . ."

It was incomprehensible to him that the glorious realization of the long-dreamed freedom should be marred by petty political differences . . . "In several weeks" . . . he was forced

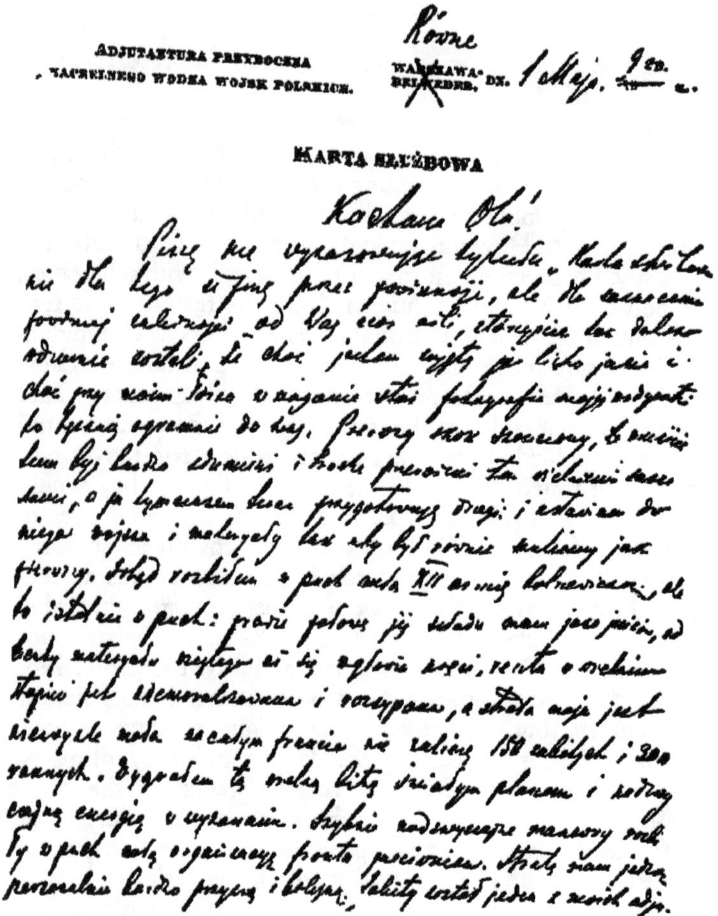

ADJUTANTURA PRZYBOCZNA
NACZELNEGO WODZA WOJSK POLSKICH.

Równe
~~WARSZAWA-BELWEDER~~, DN. 1 Maja 1920 R.

KARTA SŁUŻBOWA

Kochana Olu!

Letter written by Pilsudski from his Army Headquarters

to admit in bitter disillusionment . . . "I did not meet one man, one group or one party not carried away by an absorbing megalomania. . . ."

Faced with the utter impossibility of uniting a large national body he decided to act on his own initiative. He therefore constituted a government under the presidency of a Socialist, Daszynski, who had been President of the Lublin Government, which was thus liquidated. It was a purely provisional measure, designed to meet the urgent need for legislation, pending the creation of a Legislative Assembly, which could be representative of all parties.

The road to political unity was blocked mainly by the National Democrats. Roman Dmowski, Pilsudski's opponent in many a battle, had entered the lists once more. Since the outbreak of the Great War their paths had diverged even more widely. While Pilsudski had been leading his First Brigade against the Russians, labouring to create a Polish army in Warsaw under the German occupation, and pacing the walled garden of his prison in Magdeburg, Dmowski too had been fighting, though in a different fashion, for his weapon was a persuasive tongue. For some time he had been endeavouring to win the favour of the Allies, and as he had a great aptitude for personal propaganda, whereas Pilsudski had none, it was not altogether strange that he should have succeeded in convincing them that he and his National Democrats represented the real Poland, while Joseph Pilsudski was merely a leader from the Left, who had secured the hearing of the mob in Warsaw.

The Armistice then found Dmowski installed in Paris with his Polish National Committee, enjoying the confidence of Maréchal Foch and the other allied leaders, and having also gained a considerable following in the United States.

During that first momentous week of his return to Warsaw Pilsudski, realizing the importance of obtaining recognition for the new-born State, sent wireless messages to the victorious Allies, to Germany, and all the other Powers, notifying them that an independent Polish State had been restored, that its constitution would be founded on a basis of democracy, and defining the territories of the country which would be known

henceforth as "United Poland." To Maréchal Foch he sent
at the same time a special appeal asking for the transfer of
the Polish force which was then serving under the supreme
command of the French army. This force, numbering 430
officers and nearly 17,000 men, commanded by General Haller,
was controlled by the Polish National Committee in Paris
which the Entente Cordiale had formally recognized as representing the people of Poland.

Possibly Foch, practical realist, did not wish to add to his
responsibilities by embroiling himself in Polish politics, more
probably he was influenced by Dmowski, but whatever the
reason Pilsudski's request remained unanswered.

The news of this initial setback caused keen disappointment
in Warsaw. At a moment when Poland was in such grave
peril from her enemies even this small force, consisting as it
did of well-trained and experienced troops, would have given
valuable support. But the Allied decision could only be accepted.

In the meantime the National Democrats in Poland flatly
refused to collaborate with Daszynski and therefore Pilsudski,
determined to get together a constitution at all costs, appointed
a more moderate Socialist, Mr. Moraczewski, who succeeded
in forming a Cabinet composed of both Socialists and Radicals.
A few days later a Bill was passed granting equal rights in
franchise to both men and women. Pilsudski supported it
strongly. The women who served with the Legions, the
P.O.W. and other organizations during the war, he said, had
carried out work as important as that of the men. As they
had shared equal dangers in liberating the country they were
entitled to have an equal voice in its ruling.

The elections for the Diet were fixed for January 20th,
1919. Pilsudski ignored the signs of tension and the violent
squabbles of the rival parties, calmly confident that the good
sense of the great mass of the people would triumph. To all
the warring factions he had one answer . . . "You claim to
represent the opinion of the whole country. Only the elections
can decide that. . . ."

As the polling day drew nearer the disunity became still
more apparent. In addition to the non-Polish minorities, Jews,

Ruthenes, White Russians and others, there were some dozen political parties, each with a different program. All of them sent their deputations to Pilsudski. The National Democrats complained querulously of the growing power of the Socialists, wanted them excluded from the Cabinet. He answered that a nation could not be governed by one class alone; all must be represented. The Social Democrats demanded housing reforms, shorter hours and better working conditions. He told them that the regulations of economic conditions in Poland could only keep step with the rest of Europe, but that the Government intended to organize public work for the unemployed. The Peasants' Party and his old party, the P.P.S., supported him warmly, although some of the latter accused him of abandoning Socialism.

It was not a question of abandoning it, he replied, and reminded them that he had already put into practice the entire minimum program of the party, but the time had come when Poland must choose between the constructive socialism of the Western democracies and the destructive doctrine of Bolshevism, based on class hatred which would pull down the whole of civilization if it continued to spread. He appealed to them for the sake of their past loyalty to unite with him in building up the State which they had fought so long to liberate. . . .

"My greatest ambition is that Poland should have her first parliament, and that it should meet peaceably" . . . he told them.

To achieve national unity he was willing to sacrifice any personal considerations. He sent a delegation to Roman Dmowski as representative of the National Committee in Paris urging him for the sake of Poland to join forces at the Peace Conference. . . .

"Remembering our long acquaintance" . . . he wrote to him . . . "I am expressing the hope that under these circumstances, and in so grave an hour, some Poles at least, if not alas! all, will rise above cliques and party differences. I desire most sincerely to see you amongst them. . . ."

At the same time he invited Ignatius Paderewski, the great Polish pianist and composer, to hold the office of Prime

Minister. Paderewski accepted the offer and immediately left Paris for Warsaw. I remember that when Pilsudski first told me of this I was rather surprised at his choice until he explained his reasons. Paderewski, he pointed out, had a supreme reputation both in Europe and across the Atlantic. From the point of view of propaganda abroad, of which Poland stood badly in need, no man could be more suitable. Within the country he was not only universally beloved but he also possessed the merit of being known as a patriot but not as a party politician. The first National Government would obviously have to walk warily if peace was to be maintained between the rival parties, and Paderewski with his enormous personal popularity would be less likely to rouse hostility than any one else. The national pride in him would ensure him the co-operation and goodwill of all factions.

The opening of the Diet was fixed for February 1919, but before that there was an incident which threatened to crack the thin ice covering the political undercurrent. A section of the National Democrats attempted a *coup d'état* which was, fortunately, foiled at the last moment. Since November 29th Pilsudski had been in residence at the Belvedere, a large and gloomy palace. It was only very lightly guarded, for where his own personal safety was concerned my husband took no special precautions, even after there had been more than one attempt on his life. He used to laugh aside all fears for his safety and would go about freely and confidently amongst every type of crowd.

On the night of January 4th a plot to seize him and overthrow the Government was revealed and in consequence several armed men were caught as they entered the palace and put under arrest. Later three of them, a young man named Count X . . . and two others, were allowed to return on parole to their homes in the city for the purpose of arranging their affairs. In the meantime certain members of their party had made preparations for their escape and only waited their arrival. Two of the prisoners immediately availed themselves of them and were soon over the frontier, but Count X . . . refused to leave and instead returned to the military

authorities and surrendered to his parole. He said nothing of
the proposed escape and it was only some time later, through
the arrest of another man, that the story became known. When
it reached Pilsudski's ears he was quick to appreciate a man
who set so high a value on his word that he preferred to risk
a heavy sentence sooner than break it, even though that man
was his adversary. He used all his influence in obtaining a
pardon for the Count. It was the beginning of a long and
cordial friendship between them.

· · · · ·

At three o'clock in the afternoon of February 10th, 1919,
the Diet assembled for the first time.

The whole city of Warsaw was *en fête* for the day. Flags
were flying, bands playing. Crowds paraded the streets, laughing, singing patriotic songs, carried away on one great tide
of enthusiasm, in the realization that at last Poland's reproach
among nations had been taken away. We were once again a
free people with a parliament of our own.

The public gallery was crowded hours before the ceremony; hundreds of people had fought for admission. Cabinet
Ministers and members filled the benches in the centre, facing
a platform draped with the national flag. Just before the hour
struck a hush fell over the whole assembly, and I remember
wondering whether the people around me were feeling even
as I was the unseen presence of all those who had lived and
fought and shed their blood to give us this victory. Surely at
this moment we must be one spirit with that long chain of
patriots stretching back through the centuries, those thousands, whose very names had been forgotten, who had fallen
in the Insurrections or died in the snows of Siberia because
they had so loved the dream of this freedom which for us
had become reality.

· Then I heard a burst of cheering from the crowds outside
and a moment later Joseph Pilsudski took his place on the
platform to open the Diet. He wore the simple blue uniform
of the Legions and behind him were four aides-de-camp. He
had chosen them carefully, from the pick of his men, and each

one of them was surrounded by the glamour of some act of
special gallantry. He had always a shrewd appreciation of
the value of popular appeal, and he knew that to arouse the
pride of the Polish people in their army and in their new
State was the first step towards restoring national self-respect
which had been crushed by long slavery. For that same
reason he was insistent, in those early years of independence, on the scrupulous observance of State ceremonies and
procedure, not where he was concerned—he was always the
same, simple, unassuming and approachable—but towards the
President, the Premier and others holding high official
rank.

His speech at the opening of that first Diet was a plea
for constructive effort and for a sane and moderate policy
at home and abroad . . .

"A century and a half of fighting has been crowned by
this day of triumph. A century and a half of dreams of
a free Poland have ended in realization. The nation is
celebrating to-day a great and happy occasion, following
on a long and bitter night of suffering." . . .

Although she was surrounded by enemies Poland would
not yield a single foot of her soil, he declared, and
added . . .

"In our foreign relations there is one ray of hope, the
tightening of the bonds of friendship which unite us with
the Entente Powers. There has long been the closest sympathy between Poland and the democratic peoples of Europe and America, who do not seek glory in the conquest
and oppression of other nations, but base their policy on
the principles of right and justice. This sympathy has increased since the victorious armies of the Allied Powers
in breaking the last vestige of the power of our oppressors,
have freed Poland from her servitude. . . ."

At the end of his speech he tendered his resignation as
Temporary Chief of State.

"I confess that I was a proud man when having broken
down a thousand obstacles, I could hand my power to the

first parliament of reborn Poland" . . . he said later. But the Diet would not accept it from him. He was unanimously re-elected. The deputies of all parties cheered him with one voice as he left the hall.

The United States had given full recognition to the independent Polish State on January 30th, 1919. Before the end of February the other Allied Powers followed suit.

Pilsudski could now take stock of the position.

Poland was free. Her first parliament had met and reached unity at least over the main essentials. So much had been accomplished within three months of his having . . . "Taken the helm of the Polish ship of State" . . . as he said. But so much more remained to be done. Overwhelming difficulties confronted him. The process of establishing a constitution in a nation unused for centuries to self-government, and with no legislative traditions: of reconciling the mixed populations of the border districts . . . Lithuanians, White Russians, Ukrainians and Jews. The labour of slowly building up a country without an exchequer and without resources, and at that a country ravaged by years of warfare. France and Belgium had at least received reparations for the suffering inflicted on them; Poland, who had been the cockpit for three warring nations, was left to repair her own losses. Many of her towns were half demolished, nearly two million houses had been destroyed, 40% of her roads were ruined; 13% of her rich, cultivated fields were laid waste. Her industries were almost at a standstill, her populace reduced to sullen apathy by unemployment, privation and a virulent epidemic of typhus.

These were the obstacles which Pilsudski had to surmount. He set to work slowly and patiently, tackling them one by one.

He turned first to the problem of organizing the army. With enemies attacking the newly created State on all sides this was becoming increasingly urgent. The half-starved Bolshevik hordes were advancing further and further into the country. In Galicia desperate fighting was still going on between Poles and Ukrainians. Lwow, which had been relieved by the small force of Legionaries was still in the hands of the defenders, but the Ukrainian troops were ravaging the surrounding country. Poles and Germans were still opposing one another in the Poznan district. Unless an army could be raised without delay Poland was doomed.

To create an army at a moment's notice, without money and without equipment, seemed on the face of things impossible, but Joseph Pilsudski had so often been forced to build with broken tools. He used to pace up and down his study at night, planning and calculating. How to raise a division in one district; how to arm one in another; how to keep the training schools going; how to budget the officers' pay; how to make the Government give a willing sanction to this or that expense; how to make the nation understand that an army cannot be fed and clothed and housed on air.

At the end of two months of worrying, and organizing and breaking down obstacles, he had a force of more than 100,000 strong. It was composed of members of the P.O.W., the remnants of the Legions, Polish soldiers who had been conscripted during the war into the Russian, Austrian or German armies and a number of volunteers. Officers were appointed and training was begun. Gradually the road became easier. Arms, transport wagons, field telephones and other equipment were taken over from the German troops who were returning to their own country. An extensive recruiting campaign had successful results. By the spring of 1919 there were some 200,000 men at his disposal, and these were augmented later in the year by the return of the two Polish forces which had been serving in Russia, one which had made its way back from Murmansk in the extreme north, and the other from the south where it had been fighting against the Bolsheviks. These fully trained and experienced troops were naturally a great asset in the organization of the new army, which was further strengthened in April by the arrival of General Haller's army, which had at last been sent back from Paris with the benediction of the Entente.

To transform these diverse forces into an harmonious, smoothly-running military machine was no small undertaking, and it was rendered still more difficult by the lack of uniformity in the training of the officers. The Russian military system was entirely different from the Austrian, and consequently the officers who had trained in the Russian military schools had one conception of technique and strategy and those who had served in Galician regiments had another. Again, the combination of German-trained officers accustomed to the mental rigidity of Potsdam, and men promoted from the free and easy democracy of the P.O.W. and the Legions was not always successful.

"My studies have shown me that the Prussian system is unsuited to modern life" . . . Pilsudski wrote . . . "The whole foundation of the army should be the soldier. The Prussian system created a caste of officers separated from society by a Chinese wall and from their soldiers by a precipice. The fate of their army has proved that the fundamental principle of the army is the spirit of the soldier. When this spirit is strong the army is strong and will undergo the most severe tests; when it is broken the loss of the army is inevitable. . . ."

Twenty years afterwards the truth of his theory was demonstrated by the very men he had trained in it; when the defenders of Warsaw and the garrison of Westerplatr fought on day after day in spite of colossal odds, sustained only by that unquenchable spirit.

.   .   .   .   .

While the Allied statesmen round the Conference table of Versailles argued and debated Poland's frontiers and sought a solution to the Danzig deadlock, Pilsudski was concentrating on the more pressing problems of the new state. Foremost among them was the question of blending into one country the lands which for more than a century and a half had been split up into German, Austrian and Russian territories. While the people themselves had retained their national characteristics and remained fundamentally unchanged under the rule of their respective Partitioning Powers, their constitutions had undergone drastic alterations. The Polish provinces of Germany, Austria and Russia had been governed by entirely different legislation. Now with the uniting of the severed nation there arose the necessity of drawing up a uniform legal code, a work which involved years of patient research since every existing law in the three territories had to be carefully adjusted in order to avoid the risk of endless litigation.

Even more complicated was the question of the different foreign minorities of the frontier districts . . . Jews, Ukrainians, White Russians and Lithuanians.

Lithuania in the north had been bound by the closest ties to Poland since the days when Jagiello, the Lithuanian Grand Duke, had married the Polish Princess Jadwiga and founded the dynasty which gave Poland her greatest power and her greatest influence abroad. The Jagiellonian kings ruled all Hungary and the land of the Czechs, and the splendour of the Renaissance which spread throughout Europe reached its zenith in the Polish-Lithuanian State. The history of the two countries had been as one until the time of the Partitions, and Pilsudski, who had been born in Lithuania and loved best of all cities Wilno, where his boyhood had been spent, dreamed of reviving that heart-to-heart collaboration of the past. Between him and that dream stood the menace of Bolshevism, the sinister shadow spreading not only over the little states which had been created republics since the Great War . . . Estonia, Latvia and Lithuania . . . but to Poland and beyond to the west of Europe.

He was too true a disciple of Socialism which lies at the root of all democracy to cherish any illusions regarding Bolshevism. When Lenin himself had expounded his creed to him years before he had rejected it. He stated the case against it in an interview which he gave in 1919 . . .

"Bolshevism is a disease which is peculiar to Russia. It will never grow deep roots in any countries which are not entirely Russian. In those countries which formed part of the ancient Russia, but where the social organization is not definitely Russian, such as Poland, Estonia, the Ukraine, Bolshevism may flourish for a while but it will never be master.

"The whole base of its teaching is class vengeance. The ideal of Socialism is complete equality in rights and in laws, but Bolshevism aims at something else. It aims at overthrowing the old regime; its principal plan is the rule of the proletariat, and the oppression of those under whom it has lived hitherto, for it is born of the old Russian social regime in which men were vilely treated by their masters. . . ."

He was convinced that the only means of averting disaster to Europe from this new and dangerous evil of Bolshevism was to make a united stand. He believed that if Poland and the neighbouring small Powers formed an alliance on terms of equality they could conquer through unity, even as their forefathers had conquered centuries before when they had defeated the Teutonic Knights at Grünwald. He put forward tentative suggestions for this scheme but they met with immediate opposition from certain of the Allied statesmen, notably Mr. Lloyd George.

In the meantime Lithuania was in the power of the advancing Bolsheviks and Pilsudski decided to take matters into his own hands. If the rest of Europe would do nothing but avert their eyes in horror from the massacres going on in Russia, and hope piously for the ultimate victory of the White Army, he at least would. He began to plan the occupation of Wilno.

On the 8th of April, 1919, he wrote to Wassilewski, his representative on the National Committee in Paris:

"I hope that in the near future I shall be able to throw a little light on the political situation concerning Lithuania. You know my views in this respect. I will not be either an Imperialist or a Federalist while I cannot speak with some authority—in other words a revolver in my pocket. Since chatter about the brotherhood of nations, and American doctrines seem to be winning the day, I willingly take the Federal side."

He had been sounding Sir Esme Howard, who was representing the Entente in Poland, on the subject of a Polish effort to form an alliance with the Baltic countries. Sir Esme, however, maintained that the chief obstacle would be the Lithuanians. Pilsudski believed that if Latvia would exert pressure, Lithuania would be unable to resist. . . . "I suppose" . . . he wrote, "that both England and America would guarantee such a pact, and that they would give us Libava and Riga as an easy compensation for doubtful Danzig."

He concluded by asking Wassilewski to talk it over with Paderewski . . . "an ardent Federalist. . . ."

Eleven days later he led his victorious troops into Wilno.

CHAPTER XXI

IN THE Wilno campaign Pilsudski had to stand alone, as so often in his life.

He was taking a great risk and his only hope of success lay in telling very few people of his plans, and asking advice of no one. Discussion would have meant indecision and delay with the Bolsheviks drawing nearer every day. But he had to assume a heavy responsibility. The Russians had an immense superiority in numbers and they were elated with easy victories over the small frontier states. His own troops had been hastily got together; many of them had covered immense distances to rejoin and were weary and discouraged. In spite of their splendid fighting qualities they might well be defeated, and defeat would mean utter disaster for Poland. The morale of the people, weakened by years of war and foreign occupation, was not in the condition to stand even a single serious reverse, and the country would be delivered over to Bolshevism. He was well aware too that he could look for no help from abroad. The Allied statesmen would congratulate him warmly if he could present them with a victory over the Bolsheviks as a *fait accompli*, but they would be the first to blame him if he failed. They would await events with a bouquet in one hand and a stone in the other.

He weighed up all these considerations logically and impersonally before starting on the campaign. We discussed them together in the salon of the little house where I lived with Wanda and which was so much more home to the three of us than the Belvedere. I remember him walking up and down, smoking incessantly, and I thought that he had grown older in the last year and stooped rather more, as though his burden was a physical one. But he was very gay on the morning he left because Wanda had just walked for the first time. He laughed like a schoolboy as she staggered round the room on her little legs, very proud of her achievement, and could hardly tear himself away from her although the car was already waiting outside for him, and I had packed his bag. Wherever he went he always carried with him the children's photographs, a medallion of Our Lady of Ostra Brama, and two books which were familiar friends, "Potop" by Sienkiewicz and the Chronicles of Stryjkowski. So on that sunny April morning he set out on a campaign which appeared in the eyes of many sheer madness. He himself had no illusions over it for he wrote of his misgivings:

"I was the head of the Polish Army, and I knew well enough why I had been given the post; because no one else would take it. They all shrank from the burden. My army scarcely existed, my soldiers were only beggars. I realized that I was lacking in authority. I had only been a brigadier and from that to being head of an army is a big jump. Would I have enough experience and confidence to keep my subordinates from feeling that they knew more than I did? But I was ambitious. I welcomed this test. I wanted to prove that I could do what appeared to be impossible.

"I opened fire on Lida with a battery which could still shoot, but an unwilling, bewildered battery, obliged to go with me. For a long time I had not heard the sound of shells whistling over my head, or the bullets pattering out their song of death. Oh, Spirit of War, how strange you are! My memory went back to my Legions. I thought . . . Old friends and comrades, you who lie in your distant graves, our dreams have been fulfilled. Your Commandant is the head of an army! Be with him now. Let your spirits go with my soldiers. Give me Wilno this Easter. . . . The Russian battalions came on. The battle began. . . ."

His wish was granted. On Easter Monday the city was in his hands. The campaign which had seemed to hold so little hope was one of the most successful in his career. The plan which he followed was the one he had worked out in his cell at Magdeburg. Every detail had been stored away in that retentive memory of his. The Russians went down before his

small army like mown grass. His cavalry under Belina managed
to get round the Bolshevik flank to attack the main army in
the rear, and by an audacious ruse gained possession of the
city which they held, in spite of a tremendous enemy force,
until the arrival of the infantry.

The people of Wilno were overjoyed at their liberation.
Hundreds of the citizens ranged themselves with the Polish
troops and took part in the fighting in the streets; relays of
railwaymen brought up reinforcements under heavy fire from
the Russians. Pilsudski riding through the city at the head
of his force was overwhelmed with enthusiasm.

"I did not expect so warm and touching a welcome" . . .
he stated in a letter to Paderewski . . . "It surpassed anything one could have imagined. The people wept for joy. In
spite of the terrible state of famine in the city, they brought
out what food they had and forced it upon the soldiers. Already there are the most cordial relations between them and
the army. The only exceptions have been the Jews who under
the rule of the Bolsheviks were the governing classes. I have
had the greatest difficulty in preventing a massacre provoked
by Jewish civilians shooting and throwing hand grenades from
their windows. . . ."

Two months of Communism had reduced Wilno to utter
ruin. The public services had ceased to function; the sewers
were overflowing the streets. All money found in the banks
had been confiscated. The Bolsheviks had issued over a
thousand decrees in less than a week. Commerce was at a
complete standstill; trade was carried on by barter. The
people were starving. Typhus and other epidemics were
raging.

Pilsudski's first step was to issue a proclamation. Remembering the time-honoured ties that had existed between Poland
and Lithuania he addressed it in the old style: "To the Inhabitants of the Former Grand Duchy of Lithuania" . . . In
it he declared that the long tyranny and oppression of Germans, Russians and Bolsheviks in Wilno had at last ended . . .
"This Polish Army which I lead is bringing you freedom. I
want to give you the fullest possibility of solving your national
and religious problems in your own way, and although guns are

still thundering and blood is still flowing in parts of your land I have no intention of establishing a military occupation. . . ."

He offered them a scheme of civil administration which would provide for self-determination, based on universal franchise, aid in food distribution, and in the restoration of the country's industry, and full legal protection for all classes.

The battle for Wilno had ended in victory in as far as the sword was concerned, but in the diplomatic arena it was to rage for many years.

For the last century Wilno had been debatable ground between Poland and Russia. After the Partition of Poland Russia had extended a predatory hand and drawn the ancient city into her net, with the result that a hopeless confusion of nationalities was created. Wilno was successively claimed as Polish, Russian, Lithuanian and White Russian, but no definite decision was reached, and finally the problem was added to the long list confronting the Conference of Versailles. They were discussing it with all due decorum and the appropriate diplomatic procedure when Pilsudski, incapable of standing by while the beloved city of his boyhood remained under the heel of Bolshevism, rushed into the fray and settled matters after his own fashion.

He was prepared for the storm of criticism which broke out. He considered that he had ample justification for his actions. The destinies of Poland and Lithuania had been linked together for centuries, he said. Their association, founded in 1385 on mutual agreement, was the only example of such a union in Europe, with the exception of England and Scotland. Lithuania had shared Poland's greatness in the Jagiellonian epoch, and shared her sufferings and her bitter unavailing fight in the Insurrections of 1831 and 1863. The boundaries of a country were situated where the culture and education of another country began, and Polish influence and culture had always extended over Lithuania. Her educated classes spoke only Polish and lived according to Polish custom. The citizens of Wilno had considered themselves to be Poles for centuries. His strongest argument was that of the inhabitants of the city less than one per cent were Lithuanians.

Because of the entire friendliness of the population he was firmly resolved to abstain from anything in the nature of a military occupation, or from any suggestion of an annexation. It was unthinkable to him to use threats or force to the citizens of Wilno, his own people. He wished to invite the opinion of the entire population of the territories affected.

The inhabitants of Wilno supported him with one voice and showed their loyalty in the warmth of their welcome to his army. But the Lithuanians protested to Versailles. Their clamours put the Allied statesmen in a dilemma. Clemenceau, to whose policy a strong Poland was a necessity, sided with Pilsudski, Lloyd George opposed him. The question of Poland's boundaries, more particularly where Lithuania was concerned, was brought up repeatedly, and as repeatedly shelved.

In the meantime the Polish Army was following up the victory of Wilno. The Ukrainians were defeated and driven out of Galicia. Minsk was taken in August, Suvalki in the early autumn. The army in the north under Rydz-Smigly was fighting in conjunction with the Latvians, in a series of successful counter-attacks against the Bolsheviks. In the January of 1920 Pilsudski attended a dinner given in his honour at Dyneburg, and received the thanks of General Ballod, Commander-in-Chief of the Latvian Army, for the help which the Poles had given.

It was a year of triumph and fulfilment for him. In the month of August he realized one of his dearest wishes, the restoration of the old University of Wilno, which had been abolished by the Russians after the Insurrection and replaced by the Gymnase he had attended in his boyhood. I shall always remember his happiness because the dream of an unknown little Polish boy, smarting under the bitterness and injustice of oppression, had come to pass after more than forty years.

He faced the winter confidently, although the Russians were gathering their forces for a new attack and the Ukrainians were again massing on the frontier. . . . "We are a little army fighting on three fronts" . . . he said in an interview he gave in November . . . "And if we were to say to ourselves . . . 'Poland is only a dream: the Vistula will never wholly belong to us: we shall always be harassed and surrounded by our enemies' . . . our men, who are facing death with such courage would not have the strength to go on resisting. Our greatest strength is our faith. . . ."

The beginning of 1920 saw improvements in some aspects of the national situation and increased difficulties in others. The army had gained in strength and experience. A uniform system of training had been established; urgently needed arms had been brought from France. But the winter had been hard, unemployment had risen, and even Paderewski's liberality of ideas had not prevented friction in the Government. The dispute with the Czechs was still at a deadlock; Germany, consumed with bitterness over the Treaty of Versailles and the disposal of Danzig and the Corridor, but unable to strike back at the Allies, was concentrating all her venom against Poland. The Bolsheviks were winning the battle in diplomacy. An extensive and efficient propaganda campaign which they had launched against Poland was already having disastrous effects among Allied statesmen. The Socialist Press in England was attacking Pilsudski and clamouring for support for the Russian workers; the phrase "Polish imperialism" had been coined, and even the most moderately inclined politicians were beginning to hint that the Poles were being unreasonable.

The Russians, following up their diplomatic success, decided to put themselves in a still more favourable light with the Allies and made Poland a peace offer, although they were concentrating a large force at the Polish frontier. It was rejected, and for that rejection Poland has been severely criticized. The Allied Supreme Council adopted an admonitory tone, which they no doubt felt to be justified. Europe was sick of the very name of war. The other nations had ceased to fight, why could not Poland lay down her arms? Various motives were attributed to Pilsudski, principally that of pride, which was absurd. Unlike Hitler and Mussolini, he was utterly devoid of personal ambition, had no wish to see himself in the role of a world conqueror, and no thought of extravagant territorial claims. All he wanted was to win back for Poland that which had been taken from her. But he had another

deeper reason. His fear and distrust of Bolshevism, which he
believed would destroy any state in which it took root. He
emphasized his convictions in an interview which he gave to
the correspondent of an English newspaper in the hope that
it might promote a better understanding of Poland. . . .

"I think that the methods which have made Russian Socialism a policy of terrorism and the total destruction of social life would be unthinkable in civilized countries" . . . he
said . . . "Ask the Socialists of Great Britain whether they
would like to have Lenin and Zinoviev reorganize their Government for them on the lines of Bolshevism. I think they
would say 'No.' Do you wonder that I am afraid of the Bolsheviks coming here uninvited to reorganize the Polish Government?"

In April he signed an agreement with the Ukrainian leader
Petlura in which the Ukrainians undertook to cede to Poland
Lwow and Volyn in return for the aid of the Polish Army in
freeing the remainder of their country from the Bolsheviks.
The announcement of the pact was received with the greatest
enthusiasm by the Ukrainians, and the Poles pledged them-
selves to evacuate the New Ukraine at the end of the war.
The two armies then made preparations for a joint attack.

For the first time Pilsudski was to lead his army under the
title which had been bestowed on him of "Marshal of Poland."
No prouder name existed in his eyes. The silver baton which
was presented to him by the nation was his most valued possession. . . .

On April 25th he launched his new offensive against the
Russians, reached the Dnieper in less than a fortnight and on
May 8th occupied Kiev. Everywhere the enemy fell back before him, and he was often amazed at the small resistance his
troops encountered. From Rownc he wrote to me on May 1st:

"My dearest Ola,
"I am writing on this Field Card, not out of duty, but
to emphasize my dependence on you, my dear ones, who
are so far away from me. And although God knows I am
busy enough, and I have standing beside my bed the
photograph of my daughter-and-heir, I am longing for you.

Well, I have taken the first plunge. (You must be surprised and perhaps a little afraid of these big plunges of mine.) I am preparing the second, and bringing up troops and material for it. If it proves as effective as the first the whole Bolshevik Army will be crushed. I have made prisoners of nearly half their force, and taken a quantity of material at the base. The remainder of their army are for the most part demoralized and dispersed. My own loss has been extraordinarily small. On the whole front it amounts to only 150 killed and 300 wounded. But I have had a very sad personal loss. One of my aides-de-camp, Count Radziwill, has been killed. You know how much I liked him personally, and I valued him too as a good officer, on whom I could always rely. He was killed at Malin, that one place where we were unsuccessful. He fell badly wounded and when our squadrons drew back the Bolsheviks dispatched all the wounded without mercy. We found him after we had counter-attacked pierced all over with bayonet wounds." . . .

In June the tide turned against him. Budienny, the Russian general, brought up large forces of Cossack cavalry, and Rydz-Smigly and his men, who were holding Kiev, were forced to evacuate the city. It was the prelude to a retreat along the entire front. The Polish Army, which was now heavily outnumbered, was disastrously handicapped by shortage of arms and equipment, while the Bolsheviks were in possession of the latest big guns and munitions which the Allies had sent out to Russia for the purpose of aiding the "Whites." On August 1st the Russians captured Brest-Litovsk and marched on Warsaw.

At this blackest of hours Pilsudski appealed to the Polish people, and they did not fail him. The Government, which had been so often rent with party strife, achieved a measure of unity which was echoed by the nation. Volunteers enrolled in tens of thousands, new battalions were hastily organized. But help was also needed from outside the country, and at that juncture of her history Poland stood practically alone. The Allies were willing to supply war material, but its transport was blocked by German neutrality, and the Danzig dockers would not unload ships carrying consignments for Poland. The Hungarians sent through munitions, but most of these were seized by the hostile Czechs. Lenin's agents in every country in Europe launched a violent anti-Polish campaign which gained ground among the working-classes who were already sympathetically inclined towards the Bolsheviks.

The Supreme Council of the Allies in Paris, realizing at length the gravity of Poland's position, sent out a special Military Mission composed of General Weygand, the English General Ratcliffe, Lord D'Abernon and M. Jusserand, who arrived in Warsaw at the end of July. Pilsudski immediately offered to share the Chief Command with Weygand, who declined, saying that since he did not know the Polish troops and their commanders he preferred to act only in the capacity of adviser.

The state of affairs which developed during the next week would have been sheer comedy if it had not been so desperately serious. Each of the military experts had a different plan from which they would not deviate an inch. With the Bolsheviks advancing nearer and nearer to the city they argued and expounded their theories and finally came to a complete deadlock before any decision had been reached. My husband in describing later the events of that fateful week wrote . . .

"I had by me, *ex-officio*, at this period three important officials, namely, General Raswadowski, my Chief of Staff, General Sosnkowski, Minister of War, and General Weygand, who was newly arrived from France as Technical Advisor of the Franco-British Mission, which had been sent to Poland at this critical period. Their views on the situation were, as might have been expected, completely divergent and as the situation was peculiarly critical it appears that in my absence the discussions were not altogether amiable. Eventually they were communicating with one another only by means of diplomatic notes which they sent from room to room. In the same office on the Place Saski in Warsaw General Sosnkowski, Minister of War, endeavoured like a kindly guardian angel to reconcile their points of view which were diametrically opposed. The Marne was very frequently mentioned in all these discussions, for in them General Weygand and Sosnkowski showed an especial predilection for the Marne. Because Maréchal Joffre had endeavoured to interpose a river and a stream (the Seine and the Marne) between himself and the enemy in order to carry out the regrouping of his forces in retreat towards his left wing (i.e., towards Paris), so in our case Weygand and Sosnkowski advocated taking cover behind a stream and a river in order to cover a powerful manœuvre by the left wing in the Modlin-Warsaw area. General Raswadowski objected to this repetition of the Marne, for he was opposed on principle to anything that was said in the other room of the office on the Place Saski, and brought forward entirely different plans of lavish ideas, but he never stuck to any of them and changed them almost hour by hour. It was scarcely to be wondered at then that General Weygand, accustomed to the methodical work of the Allied general staffs, should have had to resort to diplomatic methods of communication in his relations with General Raswadowski."

The situation grew worse every day. The unity which had bound the whole nation together in the first week of preparations was shaken by indecision. A large section both of the Government and the populace began to clamour for peace, and certain of the foreign diplomatists strongly advised coming to terms with Russia. . . . "At that most critical hour there was no thought of anything but self-abasement" . . . wrote Pilsudski . . . "foreign counsels were being so far followed that a peace delegation was on the point of being sent to the headquarters of Tukachevski, Commandant of the Russian forces at Minsk. Very few believed in the possibility of our victory, the majority carried on their duties, when they did carry them on, in an atmosphere of despair." . . .

The five Russian armies swept relentlessly on, and still the military experts debated as to what line was to be adopted. . . . "While they are looking at maps and writing notes to one another the Bolsheviks will be marching into Warsaw!" . . . said Pilsudski with an exasperation that was perhaps

justifiable, and decided to act on his own initiative. On the
night of August 6th, the anniversary of that day six years
before when he had led his Riflemen over the Russian frontier,
he shut himself up in his study at the Belvedere Palace and
gave orders that he was not to be interrupted. There all
through the long hours until dawn he laboured over the plan
which has been called a brilliant feat of strategy. In describing
that night he used to say how often he had been reminded of
Napoleon's confession that when he had to make an important
decision in war he was like a woman giving birth to a child,
weak and timorous . . . "I, too, knew what that weakness
was. I was a prey to it myself."

In the morning he had his plan and refused to change it even
after the various experts had pointed out what they considered
errors. He realized that vacillation would be fatal. Faulty or
not he would stick to it. The decision was the hardest he ever
made, but he was calm and resolute.

His plan involved a considerable element of risk, for it
depended on letting the enemy concentrate his full strength
against the defences of Warsaw while Pilsudski and his army
waited for the critical moment to launch an attack on the
Russian flank from Pulawy. Correct timing was of vital importance and therefore he insisted on waiting though telegrams from Warsaw repeatedly urged him to attack.

Those days of waiting were some of the darkest in his life.
The majority of the members of the Government were openly
blaming him for the war. The Allied diplomatists alternately
lectured and criticized. He knew that many of his officers, in
spite of their unwavering loyalty to him, felt in their hearts
that he was leading them on a mad campaign and that Warsaw
was doomed. He believed in the plan of campaign which he
had formed, but there was the possibility of it failing through
insufficiency in numbers. To keep up the morale of his troops,
and also of the city, he was obliged to leave the bulk of his
army in front of Warsaw and use only a small force for his
own counter-attack. When he left to take up his position at
Pulawy he was tired and depressed. For the first time before
a battle the dread of failure weighed on him because so much
was at stake.

I had been evacuated to the neighbourhood of Cracow with
Wanda and our second daughter Jagode, who was only a few
months old, and he came to see us there before leaving for the
front. He bade good-bye to his children as though he was going to his death and was impatient with me because I would
not admit that this offensive might end in disaster for Poland.
I could comfort him because I had complete faith that our
army would be victorious, just as I knew that he would not
be killed. Some instinct always told me what was in store
for him. In the days when he was commanding his Legions I
bade good-bye to him before he left for Laski, and I felt then
that he would be wounded in the head—he was—though, fortunately, not seriously. And now before this battle the same
instinct told me that all would be well.

"The issue of every war is uncertain until it has actually
been fought" . . . he said as he left me . . . "But I believe
that it is in the hands of God. . . ."

The Battle of the Vistula which began on August 16th, 1920,
has passed into history. The Russians, despite their immense
superiority in numbers, were routed. Two-fifths of their armies
were lost; the rest fled in disorder, leaving behind them enormous quantities of war material. But the battle which was
fought on the plains of the Vistula was not the battle for Warsaw alone, or even for Poland. It had a far wider significance,
for it stopped the triumphant march of Bolshevism. It was the
battle for civilization, for liberty and justice, and for every
principle for which democracy stands. Centuries before Poland
had influenced the destiny of Europe when John Sobieski's
army drove the Turks from the plains of Vienna and gained
the victory of the Cross over the Crescent. In 1920 she influenced it again when she made her stand against the forces
of Bolshevism.

.   .   .   .   .

The rout of the Russians, begun at the Battle of the Vistula,
was followed up by further Polish victories on the Niemen and
the Szczara. The Bolshevist vision of marching to world-wide
revolution over the corpse of Poland receded. On October
18th an armistice was declared. A month later a peace

conference opened at Riga, and on March 18th, 1921, a treaty was signed which secured Poland's Eastern Frontier.

Poland was rid of the menace of Russia for the time being at least, but she had other problems to cope with. Her boundaries, in spite of all the admonitions and well-intentioned advice of the Allies, were still undecided.

The Russians on their march to Warsaw had taken Wilno once more and given a new and complicated twist to the situation by bestowing it on the Lithuanians, without consulting the wishes of the citizens. The Lithuanians immediately set up their capital there and started to oppress its Polish inhabitants who sent a desperate appeal to Pilsudski. The Polish General Zeligowski was dispatched to the rescue with his division, drove out the Lithuanians in their turn, and was given a tremendous welcome by the people. This meant, of course, that wails arose to the Allies, this time from the Lithuanians, and Pilsudski was hauled over the coals again. An official inquiry was addressed to him by the French and British representatives at Warsaw. His reply was that every community had the right to self-determination and that if a plebiscite were held the citizens of Wilno would declare themselves with one voice Poles. In the meantime General Zeligowski formed in Wilno the "Central Lithuanian Government" composed of the inhabitants, and despite the frowns of the Allies a new frontier was set up. The tumult died down: no blood was spilt, only a great deal of diplomatists' ink, and Pilsudski received still another lecture. It did not trouble him. He had accomplished what he had set out to do. Wilno was still Polish. He had kept his word to his beloved city.

The question was finally decided in January 1922, when a free and democratic vote was held in Wilno which resulted in a majority of 100 to 1 in favour of unconditional reunion with Poland. In March the district was incorporated in Polish territory, with full international recognition, and Wilno representatives were admitted to the Parliament in Warsaw. Pilsudski visited the city that had been so hardly recovered. It had suffered bloodshed and famine; the Bolsheviks had despoiled it of all its treasures of art, of everything of value, even of common necessities. But it was still the ancient city of the poets and philosophers whose lamp had lighted the road through the dark days of Poland's servitude. The city of Slowacki and Mickiewicz. He could say in his address to the citizens . . .

"I am now at that age when I can look calmly into that void from which no one returns. I know that after the many emotions which I have experienced in my stormy life Fate cannot hold many more, as great and powerful, in store for me. But there are other emotions as pure and simple as those of a child which will still fall to my share.

"To-day I am like a child on the birthday of his beloved mother. The trusting eye of a child, delighted with his mother, does not look and does not ask what gown she wears. Whether she is pretty or ugly in the eyes of others; to the child she is and remains some one wonderful and beautiful and on the day of her anniversary its heart is filled with happiness. And so like that child, profoundly moved, I cry 'Long Live Wilno.'"

The situation regarding the frontiers remained unsatisfactory. German propaganda had caused the plebiscites in East Prussia to go against Poland. There was intense bitterness between the Polish and German populations in the region of the Corridor, which was all too obviously going to remain a festering wound, doomed to break out one day. Germans and Poles were almost coming to blows in Danzig, which was our only outlet to the sea. The Allies had decided to give Cieszyn to Czechoslovakia, which Poland felt to be a deep injustice, since the majority of the inhabitants of the province were Polish. Dispute raged over Upper Silesia with its rich coal mines, and its teeming population. There too the Peace Conference decided on a plebiscite, which was held in March 1921, but in the meantime there were risings of Polish workmen which the German troops could not quell. It was only after the third rising in October 1921 that the territory was restored to Poland.

In spite of many setbacks and disappointments the year 1921 was not without its triumphs. The alliance with France in February, following Pilsudski's official visit to Paris, was a diplomatic gain of the first value. I can remember how overjoyed my husband was that Poland, who only a few years before had not even existed in the world of diplomacy, should have been sought after in friendship by one of the great Powers. During the next month our position in Europe was still further strengthened by a pact with Rumania.

CHAPTER XXII

POLAND HAD peace at last and could give herself to the work of reconstruction. In the spring of 1921 parliament passed the new constitution, which was drawn up on a democratic base. The State was to be governed by a President, a Cabinet of Ministers, a Senate whose power would be limited and a Seym, or Lower House which would include representatives of all classes and minorities.

The country was recovering from the aftermath of war. Lands which had been laid waste were ploughed and sown once more, rebuilding of the ruined towns and villages was begun, industries which had been paralysed for years were gradually reorganized.

Pilsudski dared now to look ahead into the future. So many of the giants which had threatened to crush the life out of the infant State had been slain. Bolshevism had been defeated. The quarrel with the Czechs had been settled, not perhaps very satisfactorily for Poland but at least peaceably. The mixed populations of the new frontier districts were being slowly absorbed and welded into one nation again. The barriers that had so long separated the Polish people had been broken down.

In June 1921, Pilsudski visiting the town of Torun in Pomerania for the first time since its recovery from Germany spoke of the nation no longer sundered. . . .

"Every nation has its monuments, representing the joys and sorrows of many generations: its ruins, fields of battle, towns and streets, in sight of which hearts are quickened. Poland has many of these temples of history, but to me there is no grander temple than the boundaries which once severed our country. There was a time when the Polish people throughout the whole length and breadth of the land led the same life. History grooved the soul of the nation in the same pattern. But there came a day when frontier posts were set up, posts which said 'Forget, forget! Forget your own people and the laughter and the tears you have shared. Forget even your language.' By means of this line, which seemed of so little importance since the smallest animal could run across it, we were to be made different physically and morally, different in mentality and in our character, so that if need be we could fight one against the other. Three great powers expended time and energy to make these frontiers strong, and the efforts of many generations of Poles were needed to destroy their work. There is no greater historical temple to me than these frontiers by which we are no longer divided.

"The message which came to us from these frontier posts not so long ago was 'Forget.' To-day the message is 'Remember.' And that 'Remember' is not an empty word. It means work, and still more work until this ditch of which the enemy wanted to make a precipice is filled." . . .

The ditch had been dug deep and years of slow and patient toil went to the filling of it. In looking back on that process of rebuilding Poland I can only think of the comparison of some one who has been paralysed for a long time learning to walk again. We would go forward a few steps and then stand still, tired and discouraged at realizing the distance we had still to cover. Or we would collide with some obstacle we had not even seen because we had been too ambitious. We walked haltingly because movement depends on co-ordination and it takes time and long practice to acquire co-ordination. Constitutions are based on tradition, and we had had no tradition as a self-governing people for a century and a half. We were without experience in economics, constitutional laws or finance, and so inevitably we made mistakes, and we had no smoothly-running state machinery to stand the strain of them; only an empty exchequer and a non-existent credit.

Our worst handicap was our lack of revenue. In those first post-war years when international finance fluctuated wildly and the currency of nearly every nation in Europe depreciated Poland's position was almost desperate. The German mark, the Austrian crown and the Russian rouble fell to a fraction of their former value. Poland with her frail economic structure and with no powerful foreign interests to support her could not hope to hold up the zloty. It sustained a serious drop in 1920 and in consequence prices rose and unemployment increased. It was almost impossible to budget successfully. National expenditure was high in a country which had nothing to start with, no social services, not even a police force. Hospitals and schools had to be instituted, pensions paid to soldiers' dependents and to disabled men, and the necessary funds could only be raised from a people which was almost bankrupt. The question of capital was an ever-present skeleton, and one which was particularly ill-adapted to the Polish temperament, which is lavish to a fault. In the first flush of enthusiasm and pride in our newly-created State there were some disastrous experiments. Every government department was infected with our national characteristic of lofty aspirations, and gave rein to them. Ambitious schemes were begun and had to be abandoned half-way through because there was no money to complete them. We wanted to beautify our cities and so we put up magnificent buildings and then when the last available zloty had been spent on their adornment there would be nothing left to make roads leading to them. The unfinished canal outside Warsaw is still witness to our inability to reconcile our ambitions with our limitations in those early days. Originally intended as a grandiose scheme for a great waterway, which would revive the mediæval trading glories of the Vistula and bring the ships of all nations to our capital, it was left not even half constructed after the painful discovery that it would cost more than the entire year's revenue. Since then it has remained a desolate waste, given over to weeds and stray cats. My husband used to say that the sight of this national monument so depressed him that he always turned his head away when he passed it in the car. It reminded him of his father's passion for building and its disastrous effect on the family exchequer.

The war having ended the opinion both of the Government and the nation trended towards drastic economy in the army,

to the alarm of Pilsudski, who realized the folly and the danger
of such policy. No one, he said, could be guileless enough to
suppose that Poland would remain on good terms with either
Germany or Russia unless she was strong enough to defend
herself against them both. Germany made no secret of her
resentment over the Corridor. The Treaty with the Bolsheviks
would hold good just as long as Russia was unsure of herself.
. . . "When she is weak she is ready to promise anything,"
he said. "But she is equally ready to break those promises the
moment that she feels herself strong enough to do so." Despite
Lenin's protestations of universal brotherhood and widespread
propaganda to the workers of Poland her mentality had undergone little change since the days of Ivan the Terrible. He
quoted his own maxim. . . .

"Whatever government Russia has becomes an imperialist
government, because she herself is essentially imperialistic.
She has only exchanged the imperialism of the Czars for the
Red imperialism of the Soviets." As far as Poland was concerned her only hope was to make herself strong in arms.

He succeeded in convincing the Seym and managed to avert
an actual reduction of the army, but he had to wage one long
and persistent struggle to obtain the necessary grants for it.
All expenditure, even on such obvious necessities as boots and
clothing for the troops, assumed mammoth proportions in the
eyes of the Government, so that he had to beg and plead, and
keep up a continual propaganda for the army, always present-
ing it to the people as a part of the national life. There were
times when he despaired of making a nation which had had no
army for more than a century and a half military-minded. It
was a thankless task, and one which caused him to be often
misunderstood, for his enemies constantly brought the charge
of war-mongering against him.

His duties as Chief of State covered a wide field, wider indeed than he wished. He had no liking for many aspects of
political life, and was impatient of the petty details attendant
upon his position. He fulfilled them because some one must
hold the State together and he knew, quite dispassionately and
without vanity, that at that critical stage he was the one man
who could do it. When I look back on those days I think of

him always as teaching the country self-government. Slowly and with endless patience he revived the constitutional life which had lain dormant for so long, built up the relationship of mutual responsibility between the people and the Government.

He worked tirelessly and unendingly, very often eighteen hours out of the twenty-four. The short vacations which he used to take for Christmas or Easter when we went to Spala were his only opportunities for relaxation, and even there we had always visitors, members of the Government, or foreign diplomatists with whom he wanted to discuss affairs of State. But he was happy there in the snow-clad forests which he loved.

The close of the year 1922 marked a crisis in his life. It had been universally expected that when the election for the Presidency was held on December 9th, he would be chosen. There was consternation then when at the meeting of the Seym on the fourth he announced his decision not to stand.

For some considerable time there had been constant grounds for complaint between him and the Seym, but he had either ignored them altogether or glided lightly over them, for he was easy-going where trivial matters were concerned and his keen sense of humour carried him through the quarrels and recriminations which seemed incidental to Polish politics at that juncture. But now a more important issue was at stake.

During his four years as Chief of State he had successfully carried out the duties of a President, but since March of the previous year when a new Constitution had been established, he had found his task increasingly difficult, for he had been hampered by a hundred and one petty regulations. He could not even give an order unless it had been countersigned by one of the Ministers; every speech he delivered had to be written out beforehand and submitted for approval; he was expected to represent the Polish Republic on all occasions, yet he could not express his own opinions or work for the State according to his own ideas. He was sick of the incessant arguments over trifles and delays over important matters. He felt like a child, alternately petted and criticized. So he told the Parliament to elect another President. . . . "Choose a man with a heavy step and a light hand" . . . he advised them. . . . "There will be mires and swamps to cross, and a man with a light step will cross them too quickly, and therefore he will be no help to others. For the rest: a light hand is needed in order to compromise. Compromise is perhaps an unfortunate word, for to many it is synonymous with treachery. But nevertheless it is allied to the very essence of democracy. It consists of admitting that if my will and my preferences can manifest themselves in the State others also have the same rights. . . . Only a light hand can carry out successfully a compromise of this sort. A heavy one will be useless for it will be too ready to resort to compulsion."

Gabriel Narutowicz, the President who was elected by the National Assembly of the Seym and Senate on December 9th, had indeed the qualification of a light hand, for he was a gifted diplomatist and a man of wide culture. Descended from an old Polish family with estates in Lithuania he had studied extensively in his youth, principally in Switzerland, specialized in science and engineering and finally turned his energies to politics. Between him and my husband there existed a warm affection, for although they were totally unlike in temperament each could appreciate the other. Narutowicz, who was a gentle scholar, unassuming as a child, shrank from the responsibility of the Presidency and would have refused it but for his stern sense of duty. He had already proved an able Minister of Foreign Affairs, and although, as a staunch supporter of Pilsudski's policy, he would meet with opposition from the extreme Right, it seemed probable that his appointment would be approved by the nation and that the choice would be a happy one.

He was so distressed before the election that my husband asked me to visit him that evening as he was too busy to do so himself. On arriving at the simple little house where he lived with his nieces I found him in poor health and suffering from a deep depression which he tried in vain to shake off. He confided to me that he had a strange premonition which warned him not to accept the Presidency. He was convinced that trouble would come of his appointment, and apart from that, he did not feel strong enough to undertake so great a responsibility.

I told him that my husband had the greatest confidence in his tact and judgment and that he believed he was the right man to guide the nation through a difficult time. After we had talked a little while he grew more cheerful and even spoke of the arrangements he would make at the Belvedere where he would have his office . . . "I shall not take over the Marshal's study," . . . he said with a smile . . . "I shall keep that exactly as he leaves it so that I can be constantly reminded of his example."

I left this loyal friend and kindliest and most gracious of men with the promise that I would visit him next week. To my sorrow I was never to fulfil it for a few days later he was assassinated.

The news of his appointment was followed by a violent outburst of hostility from the National Democrats. Popular feeling was inflamed against him by reports that he was a Jew. There was not the slightest foundation for them, but none the less they gained currency. A twelve-hour strike was organized in Warsaw as a protest, and when the new President drove through the city to take the oath crowds blocked the streets yelling and booing. Even boys of fourteen pelted his carriage with mud.

By accident I was caught in one of these crowds, wedged tightly between an old peasant who was deaf and kept asking me plaintively what all the fuss was about, and a fat woman of the servant class. She was scarlet in the face, jumping up and down and waving her arms as she shrieked abuse of "the dirty Jew Narutowicz." I told her that I knew the family of the new President and that he had not a drop of Jewish blood, but I only wasted my breath for she continued to shout "We will not be governed by the dirty Israelites," until those around took up the cry and howled threats and curses as loudly as she. The crowd was in an ugly temper, obviously worked upon by agitators. The atmosphere was heavy with the approaching storm.

Two days later, on the morning of December 16th, my husband left our house in the Ulice Koszykowa (he had already handed over his official residence at the Belvedere to Gabriel Narutowicz) to go to the office of the General Staff. I remem-

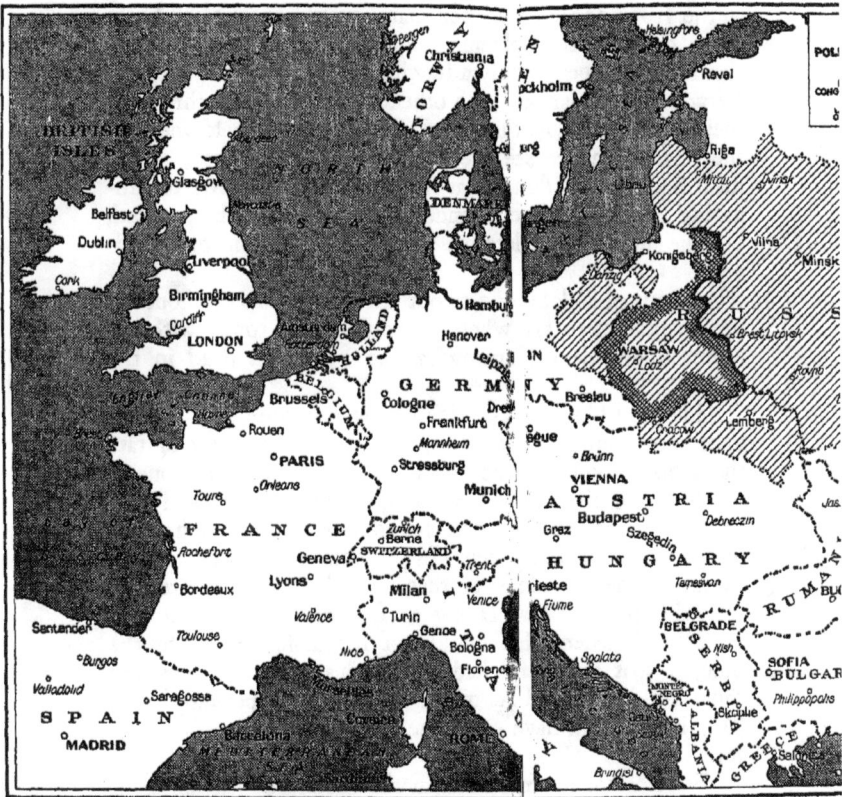

ber that he was in good spirits, laughing with the children, because he had laid down so many of his worries. He had been gone only a few minutes when the back door bell rang. Some instinct made me warn the maid that she was not to admit any stranger. Presently she came back to report that the visitors had been three young men who had asked to see the Marshal. She had replied from behind the door that he had already left the house and would not be home for some hours. Before they could reply she had shut the door in their faces.

She had scarcely finished speaking when there was a ring at the front door. I told her that I would answer it. There was a chain on the bolt and I slipped it firmly into place so that the door opened only a few inches. Through the aperture I saw a young man and two others behind him. All three had their right hands in their coat pockets. They told me that they had called to see the Marshal and I answered, as the maid had already done, that he was not at home. After lingering for some time outside the house they disappeared, but the incident had left me with a vague feeling of uneasiness.

An hour or so later one of our friends came to the house in great agitation to ask where he could get in touch with the Marshal. President Narutowicz had been shot dead in the street.

This cold-blooded assassination was a source of lasting grief to my husband. It seemed to him a cruel irony of fate that a man who had loved Poland so passionately, and done so much during his term at the Foreign Office to increase Polish prestige among other nations, should have died by the hand of one of his own countrymen. His personal sorrow was doubled by the murderer's admission that his bullet had been intended for Pilsudski, but that failing to find him that day he had shot the President. He could not reconcile himself to the thought that his friend had died in his stead. "If only the shot had been fired at me" . . . he said repeatedly. . . . "My luck would have saved me, as it has so often done before."

His grief found expression in the brochure "Memories of

Gabriel Narutowicz" which he wrote in the following year.
Was there a touch of envy in its concluding words?

> "You did not fight with us. You did not know the
> misery of servitude. The struggle did not rob you of the
> sentimentality of your youth; your spirit was not sullied
> by the mire of slavery. You kept among your Swiss
> mountains the dreams of your childhood and your
> youth; your childish faith in humanity, and in its good
> will." . . .

A few days after the assassination of Narutowicz the National Assembly elected another President, Stanislas Wojciechowski, who had collaborated with Piłsudski in the publication of the *Robotnik* in the old days of the P.P.S. Sikorski
became Premier and my husband took over the office of Chief
of the General Staff. He was free now to devote himself to
the work he loved. The army was his creation, and whatever
disadvantages might be attached to it, his heart was always
with it. He watched over it like a proud father, fought its
battles fiercely in the parliamentary arena, where it could not
fight for itself, and was never happier than when he was thinking out schemes for increasing its efficiency or contributing
to its welfare. It was therefore with much misgiving that he
saw it being dragged increasingly within the sphere of party
politics. The trenches had seemed preferable a thousand times
to the constitutional battlefield in which he now found himself;
the political intrigue with which he was surrounded disgusted
him. As the years of peace lengthened and the terrors of war
receded into the background the Government showed less and
less inclination to make his task easier.

A crisis was reached in May 1923, when the Witos Government, which was closely allied with the National Democrats,
came into power. With the murder of Narutowicz still festering in his mind he refused flatly to defend such a government
and gave in his resignation. At the same time he published
several newspaper articles openly attacking the evils which
were cropping up like weeds on the soil of Poland. The nation
was being nourished on deceit and hypocrisy, he wrote, therein
lay its weakness. . . .

"A nation whose life is built on lies will always be weaker than one whose life is built on truth. Truth is the strength and the power of the spirit . . ."

In response his enemies launched a violent attack on him. Accusations without a vestige of foundation were whispered against him. He was even stated to have been in the pay of both Germany and Russia . . . he, whose every breath, whose every thought was for Poland and for Poland alone. But as some attacked him others defended him with equal vehemence, and so fierce controversy raged, both in the army and outside it. On July 3rd a banquet was given in his honour by over two hundred of his political friends. The speech he made that night has been called the most memorable in his career. It must certainly, I think, have been one of the frankest ever made by a statesman. . . .

He began by painting one of his vivid word pictures of his sudden rise to power. A man named Joseph Pilsudski had walked out of the railway station one day in November 1918, wearing the uniform of the Polish Legions, a man who was on his way back from a German prison, as were many other men at that time. But this man, because he was Commandant of the First Brigade became in a few days Dictator of Poland. . . . "The new Poland as its first symbol chose, rightly or wrongly, a man dressed in a grey uniform, worn and stained in the prison of Magdeburg."

After a few months as Dictator, he continued, he had opened the first parliament and handed over his power to it. He stood before it in the same uniform, wearing the sword which his officers of the First Brigade had given him. And the parliament had made him Chief of the Polish State and Commander-in-Chief of the Polish Army. Everything was in his hands. . . . "Yet there was a shadow which encircled me, which went before me, which remained behind me. On the battlefield, at work in the Belvedere or caressing my child this shadow pursued me always. The shadow of a monstrous dwarf on crooked legs, spitting out his filthy soul, spitting at me from every side, sparing nothing sacred, neither my family life nor my friends, following my steps, distorting every thought." . . .

This dwarf was not a mere metaphor. He who represented

the nation had been called a thief, a traitor who had sold his country to the enemy. That was the hateful soul of the monster that had pursued him.

He went on to give the reasons which had caused him to resign. He had left the army because as a soldier he would not draw the sword in the defence of those men whose agents had first thrown missiles at the newly elected President in the streets and then completed their crime. He ended . . . "I am not a public prosecutor. I only look for the truth. As for myself, I ask you to remember me, and at the same time I ask for a long, long rest, so that I may breathe the air, so that I may be as free as you, and as gay as were my comrades of the First Brigade." . . .

He did indeed need a rest. He was fifty-six, and the strain of the last few years had taken toll of even so boundless a vitality as his. He only wanted to retire quietly with me and the children to Sulejowek, the pleasant little villa some fifteen miles from Warsaw which had been presented to him by the army. The Seym voted him a pension of the equivalent of £600 a year, but he refused to take it and gave it over to the endowment of Wilno University. He had never cared for money. His tastes were simple, and if he took up his writing again he could earn enough to enable us to live quite comfortably, though perhaps not luxuriously.

.   .   .   .   .

We remained at Sulejowek from July 1923 until May 1926, and because they were some of the happiest years we ever spent together I must try to draw the picture of a house in the heart of a pine forest, a neat little white house with a red roof, set back in a garden that was full of flowers nearly all the year round. On either side of the porch were tablets bearing the inscriptions . . .

"The Soldier of the Reborn Poland Offers This House to His Commandant" . . . and "May the sun of this restored country shine upon the walls of this house for many long and illustrious years." . . .

My husband was deeply attached to this house both for

itself and for what it represented, thousands upon thousands of zlotys spared from none too generous army pay. There was a story behind it.

At the end of the Great War a fund was started among the Polish people for the purpose of buying Pilsudski a house and estate as a memento of his services to the nation. Donations poured in from all parts of the country and in due course a substantial cheque was presented to him. But instead of putting it to the use for which it had been intended he gave it for the relief of widows and orphans of men who had fallen in the war. The army on learning of what had happened determined that their Dziadak * should have his house, come what might, so they opened another fund secretly among themselves, and said nothing to him until all arrangements were completed. The site was chosen and in due time the house arose. The sun did indeed shine upon its walls, penetrating into every room, and the bees hummed in the garden all summer. And this little white house, which seemed to have absorbed something of the warmth and friendliness which had gone to its building, became our home. After all the tempestuous troubles we had known it was a haven, the first place where we could live the simple family life we had always dreamed of.

I want now to draw the portrait of my husband, not as the Marshal of Poland, but as we saw him in those days of Sulejowek, and because the impressions of the very young are always vivid and clear-cut, I called my daughters and asked them . . . "What shall I write of your father?"

Wanda said . . . "You must write of how gay he was. How he used to laugh."

And Jagode, the younger, added . . . "And how he used to make us laugh."

It was true. That unquenchable gaiety which could find humour even in the midst of disaster, and always sought to turn a heavy moment into a light one was inseparable from any picture of him. The house at Sulejowek used to ring with laughter when he was with the children. He would tell them stories by the hour, for he had an unlimited repertoire. Sometimes fables and fairy tales which he seemed to enjoy almost

* Dziadak—"Grandfather," the nickname given him by the Legions.

as much as they did, and which kept them so spellbound that
they could hardly be dragged away at bedtime, because the
most exciting moment of the plot had just been reached:
sometimes stories of his travels in Japan or Siberia. He had so
rich a fund of his own experiences, and even the darkest hours
of his life were transformed for their ears into comedy. When
they grew older he showed them not the horrors of war but the
adventures of his years with the Legions, the humour of the
different types of men in the ranks, the peasants in the villages
through which they passed; reproducing each character with a
perfection of mimicry that would have earned him fame on the
stage. These hours of story-telling were a constant delight to
the children; to them their father was the gayest and best-
loved of all companions, for although he was over fifty when
they were born he could always tune his mind to the tempo
of theirs. He had a great understanding of children, even the
shyest child responded to him. This love of childhood was one
of the strongest motives in his life. He strove to free Poland
not so much for his own generation as for those who would
come after: in the carefree laughter of Polish children who had
come into their own at last he had the reward for his lifework.
The first reforms he introduced in the new State were those
affecting its children; they had always the foremost place in
his considerations.

I remember that in the early autumn of 1924 he was asked
by a Warsaw firm to make two speeches for the gramophone
so that a record of his voice could be kept. . . . "The second
will be best" . . . he said. . . . "I shall have had time to
practise on the first one."

The young representative of the firm who did the recording
had expected some weighty discourse on philosophy or history,
but instead Pilsudski spoke to the children. Because I am very
fond of this record and because it is very typical of him I
quote it. . . .

"I am standing in front of a queer tube and thinking
that my voice is soon to be separated from me, and go
somewhere into the world without me, his owner. People
have funny ideas! It is really difficult not to laugh at this

odd situation in which the voice of Mr. Pilsudski will
suddenly find itself. I can imagine the funny moment
when some good fellow will turn a handle, press a button,
and a tube will start talking instead of me. I should like
then to see the children who will gather to listen to this tube
talking with a human voice. And I think that among those
children there will be also my own children who will certainly think that their daddy is somewhere behind the tube,
playing at Hide and Seek with them. Then I must laugh
heartily that this poor voice separated from me has suddenly ceased to be my property and belongs to I know not
whom or what: to the tube or to a joint stock company.
But the funniest thought is that when I shall not be here
any more the voice of Mr. Pilsudski will still be sold for
three grosse somewhere at county fairs, almost by the
pound like gingerbread, and by the ounce like some sort
of sweet.

"They say it is going to make me immortal. So if my
wanton thought can link a tube with eternity I want to
make sure that this voice of mine shall utter one beautiful
truth; the truth of laughter.

"Laughter is the element of happiness, and the more
light-hearted and sincere it is the more frequently we call
it childlike; the more happiness that is in it, the more of
heaven we have on earth. As a good soldier I knew how to
laugh merrily, even in the midst of danger. And while I
am standing before this little machine one thought continually returns to me . . . that I would immortalize not
a voice but laughter.

"We welcomed the restored Poland not with the ringing laughter of restoration but with acidity and the morbid
peevishness of dyspeptics. So I beg you with this voice
from the tube, all of you who are parents, when you cannot
laugh yourselves, put away the discussions of the peda-
gogues, when the jolly silvery laugh of happy children rings
through your house. Let the Polish children laugh with
this laughter of restoration even if you do not know
how to." . . .

CHAPTER XXIII

Those three years at Sulejowek were passed in rest and quiet contentment. My husband had always been happiest in the country; he had never had any liking for the life of cities. In the peace of the garden in summer where the stillness of the forest around us was only broken by the drone of the bees among my sunflowers, and the laughter of the children playing with their friends on the lawn, he could relax for the first time in many years.

Our daily routine was nearly always the same. He slept late in the morning and rarely came downstairs before noon, when he had breakfast, read his letters and newspapers, and walked in the garden with the children. Dinner was at two-thirty and afterwards he used to spend the afternoon reading on the veranda, generally works on military topics, travel or history. Tea, which was at five o'clock, was his favourite meal of the day. He was very fond of sweet cakes and Adelcia, our cook, who was devoted to him, used to make them in great variety for him. His tastes in food were simple. He drank a little wine, generally Hungarian, ate large quantities of sweets and chocolates, and preferred our Polish national delicacy of smoked meat to the most elaborate cuisine. After tea he walked in the forest or up and down one path in the garden which he specially loved, a long avenue of lilac and acacias. I always knew by looking out of the window whether he could be disturbed or not. When he was deep in thought, composing one of his speeches, he walked with his shoulders hunched and his hands clasped tightly behind his back. At other times he liked to have the company of the children, or to watch me working in the garden. Gardening was almost the only pursuit which we did not share. He was passionately fond of flowers but had no instinct for growing them. I can only remember his making one attempt to acquire it and that was at Sulejowek when he spent a whole afternoon in digging, and was so stiff

321

the next day that he could hardly move. After that he left the care of the garden to me.

Much of his best literary work was produced during those years at Sulejowek, including the "History of the Year 1920," and "Memories of Gabriel Narutowicz." His writing was always done at night when the children had gone to bed and the house was quiet. He hated writing and so he used to dictate everything, occasionally to one of his friends but generally to me. We would shut ourselves up in his study every evening at about eleven o'clock and work, sometimes without a break, until two or three in the morning, I seated at the desk scribbling at top speed, he pacing up and down, smoking cigarette after cigarette, dictating so smoothly and rapidly, with never a pause to contradict himself, that I could scarcely keep up with him. Then when the work was finished for the night I would make tea and we would drink it together, while we talked. I shall always cherish the memory of summer nights in Sulejowek when we worked and talked together, alone in a sleeping world, while the nightingales sang in the acacias and the sweet scent of lilac was wafted in through the open window.

In the winter when the evenings closed in early and it grew too dark to walk in the forest and the garden after tea, he used to find recreation in a game of chess with any of his friends who happened to be visiting us, or in playing Patience. He had several different kinds and if the cards would not work out he would try each in turn.

It was during this same time that he began to take an interest in psychic experiments, particularly the transference of thought. He obtained some extraordinarily successful results with one of his friends, and was able not only to exchange messages with him, but even to report accurately a conversation which had taken place at his house which was some considerable distance away. Experiments in automatic writing were equally interesting, and he would, I think, have penetrated more deeply into the study of the occult but for the fact that he considered it a subject not to be lightly embarked upon. He had a profound belief in the immortality of the spirit.

Fête days, which in Poland are not birthdays but the festival of the patron saint after whom every child is baptized were great events at Sulejowek and were eagerly looked forward to by the children. My husband always managed to think of some surprise for them and never failed to choose their presents himself, although as a rule he loathed shopping and could only with difficulty be prevailed upon even to go to his tailor. But the buying of birthday presents was another thing and no matter how busy he was he always found time for it.

His own fête days always brought a stream of visitors to the house from early morning until night. Relatives and personal friends, deputations from the army, former members of the P.O.W., ex-soldiers of the Legions, representatives of various social organizations, all of whom had to be received personally. By the end of the day the salon was full of flowers, and fruit and presents of every description. But the tributes which gave him the most pleasure were those which came from hundreds of simple people, Legionaries, peasants, and workmen, many of whom had walked long distances to see him.

The peasants' presents always took the form of produce from their own little holdings, eggs, butter, cheese or homemade wine, and very often live stock. I can remember one fête day when they included two dogs, a dozen or so of rabbits, a lamb, a deer, a fox, a goose and a fierce fighting cock. My husband was so touched at the kind thought of the donors that he refused to get rid of any of them for several weeks, during which time the lamb manifested a most unfortunate predilection for the carpet in the salon, the deer devoured all my early spring flowers, the fox in his anxiety to create a lair for himself dug up most of the seeds that I had just planted with great care, and the cock attacked visitors. After that homes were found for most of them, but the lamb and the goose remained, and became inseparable companions. It was the oddest sight to see them walking about the garden, the lamb adapting its gambols to the sober pace of the goose, or sleeping in the sun curled up together, the goose's head tucked firmly into the lamb's neck. It was the strangest case of friendship between animals I have ever known, but evidently it sprang from genuine affection, for when the lamb grew up and had to be given to a neighbouring farmer the poor goose was inconsolable, refused to eat and pined away.

A permanent member of the household at Sulejowek was Pies, my husband's enormous wolf dog, who in spite of his size was the gentlest and most lovable of creatures. He had however one grievous blemish on an otherwise perfect character. He could never be trained. He was sent away to three different establishments in succession, each of which guaranteed to achieve the desired results, but immediately he returned home he lapsed into his old and bad ways. At length my husband said that so obstinate a scholar should be left in peace, and his education was abandoned as hopeless In spite of this he gave implicit obedience to his master, and was a perfect companion for the children. He seemed to consider it his special duty to watch over them, with results that were sometimes embarrassing. In his zeal to protect them he would not let other children approach them, and small visitors to the house used to be terrified when he laid a heavy paw on their shoulders, pulling them gently away from his charges.

My husband's favourite pet was Kasztanka, the beautiful Arab mare who carried him through all his campaigns. She was given to him on the day he led his Strzelcy over the frontier to the war, in August 1914, and ever after she was his devoted companion. She was intensely nervous, hated gunfire in spite of her long experience, and could not be controlled by any one else. But between her and her master there existed an almost human understanding. She reached an honourable age and was finally put out to grass, but she was brought to visit us at regular intervals, and it was sweet to watch her nuzzling her soft mouth into my husband's hand, and rubbing her neck against his shoulder in the joy of greeting.

Kasztanka had a son named Niemen, a powerful white Arab, who was originally intended to succeed her as my husband's charger. But alas! Niemen had inherited only her beauty, nothing of her fire and intelligence. He was the laziest quadruped who ever cropped grass, and no matter who attempted to ride him could never be urged into anything more than a jog-trot pace. He grew fatter and fatter and was finally left to his inglorious ease in the fields at Pikiliszki.

In the meantime clouds were steadily gathering over the political horizon in Warsaw. In December 1923 the Witos Government fell. Ladislas Grabski became Prime Minister, and Sosnkowski, one of my husband's oldest friends and collaborators, was appointed Minister of War. Pilsudski was invited to return to the High Command but refused to do so unless the conditions attached to the post were completely revised. During his term in office he had been handicapped on every side. Despite the fact that he would be responsible for the army in the event of war he had been allowed only a limited voice in such important questions as military training and education, and even regarding the promotion of officers.

Although he insisted on remaining aloof from all active political work he was kept in constant touch with events in Warsaw. During the whole time we were at Sulejowek there was a continual procession of visitors to the house, ministers and politicians who wanted his advice, army officers who would not let him retire into oblivion, and brought him their problems. He still took a prominent part in the organization of some charitable societies connected with the army. I remember his speaking at Warsaw in the winter of 1925 when he opened the newly created Association of Soldiers' Families. His own great love of his home and children gave tenderness to his words to this audience of women, each of whom had sent a husband to the war.

He began by telling them that he had been invited to open their meeting because as the late Commander-in-Chief of the Polish Army he had given the orders which had sent the men they loved to face death. . . .

"Often when I thought of you and of the blood which I must cause to be shed I knew black days, and black hours, in which I judged myself. But the shedding of blood belongs to black hours.

"There were moments of joy and triumph. But when I thought that the bulletins of victory were read by many whose hearts did not beat joyfully but in fear and anxiety as they scanned the numbers of regiments and divisions to find one, that of some one dear to them who was exposed to the bullets which must claim their victim. In those black hours I searched my conscience to justify this shedding of blood. I could only hope that some day the case would be taken into account before a higher tribunal than ours, judged by another wisdom. There are wounds which can only be healed in the grave, and there are scars which cannot be obliterated. In those black hours I thought of the women who stayed at home, who did not hear the fluttering of the banner, and had only uncertainty and fear for those who had gone away."

1925 was a year of varied fortunes for Poland. Her fate was once again debated, this time at Locarno, whereon the longing eyes of a war-weary world were focused. Unhappily Pilsudski had already acquired there the reputation of a warmonger, which had been previously bestowed upon him in Berlin. Warsaw and Moscow, and the Western Powers hesitated to guarantee the frontiers of Poland.

It was a sore point with my husband. In 1923 Poland had asked to be admitted to the membership of the Council of the League of Nations, but her request had been refused, although Germany was duly installed there, for at that time the sentimentalists of every nation were preaching the necessity of extending a helping hand to the German people, a state of affairs which would no doubt be ideal, said Pilsudski, but for the mentality of Germany, who would keep to her pose of penitence as long as it suited her purpose, and then change it.

"She has just plunged Europe into one war. She is quite capable of doing it again in twenty years' time . . ." he prophesied. But because even statesmen are deceived with fair words every one believed in the good intentions of Germany, and distrusted the blunt realism of Pilsudski, who desired peace perhaps more passionately than any one in Europe since it was vital to Poland's very existence, but who admitted frankly that he wanted his country to be sufficiently strong in arms to resist attack.

"For centuries men have proclaimed peace with their lips and yet continued to make war" . . . he used to say. . . . "Why should we suppose that human nature is going to undergo a complete change?" . . .

He gave a candid statement in an interview which did not increase his popularity at Locarno. . . .

"If this universal desire for peace is to be relied upon, why should preference be given to those who disregard it and persist in organizing their aggressive forces? I am afraid that I have not the faith to believe that when one nation is attacked every other will hasten to its aid. If all of them continue to arm it is proof that all are afraid. Why should Poland be more obedient in guaranteeing peace, when no other country sets the example by decreasing its armaments?"

He insisted that the only practical means of enforcing peace in Europe was for the League to maintain a standing army to which all countries would contribute and which would be at the service of any victim of aggression.

The internal situation in Poland was no less complicated. The Skrzynski and Grabski Governments had introduced grandiose schemes of finance and economy but they had not known how to carry them out, and it was utterly impossible to arrive at a budget. The zloty fell lower and lower every day. Those who received monthly salaries were obliged to turn them immediately into goods before their purchasing powers dwindled still further. Shopkeepers altered their prices every few hours, financiers speculated wildly in foreign exchange. There was poverty everywhere, the unemployed in the big industrial towns were reduced to the verge of starvation.

Pilsudski who had nursed the new Poland through the first most difficult years of its existence grew increasingly alarmed as he saw discontent spreading through the country. Even more serious was the dissatisfaction in the army. The whole military system was badly organized. Both officers and men were seething with resentment. Scarcely a week passed without officers, many of whom were his old Legionaries, coming to him at Sulejowek, singly or in deputations, to lay their grievances before him and ask him to take action on their behalf.

On November 13th the Grabski Government, having lost the confidence of the nation, was forced to resign. On the following afternoon Pilsudski called upon President Wojciechowski at the Belvedere and handed him a declaration asking him to protect the interests of the army.

The next day, the anniversary of his return from Magdeburg, brought my husband a tribute which he valued more than any others he had ever received. The officers of the Warsaw garrison, numbering about a thousand and including several generals, marched in a body to Sulejowek to demonstrate their loyalty and appreciation. General Dreszer, who acted as their spokesman, in explaining the purpose of their visit, said:

> "On the anniversary of your wedding with the State seven years ago we come to remind you of the time when you returned from a German prison, and found Poland apparently lifeless. Broken hearts and nerves strained by slavery became a background for disputes, quarrels and the play of petty ambitions. With you came salvation. You took boldly the highest, albeit the unwritten power of dictator into your hands. You restored to us Poland's long forgotten glory; you crowned our banners with victory.
>
> "To-day we are once again in the midst of doubt and trouble. We ask you not to leave us in this crisis, for you will desert not only us, your loyal soldiers, but Poland. We offer you our grateful hearts, but with them we also offer you our swords." . . .

Pilsudski in reply quoted the words one of them had used in a recent report . . . "Honour is the army's god: without it the army crumbles," and added that in the black hour through which the State was passing he had tried to defend that maxim before the President. He had asked him to defend all that the army stood for. . . . He ended by an appeal . . . "Collaborate with me in protecting the dear service of our country. . . ." They left him with renewed promises of fidelity to the State.

The one thing which he had striven to avoid had come to pass. The army was being used as a pawn in the political game, controlled by deputies who had no knowledge of its organization, no care for its welfare, and no interest except self-advancement.

In the early part of 1926 he was repeatedly asked to take

up his former post again, but he steadfastly refused to do so unless radical changes were made. . . . "Only a fool or a self-seeking schemer would accept the Chief Command under the present conditions . . ." he said. The Poles had long lost their military tradition. Of the six hundred members of the Senate and the Seym not more than twenty had seen active service. How then could they be considered as qualified to direct the life of the army? Some of them were already urging its reduction, and complaining that the money expended on it would be better employed in the development of building.

The discontented regiments were clamouring for his return, but he issued stern and uncompromising orders that there was to be no agitation in the army on his behalf. Above all things he would never be a cause of trouble and dissension in the State. He remained at Sulejowek, quietly confident of his own point of view, but resolved to take no steps to force the situation in any way. It was obvious, however, that a crisis was approaching. The budget showed no improvement, and the Finance Minister's proposal to increase the already heavy taxes only served to heighten the general depression. The Government split up, various unsuccessful attempts were made to form another, and finally, on May 10th, Witos once again became Premier. Dissatisfaction spread still further among the people. There were violent outbursts in a large section of the Press, riots broke out in many parts of Warsaw.

A newspaper reporter interviewing my husband asked whether his return to the army would be delayed by the change of government. . . .

"Of course . . ." he answered with his usual frankness . . . "I shall do nothing to support such a glaring transgression of the moral interests of the State and the army. I shall, as before, make war against the chief evil of our State, the mastery of Poland by ungovernable groups and parties, which consider only pence and profits. . . ."

The newspaper in which the interview appeared was immediately confiscated.

In the meantime the tension increased both in Warsaw and in the army. Several regiments were on the verge of mutiny. Pilsudski realized that the State whose creation had been the

work of his whole life was being destroyed by the gangrene
within it. After a consultation with the officers at Rembertow
(the military barracks outside Warsaw) he agreed to lead a
demonstration against the Witos Government, in the hope of
forcing it to make some reforms, at least in the case of the army.

At seven in the morning of May 12th he left Sulejowek
for Rembertow, telling me that he would be home in time for
dinner at two-thirty as usual. At one o'clock he telephoned to
say that his plans had been changed. The demonstration was
to take place that afternoon; they were marching to Warsaw
immediately, and I must not expect him home before night.
At that time neither he nor the officers and men of the few
regiments who followed him intended anything other than a
peaceable demonstration.

They marched through the Praga suburb and arrived at the
city itself, which is approached by two parallel bridges. Pilsudski decided to cross the Poniatowski Bridge, but his way
was barred by President Wojciechowski at the head of troops
who had been rushed to the scene. The president refused to
parley and ordered his men to attack. Pilsudski, not wishing
to fire upon his former friend and President, retired with his
troops, quietly crossed another one of the bridges and occupied all the centre of the city.

Fighting broke out in the streets. Pilsudski's men were unprepared, the majority of them were even lacking in ammunition until they were able to seize supplies in the city, and they
were hampered by the fear of injuring the citizens. But they
had implicit trust in their Commander, and they were fighting
for an ideal.

That night Pilsudski gave an interview to the Press in which
he said· "Although I have always been opposed to violence, a
fact which I proved when I was Chief of State, I have brought
myself after a severe struggle, to a trial of strength with all
its consequences. All my life I have fought for honour, virtue
and all those forces which make a country strong: not for
profit either for myself or for those about me. If the State is
to live there must not be falsehood, iniquities and injustice. All
must work for the good of the whole. . . ."

The fighting did not last long. More than three-quarters

of the populace was behind Pilsudski; the Government troops had little heart in opposing him. All those in Praga came over to his side; Rydz-Smigly and the Wilno garrison joined him and regiments arrived from several parts of the provinces. One cavalry regiment covered eighty miles in a day, but it insisted on going into action. A young pilot of the Air Force landed his machine at Sulejowek and came to the house to ask where he could join my husband. He had flown from a distant aerodrome to offer his services. By the morning of May 14th, the Belvedere was in Pilsudski's hands. The Government fled to Wilanowa, and from there President Wojcie-chowski sent in his resignation.

In the meantime I had remained at Sulejowek with the children during what were the most anxious days of my life. On the second morning my husband sent a guard of forty men in case we were attacked. They brought me a note from him in which he explained briefly what had happened, and after that I could only wait until the evening of the third day when I could endure the suspense no longer and went to Warsaw. To my intense relief I found the fighting over and the city comparatively calm. My husband was already in the General Staff Office. I was appalled at the change in him. In three days he had aged ten years. The flesh seemed to have fallen from him; his face was parchment white and the skin had taken on a strange transparency, almost as though it was lighted from within. His eyes were hollow with fatigue. Only on one other occasion did I ever see him look so ill, and that was within a few hours of his death.

When we were alone together he broke down in telling me of the battle that had taken place, and I realized what it had cost him. Because he believed it to be his duty he had fought against Poles, even against the men who had followed him so blithely to the wars with Russia. He had won, but there was no triumph in the moment of victory, only bitterness. Those three days of civil war left a mark on him for the rest of his life. He was never so calm as before, never so completely master of himself. Thereafter he carried always a load.

He held absolute power in his own hands now. He was

virtually the Dictator of Poland. He could have assumed the title and prerogatives at any moment. He was repeatedly urged to do so by all the different parties. The Royalists of the Right even went so far as to approach him with the suggestion that he should be crowned King. He countered it with a flash of his dry humour . . . "A monarchy should be hereditary, gentlemen. If you will establish one where the succession descends through the female line only I will consider it. . . ."

To the Socialists of the Left, many of whom were his old comrades of the P.P.S., he explained seriously that he had no ambition to be dictator. . . . "Why should I be? I am a strong man and I like to decide matters myself. But when I study the history of my country I cannot believe that we are a nation to be governed by the stick. In any case I do not like the stick. Our generation is not perfect, but it has rights which must be respected, and the next generation will be much better. I could never be in favour of a dictatorship for Poland. . . ."

He used to say that any nation weak and spiritless enough to put itself voluntarily under the heel of a dictator deserved its fate. . . . "Dictatorships always end disastrously. History has proved that. One of two things always happens. Either the dictator dies, leaving no one to replace him, and the nation which has become accustomed to complete submission to one man's will collapses; or else the people grow tired of him and throw him out. With a monarchy it is different for the nation is faithful to the constitution, not to the man. No mortal man can command eternal fidelity from even one person, let alone millions." . . .

In those weeks of power there were suggestions from the leaders of the Left Wing that he should rid himself of some of his political adversaries by the simple expedient of having them put to death. When he refused several of those in favour of the idea even came to me asking me to use my influence with him. He answered that he would be very sorry to create such a precedent for there would be no end to the hangings in Poland if every political party which happened to be in power adopted such a form of vengeance.

He was determined to give full legality to the overthrow of the Government and therefore, in accordance with the law providing for the absence of the President, he asked Matthias Rataj, Speaker of the Seym, to take over the office of Acting President. Casimir Bartel, who had risen from a simple railway worker to be Professor and Minister, and who was one of the most popular men in Warsaw, was appointed Temporary Premier. A Cabinet was then formed pending the election of a President by the National Assembly of the Seym and Senate, and Pilsudski became Minister for War.

On May 21st he was elected President by a majority of three to two. He refused to accept the office. He had only stood because he wished to obtain parliamentary approval for his actions of May 12–14. The result of the voting was in itself ample justification. He held the confidence of the Seym. In a letter to the Speaker he explained his views. He was grateful to the Parliament for legalizing his actions, as in February 1919. The fact that the verdict was not unanimous this time was a hopeful sign. There might be less falsehood and treachery in Poland. But he considered that the office required a man of a different type, and that he for his part could not live without fruitful work.

A new election was held next day and Professor Moscicki, the well-known scientist, and Pilsudski's friend of many years' standing, was chosen in his stead. The choice was a most happy one for Poland, for no man could more ably have represented the country both at home and abroad. For my husband it was the beginning of a harmonious collaboration which lasted until his death.

The storm which raged so fiercely in the summer of 1926 gave place to a period of calm and tranquillity. The zloty was stabilized, commerce and industry began to show signs of improvement, a bounteous harvest raised the hopes of the peasants. In the autumn there was a passing phase of tension when Bartel was forced to resign from the Premiership because of the intense opposition of the National Democrats in the Seym. Pilsudski countered it by becoming Premier himself. He hated the post, for it would encroach upon the time he wanted to give to the army, but it was the only means of putting a check to the party squabbles which were ready to break out with renewed force, and which would prevent the Government from devoting its entire energies to the regeneration of the country. As far as he was concerned he already had the two posts which he had chosen in preference to any, since they represented the custody of the army, the High Command and the Ministry of War. Except for two brief Premierships, he held no others until his death. He wanted no official rewards, he detested publicity of any sort and shunned the limelight. All that he wanted was to work for the State and to see that others did the same. He was fond of the quotation . . . "Love should be a reality every hour; it should not need expression in words. . . ." He never applied it to his own love for Poland, yet I have sometimes thought how true it was of him. Love of his country came before all else; it was for ever present in his mind; and because of it he took upon himself tasks that were often uncongenial to him. He had no real wish to rule, but only to teach others how to rule.

I remember the scene at the opening of the Seym on March 27th, 1928. It was a solemn occasion with all the newly elected deputies assembled for the first time, and the public galleries were crowded with spectators. Pilsudski as Premier had to read the President's address, and knowing that the Poles were rather inclined to treat their President too casually he always insisted on a punctilious observance of ceremony during the formalities.

There was dead silence when he rose to read the address, but before he had spoken even the opening words there were shouts of "Down with the Government" from the Communist members on the side benches. My husband swung round upon them, grey eyes flashing above the grey blue of his uniform, and his deep, resonant voice rang through the hall . . . "Silence, or I will have you turned out. . . ." He began to read the address, but again he was interrupted.

"You heard what I said. You will be turned out. . . ."

For a moment he dominated the clamour, then it broke out anew. This time he turned to the Minister for Home Affairs, Skladkowski, who stood behind him. . . . "I must ask you to have them put out. . . ."

Skladkowski left him to return a few minutes later with several policemen, who flung themselves on the interrupters. The latter put up a violent resistance, whereupon the remaining Socialist members shouted their protests. For a few minutes the house was in an uproar.

Pilsudski waited calmly until the arrested men had been removed, then he turned to the occupants of the Socialist benches and sternly warned them that unless they were quiet he would adjourn the parliament. When at length peace was restored he read the President's address which dealt with the immense improvement achieved by Poland during the past twelve months, both in regard to home affairs and in relations with other European Powers. It was an encouraging statement, and it was applauded even by the Socialists. Pilsudski had gained the day. But the strain had been great, and he was too tired even to find relaxation in his usual game of Patience that night.

CHAPTER XXIV

My husband was given his former residence at the Belvedere Palace on his return to office in 1926 and this time I too moved in there with the children. I can still remember my first impressions of its sombre grandeur and that I wondered whether anything would make it look more like a home and less like a museum. A succession of owners had left the imprints of their conflicting personalities on it. The main building was seventeenth century, and its florid baroque had probably been the last word in elegance when Krzystof Pac, the Lithuanian Chancellor, had established his family there. A hundred years or so later it had passed into the possession of Stanislas Augustus, last King of Poland, who restored it in the Polish Empire style, and installed the pottery which was his favourite hobby. It gave its name to the exquisite pieces of Belvedere porcelain which found their way, accompanied by one of the King's gracefully penned notes, into nearly all the royal houses of Europe. Its next royal owner, the Grand Duke Constantine, most hated of all Poland's Russian Viceroys, completed the restorations of his predecessor and added his own version of embellishment. It was said that his restless ghost used to return to the scene of his cruelties and wander through the gardens and salons to the study where he had signed the orders that sent hundreds of Poles to die. I myself never saw this apparition, but many people claimed to have done so, including one of my husband's aides-de-camp, on the night of the anniversary of the Insurrection of 1830. Even my husband, who was the least superstitious of men, used to admit that he often heard steps outside his study, and yet when he opened the door there was no one in sight, and when he slept there he used to keep a light burning all night.

At first sight the succession of lofty and imposing salons, each opening out of the other, and all painted a dull sombre grey, was depressing, but after the Palace had been redecorated in warm clear tones and brilliant lighting had been installed the effect was much happier, and the children loved the big gardens with their avenues of lime and chestnut trees.

We gave many receptions at the Belvedere, generally in the afternoon, for my husband hated formal functions and lengthy official dinners, and always said that the intimate atmosphere of a "five o'clock" was a much better background for diplomatic relations. He had a great dislike for ostentatious entertaining, and except for official occasions he preferred to surround himself with members of his own family whom he used to invite for week-ends at Sulejowek or Pikiliszki. The love of family life was very strongly marked in him, and not one of his relations, even those with whom he had quarrelled in his youth on account of his political views, was ever forgotten. In friendship he gave that same loyalty. He never believed evil of his friends and would defend them passionately if others attacked them. But at the same time he never allowed himself to be influenced by personal considerations in his choice of a man for some particular post. All that concerned him was his capability for filling it, and so he made appointments irrespective of parties or politics. Several of the men he promoted had actually opposed his rise to power, but that fact made no difference to him. He never bore any malice towards them. The one question of paramount importance in his eyes was whether they could be of use to the State.

The close of the twenties saw the real beginning of the regeneration of Poland which had so long been his dream. By that time the administration of the army had been reorganized and put upon a sound basis, and he had induced the Seym to grant higher pay to the officers.

The Constitution was still a vexed question. Hurriedly drawn up in 1919, in the first confusion of the new State, it had been finally passed in March 1921 after a great deal of quibbling over side issues and not enough investigation of its main clauses. Consequently it was too loosely framed. The functions of President, Government and Parliament were never clearly defined and therefore there was continual, and sometimes ridiculous, friction between the three. They were always, as Pilsudski used to say, treading on one another's toes, and much of their time was spent in reversing each other's decisions.

The President was the most seriously handicapped, for while he was nominally the head of the State his actual power amounted to nothing. He was, in fact, in the unhappy position of being placed in the centre of a perpetual tug of war between the Seym and the Government.

Pilsudski had long called attention to the disadvantages of this Constitution and had aimed at changing it. During his retirement at Sulejowek he drew up plans for a new one, but nothing could be accomplished until he had a majority in the Seym. In 1929 his supporters submitted to the House the projected scheme of alteration, but it was not until the last year of his life that he had the satisfaction of having it passed.

In the meantime the economic life of the country continued to improve. New industrial enterprises were started. Foreign export developed to such an extent that the docks of Danzig were not sufficient for our overseas trade and a new port was created at Gdynia which, with its modern wharves and equipment, was soon to rank as the first Baltic port. Within a few years it had been transformed from a peaceful little village to a town of 120,000 inhabitants. Between the two ports there was constant rivalry and the percentage of export by sea rose from 7 per cent in 1922 to 50 per cent in 1930, and finally to 77 per cent in 1938. We had at last a merchant fleet of our own. Coal from our mines in Silesia, timber from our forests, textiles from the looms of Lodz and Bielsk went all over the world. Renewed prosperity brought improvement in the general standard of life. The sum paid into the Postal Savings Bank, which in 1928 had been 167,000,000 zlotys, reached in 1937 a total of 917,000,000 zlotys.

In those years of regeneration my husband realized many of the plans which we had first discussed so long ago in the gardens of Kiev. One of his first measures on taking over the reins of government in 1918 was a decree establishing an eight-hour working day with seven hours for miners, and paid holidays varying from eight to fourteen days a year. At the same time he introduced a scheme for health insurance and prohibited the employment of children under sixteen. These decrees were the preludes to a series of social reforms which gave Poland in many matters concerning working conditions a leading place among European nations. Special tribunals were set up to deal with disputes between employers and their workpeople, others for arbitrating in cases concerning land and agriculture. Unemployment was relieved by means of grants in some cases and organized public work in others. A special service was instituted to provide medical attention for working women and children of sixteen to eighteen.

In those first years of freedom there was nothing to build upon. The country was completely without resources in any branch of social life. Money had to be raised for schools and higher education. Schemes had to be organized for the relief of the aged and incapacitated, sanatoriums, hospitals and convalescent homes had to be built. It says much for our constructive ability as a race that we were able to do it. The women of all classes worked unsparingly in every type of social welfare. It was a proud day when I presided over the first Women's Congress to be held in independent Poland, at which forty different women's organizations were represented by 250,000 delegates drawn from all classes—landowners, peasants, women barristers, police and judges, doctors, deputies, and factory girls. To us who twenty-five years before had been forbidden even to speak our own language it was a great event.

The most difficult problem was that of the peasantry, who were forced to bear the brunt of the nation's poverty and unemployment. With a birth rate that rose steadily (in the years between 1921 and 1938 the population increased by nearly eight millions) * the economic system was not sufficiently organized to find a place for them. Their holdings could not yield them a living; the industries, rapidly as they were developing, were still not large enough to absorb them. A scheme of industrial centres seemed to be the most practical solution to the problem, and was beginning to give admirable results when the war broke out last year.

. . . .

The years from 1926 until my husband's death passed in an almost continuous round of work for both of us. The women's organizations in which I was interested occupied my days from

* Population of Poland in 1938—34,500,000.

9 A.M. till 3 P.M. and then again from 5 P.M. until 8 P.M. and between those hours I had the care of the house and the children. Except for meals we scarcely saw one another until the evenings but we always kept three precious hours between 10 P.M. and 1 A.M. to spend together, no matter how busy we were. We used to sit in his study to talk over the events of the day, and then he would leave me and go back to his work until 3 or 4 A.M. He had no time for relaxation in those days, even the chess-board was put away except for week-ends at Sulejowek. Fortunately he had trained himself to snatch five minutes' sleep at any time in the day. He would relax completely in his chair and awake rested and with renewed vitality. Had it not been for those odd moments of repose I do not think that even his iron constitution could have stood the strain.

Foreign relations were a continual source of anxiety to him. We lived perpetually in the shadow of war either with Russia or Germany. For many years small groups of Soviet troops continued to harry the eastern frontier. The Germans clamoured incessantly for the return of Danzig and the Corridor and sent their agents to stir up trouble in the Free City, though the populace, to whom Polish commerce had brought prosperity, were now on a completely friendly footing with Poland and desired no break in the relationship. Pilsudski, who longed for peace above all else, foresaw the inevitability of war, and his one object was to postpone it until such time as Poland should be strong in her own defences. . . . "Every day when we are not at war is a day gained" . . . he used to say, and he never ceased to urge upon the Government the necessity of rearmament, and the fallacy of complacency. . . . "To be conquered and not surrender, that is victory. To conquer and rest on one's laurels is defeat. . . ."

He welcomed the advent of Hitler to the German Chancellorship in January 1933, because in those early days of power Hitler's gospel was one of peace and the Germans had been most vociferous in their demands for Danzig under Stresemann. The new Chancellor, on the contrary, seemed desirous of manifesting his goodwill.

A few months later we were spending a short holiday at Pikiliszki when the news reached my husband that the Germans were concentrating troops at the frontier. Without losing a moment he hurried to President Moscicki, dispatched several regiments to the Westerplatte and mobilized the Fleet.

Those were the days before Goering preferred guns to butter and therefore there was a conciliatory note from Hitler, regretting the unfortunate misunderstanding. He had no designs upon Poland; on the contrary, he would be glad to establish friendly relations between the two countries. It was a diplomatic victory, but it did not deceive my husband. . . . "It will give us longer to prepare our defences . . ." he said to me afterwards . . . "But it is only a question of putting off the evil day. While Germany looks towards the Corridor and Russia has her eyes on the west there can be no lasting security for us. . . ."

In the following year the ten-year pact of non-aggression was signed between Poland and Germany. He was jubilant over it. "I suppose that means that for ten years we shall not have war . . ." I said. He shook his head. . . . "No, no. It only means that Hitler has postponed it. Poland is not so weak as all that, nor is Germany as strong and united as he will wish to make her before he takes upon himself the risk of a war. The respite will give us time to organize our lives, but after that we must be ready to defend ourselves. We have no other alternative. . . ."

After Hitler's recovery of the Saar he warned certain foreign diplomatists on the subject of German rearmament for he was convinced that it could only have one outcome, but unfortunately for Europe his warnings were not heeded.

The last twelve months of his life brought him the harvest of all that he had sown. Poland was free. She was a solid, self-governing nation with a well organized army and a balanced budget. Her ships sailed the sea, her trade was bringing her prosperity, her people were thriving and contented. She had pacts with Russia and Germany. Her future seemed assured of peace for some years at least.

The new Constitution had been signed. The nation had reached real unity at last. As he said. . . .

"We will stand together, as always, ready to give our lives for our country, and the fights we have had in the past will not divide us, but will draw us together, like the memory of a violent quarrel between brothers who love one another and love their family. . . ."

In the autumn of 1934 his health began to fail but he carried out his full program, even to setting problems in military tactics and strategy for his officers at Wilno and near the Czech frontier, and reading all their reports himself. It was tiring work and he came home haggard and exhausted. But by Christmas he had recovered and for the first time in many years he escaped influenza. He talked no more of resigning and made plans for the future.

January was saddened to him by the death of his sister. A strenuous fast which he imposed on himself robbed him of his resilient vitality. During the month of March the slightest exertion became too much for him. But he made a great effort and rallied to a semblance of himself for Mr. Anthony Eden's visit to Warsaw in the beginning of April and he was pleased with the satisfactory results of their conversations together.

We were to have spent Easter at Sulejowek but he was not well enough to leave Warsaw. He passed the time instead in an easy chair on the veranda reading a great deal, playing Patience and feeding the pigeons, but he was so obviously growing weaker that I asked the doctors who were attending him to send for a celebrated professor from Vienna. At first my husband refused to listen to the suggestion, told me that it was my imagination, and that all he needed was a holiday. He insisted on going to the office, even though he was too ill to work and a bed had to be made up for him there. He was tormented by the fear of another cut in Poland's territories. . . . "We can only just exist within our present limits . . ." he said repeatedly. . . . "If they slice our boundaries down to the Bug we shall lose everything. . . ." He used to sit at his desk anxiously studying the map.

The specialist who came from Vienna diagnosed a cancer which had already attacked the liver, but he kept his verdict from every one except the doctors who consulted with him, and my husband remained convinced that he would soon be well. The end came so quickly that he did not even realize it.

He died on Sunday, May 12th, still in harness, receiving the ministers and giving them instructions to the last.

On the Friday, two days before he died, M. Laval was in Warsaw, and although my husband was not well enough to see him, Mr. Beck, the Minister of Foreign Affairs, came to the Belvedere to report the conversations that had taken place. They worked together for an hour and Mr. Beck was delighted to find him apparently so much better. The next morning he laughed and talked animatedly with one of his generals who came to visit him, but later in the day he had a sudden haemorrhage from which he never rallied. The next evening his life drew to its close, very quietly and peacefully.

When the news spread through the city the people were stunned. They had not even known that he was ill. They had believed that he was suffering from a diplomatic indisposition because he wished to avoid discussing the Eastern Pact with Laval. The news found them utterly unprepared, and men as well as women wept openly in the streets when they heard it.

The whole nation mourned him. Reverent crowds lined the street as his body was borne with military honours from the Belvedere Palace to the Cathedral to lie in state for a week. Thousands, from the highest to the lowliest, filed past to look their last upon him. And afterwards his soldiers too took farewell of him at the solemn ceremony of the last review.

He was laid to rest at the Wawel in Cracow with the kings and heroes of Poland, but his heart is buried, in fulfilment of his last wish, at the feet of his mother in Wilno, in the same cemetery where so many of his soldiers are laid.

It was night when he was borne on his last journey from Warsaw to Cracow, but all along the route of the funeral train his way was lighted by the flames from the fires of wood which the people of the countryside had gathered to do honour to his passing.

"When I stand before a coffin I must speak of death, of the omnipotent mistress of all that lives. All that lives dies, and all that dies has lived before. The laws of death are irrevocable. They are as though their purpose is to

state the truth that what has risen out of dust into dust
must return. When we drop a stone on the surface of still
water, rings arise which spread, and slowly subside. Like-
wise men live after they have passed through the narrow
gateway of death; the rings of their life slowly subside and
disappear, leaving behind them emptiness and even oblivion.
The laws of death and the laws of life which are interwoven
are irrevocable and merciless. There have lived multitudes
of men and all have died. Generations after generations
living an everyday life, ordinary or extraordinary, pass into
eternity leaving behind them only vague recollections. Yet
there are men and there are human works so strong and so
powerful that they gain victory over death, that they live
and are present among us. . . .

"The narrow gates of death do not exist for some men.
When I count the layers of open earth and see the highways
of the past along which humanity has marched and along
which history now steps forward, I see hard roads which
men, entering upon life by generations and dying by
generations, have strewn with their life as with their death.
Generations have left traces by their skeletons and their
daily work and by their daily rest have strewn lasting and
eternal highways. But everywhere where the highways
have turnings, where the road bends, where there is human
hesitation and fear, huge boulders stand like finger-posts,
testifying to the great truth of existence. Huge boulders
stand lonely, but they bear names, while men perish leaving
no name. . . ."

Thus spoke Joseph Pilsudski as he stood in that same Wawel
beside the coffin of Slowacki, the patriot poet whom he had
caused to be brought from France to lie in Polish soil. And
on his own tomb are inscribed the words of Slowacki. . . .

"He who has chosen the nest on the heights of the eagle
rather than the hearthstone will know how to sleep when
the horizon is red with the storm, and the mutterings of
demons are heard in the wind among the pines. Thus have
I lived. . . ."

INDEX

S

Sabashnikov, Dr. Ivan, 178
Sawicki, Colonel, 191, 194, 195
Scallon, Russian Governor, 133-4
Siedielnikow, Alexel, 177
Siemiradska, Madame, 93, 96
Sieroszewski, Waclaw, Polish
    novelist, 218
Sigismund I, King, 69
Skladkowski (Minister for Home
    Affairs, 1928), 334-5
Skrzynski, 327
Slaweck, Walery, 115, 187, 188-9,
    191
Slowacki, 77, 85, 120, 155, 157, 303,
    344
Sobieski, King John, 66, 82, 118,
    301
Social Democrats, 144, 226, 280
Sosnkowski, General Casimir, 115,
    182, 197, 221, 222, 261, 265, 266,
    269, 298, 299, 325
Starzynski, S., Mayor of Warsaw
    (1939), 31
Strabrowski, painter, 130
Stresemann, 340
Strzelcy (Union of Riflemen),
    199, 203, 204, 205, 206, 213-18
Sulkiewicz, Alexander, 99, 164
Sulkiewicz, Mendelssohn, 99, 164
Supreme Council of Allies, 298
Swetochowski, writer, 96
Swirski, Count, 187-8
Szwarce, Bronislaw, 163

T

Thorn, Treaty of, 69
Tukachevski, Russian Comman-
    dant, 299

U

United States of America, 260
    278, 283, 284, 289

V

Vistula, Battle of (1920), 301-2

W

Warsaw, 21, 22-7, 31-6, 73, 74, 75,
    94-5, 97, 104, 133, 188, 239
Wassilewski, 288
Weygand, General, 298, 299
Wilno, 45, 46, 48, 49, 191, 207, 287,
    288-9, 290-5, 302-3; University
    of, 47, 150, 154-5, 294, 317
Wilson, President, 259
Wislicki, Statute of, 87
Witos, Wincenty, ex-Premier of
    Poland, 329
Wojciechowski, Stanislas, ex-
    President of Poland, 165, 169,
    315, 327, 330, 331

Y

Yodko, 99

Z

Zeligowski, General, 302
Zelinsky, Jan, 146, 147
Zulinski, Thaddeus, 229, 239

Printed in the USA
CPSIA information can be obtained
at www.ICGtesting.com
LVHW010007030124
767724LV00052B/507